The Thames Torso Murders

The Thames Torso Murders

M J Trow

First published in Great Britain in 2011 by
Wharncliffe Books
an imprint of
Pen & Sword Books Ltd
47 Church Street
Barnsley
South Yorkshire
S70 2AS

Copyright © M J Trow 2011

ISBN 978-1-84884-430-8

London Borough of Richmond Upon on Thames	
WH	
90710 000 071 497	
Askews & Holts	
364.152 TRO	£19.99
	9781848844308

The right of M J Trow to be identified as Author of this Work has been asserted by him in accordance with the Copyright, Designs and Patents Act 1988.

A CIP catalogue record for this book is available from the British Library.

All rights reserved. No part of this book may be reproduced or transmitted in any form or by any means, electronic or mechanical including photocopying, recording or by any information storage and retrieval system, without permission from the Publisher in writing.

Typeset in 11pt Ehrhardt by
Mac Style, Beverley, E. Yorkshire

Printed and bound in the UK by CPI

Pen & Sword Books Ltd incorporates the imprints of Pen & Sword Aviation, Pen & Sword Maritime, Pen & Sword Military, Wharncliffe Local History, Pen & Sword Select, Pen & Sword Military Classics, Leo Cooper, Seaforth Publishing and Frontline Publishing.

For a complete list of Pen & Sword titles please contact
PEN & SWORD BOOKS LIMITED
47 Church Street, Barnsley, South Yorkshire, S70 2AS, England
E-mail: enquiries@pen-and-sword.co.uk
Website: www.pen-and-sword.co.uk

Contents

Foreword by Professor Laurence Alison	vii
Acknowledgements	xi
Map	xii
1. Messing about on the River	1
2. The River of Death	13
3. 'Found Dead': Rainham, May 1887	25
4. Jack	35
5. The Whitehall Mystery: Scotland Yard, September 1888	45
6. The Frankenstein Connection: Horsleydown, June 1889	57
7. The Women of Moab and Midian	67
8. The Pinchin Street Torso: Whitechapel, 10 September 1889	75
9. 'Dealers in Horror': Battersea, 5 September 1873 and Putney, June 1874	85
10. The Girl with the Rose Tattoo: Tottenham Court Road, 23 October 1884	99
11. Men Behaving Madly	107
12. Other Times, Other Crimes	119
13. The Habitual Homicide	133
14. The Cat's Meat Man	141
Notes	157
Bibliography	165
Index	167

Foreword
by Professor Laurence Alison

I occasionally get asked to contribute to so called 'cold case reviews' – cases that, for various complex reasons, have remained unsolved and without a conviction for many years. Not infrequently the impetus has come from advances in DNA or other 'hard science' forensic methods. A diligent and conscientious Senior Investigating Officer can make great strides and resolve and successfully convict in cases that are sometimes over two decades old. Psychologists, profilers, or behavioural investigative advisers are occasionally asked to advise on narrowing suspect searches, 'building' search matrices or suspect lists, or provide input with regards to the use of the media, leaflet drops or where to prioritize an area for buccal swabbing. As such, the 'softer science' advisers are there to assist (broadly) in the decision making of the SIO and in regards as to where he or she should put his or her resources. There are several recent cases that have been extremely successful 'revisits' to cold case reviews and recently I wrote a book about the Rachel Nickell murder, the murder of a young woman, solved some eighteen years later by diligent modern methods of policing.

However, it is exceptional to be asked for consultation on cases in the 1880s! In such cases, it was not even possible to establish fingerprint evidence and scientists were only just able to distinguish whether blood was human or animal.

I had the pleasure of working with Mei on his Jack the Ripper documentary for Atlantic Productions in which he proposed a mortician's assistant, Robert Mann, as a plausible suspect. I frequently am asked to comment on new 'Jack' suspects and must confess I have an interest in those murders partly because of their unusual and psychologically disturbing features and partly because of the atmosphere of Victorian London that surrounds them. Having lived in London myself for many years the history of that city and the narratives around crime, police and policing that surround it hold a peculiar fascination. Normally I reject making a contribution to TV documentaries but in Mei's case it was rather different. It was very gratifying working with a historian and crime writer who wasn't rabidly promoting and promulgating the notion that his/her pet suspect was *the* definitive answer to the Jack mystery. Instead, Mei, diligently worked through the socio-historical context, and in the spirit of Occam's razor 'deleted' out (quite rationally and systematically) all the ridiculous suspects (Queen's surgeons, painters, etc.) and provided a plausible and, moreover, psychologically coherent suspect. I must confess there are several aspects to Mann that do not fit with sexually sadistic murderers and there is no compelling circumstantial evidence or reason to believe that Robert Mann must be Jack but Mei acknowledged that point and was happy to discuss these issues and acknowledge that nothing was black and white, cut and dried.

Psychologists work with probabilities and not certainties (as do profilers) and as such definitive answers do not sit well with them. So Mei was a breath of fresh air. He is interested in motive, research, empirical approaches, statistical mechanisms, geoprofiling, crime scene analysis and methods of working that are outside of his direct area of expertise. What he does so cleverly is critically evaluate those areas and successfully weave them into his own, considerable knowledge of the relevant social historical issues.

The same is true for this book. He was willing to listen, but sometimes reject my musings and incorporate them (not uncritically I may add) in this bizarre series of so-called torso murders. I must confess it was not a series of crimes that I had heard about and, of course, as he notes, they were superseded by the Ripper murders in terms of press coverage and notoriety.

Unlike the Jack murders though there is something disturbingly clinical and cold about them and what I found most fascinating was what was *not* present. No apparent motive (sexual, financial or retributive), a lack of anger, a lack of sadism. No obvious gain and no real knowledge of why these victims were selected. It was hard to establish what the offender was 'getting out of' this grisly, high-risk series of offences. The removal of body parts, the disposal of them at various locations and the consistent non occurrence of the heads are all (mercifully) unusual features – as unusually rare as the acts of sexual sadism in the Ripper cases but in many ways far harder to understand (at least psychologically).

My view was that a central psychological signature was the instances of display of body parts. Signatures are commonly considered those psychological features that are irrelevant to the commission of the crime but are psychologically relevant aspects. Thus, binding a victim may be functional in so far that it disables and controls them but an act of piquerism or dressing victims in a particular way. I will leave the reader of course to follow through Mei's compelling account of this series of offences and allow the reader to develop their own interpretations (as I am sure is Mei's intent) prior to his own particular views; suffice it to say I would encourage the reader to examine what is absent in terms of the behaviour and what this may tell us about the offender.

Finally, a word about the significance of socio-historical context. Psychologists rarely if ever consider such matters. Why would they? They deal with the here and now. But what is so important and instructive about working with a historian is seeing how the psychological function of any given behaviour can vary so considerably. Take for example the act of beheading. To the 'civilized' contemporary Western mind this is an act of utter barbarism, cowardice and brutality. However, it once was a method of execution reserved for royalty and seen as a quick, some might argue honourable death. We know that our 'torso' murderer beheaded his victims. This is a difficult act to inflict on a victim (both technically and because of the revulsion) and, certainly, forensically, will have made this investigation especially difficult for the police. The strength of Mei's work lies in the integration of psychology, forensics, functionality and the socio-historical context surrounding this behaviour and I'd struggle to think of another author that would be able to make such a sensible series of possible interpretations of this complex, horrific case.

Acknowledgements

I would like to thank everyone too numerous to mention who has been generous with their time and expertise in the writing of this book, but especially Rupert Harding and his team; Professor Laurence Alison of Liverpool University; Eloise Campbell for her excellent photography and company; Neil Paterson of the Historic Collection, Metropolitan Police; the staff of the Guildhall Library; the staff of Colindale Newspaper Library; and as always my wife Carol, for her medical insight and for being the only woman in the world who doesn't mind typing out tales of dismemberment!

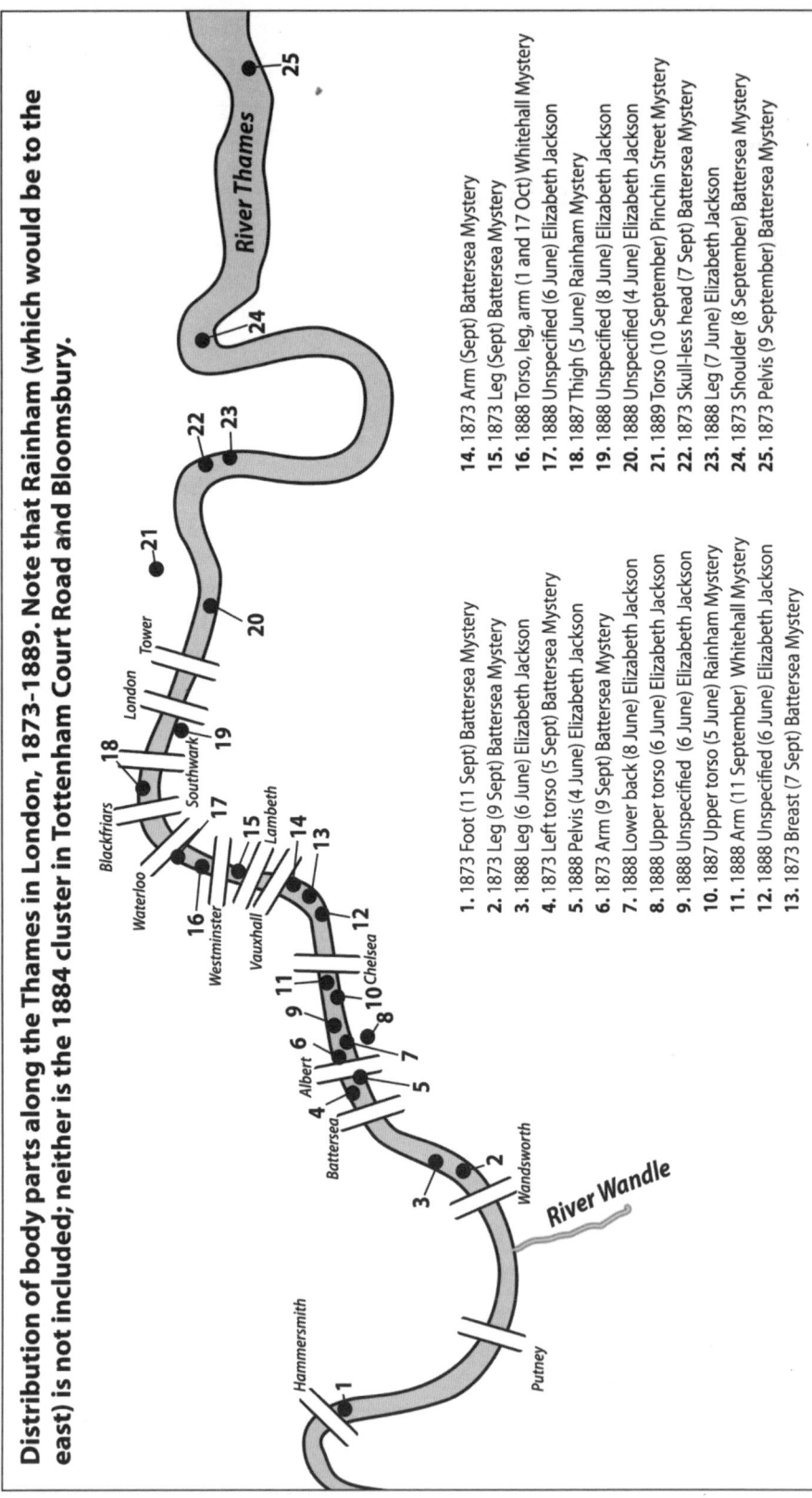

Chapter 1

Messing about on the River

TWENTY bridges from Tower to Kew –
(Twenty Bridges or twenty-two)
Wanted to know what the River knew,
For they were young, and the Thames was old
And this is the tale that the River told: –[1]

On 21 June 1888, only weeks before a series of appalling murders began in Whitechapel, the failed actor and writer Jerome Clapp Jerome married the recently divorced Georgina 'Ettie' Morris. The couple spent their honeymoon in a little boat moored on the Thames. The result of this, in the following year, was Jerome's only literary success *Three Men in a Boat*, an affectionate and occasionally riotous look at young friends messing about on the river.

Two years earlier, Charles Dickens,[2] son of the great novelist, produced his unconventional handbook, the *Dictionary of the Thames*, which charts the same ancient waterway and in the same spirit of leisure and laughter. The Thames of Jerome and Dickens, always set in the river's largely non-industrial reaches above London Bridge, is one of endless sunshine, punts, pleasure steamers and cream teas. The dress is swirling parasols and bustles, straw boaters and striped blazers.

Let us take a trip downstream with these men. Let us do it on 11 May 1887.

Jerome's oarsmen started at Kingston and worked upstream, past trailing willows and open fields, the sort of countryside that would be captured years later by Kenneth Grahame in his *Wind in the Willows*. We will take the opposite direction, downstream to the Port of London, then the busiest docks in the world. The Oarsman's and Angler's Map of the River Thames, published in 1893 forms a snapshot of the life of the late Victorian river. The whole thing is 9 inches wide and nearly 9 feet long, charting the twists and turns of the Thames with the principal road and rail links that lay on both banks.

At Kingston, in a nod to history, the map refers to the stone near the marketplace where Saxon kings were crowned. Recommended hotels were the

Griffin and the Sun. R J Tuck and A Burgoine ran the principal boatyards, with all manner of skiffs, punts and larger craft for hire. The town's population was about 17,000 and, although it was linked via the London and South Western Railway to the metropolis itself, was still serviced by the Guildford Coach, the horse-drawn attractions of which were enjoying something of a revival at the time. For a meagre 17s 6d, a nostalgic passenger could travel the 'Old Times' route via Richmond, Barnes, Hampton Court, Weybridge and Chertsey, 'thus taking in all the best views of the river'.[3]

Kingston housed the East Surrey Territorial Regiment and a number of Volunteer units. It had a High Steward, mayor, eight aldermen and twenty-four councillors. Dickens waxes lyrical for two pages over the town's history, from the Celtic chieftain Cassivelaunus, through the Saxon witanegemot (council) of King Egbert, through to the second Civil War in 1648 when Lord Francis Villiers was killed there in a skirmish.

The place was growing in 1887, largely as a dormitory town for London. Parks had recently been laid out, and the grammar school rebuilt. The thriving banks in the town were the London & County and Shrubsole & Co, a faint reminder that the financial capital of the world was only twenty miles away. Kingston had its own rowing clubs, of course, and the amateur regatta, held in July, was enthusiastically attended. Regattas were, rather like the music hall, great levellers. Even if the majority of oarsmen were upper and middle class, the families who ate their packed lunches and cheered from the banks were just as often the hoi polloi from the working-class areas of the town.

The Thames flowed north above Kingston where the first wooden bridge was built to link the town with Hampton Wick in 1219. The water here was known in pre-industrial times for its purity.

Rudyard Kipling assumed[4] that Teddington was Tide End Town, because here the tidal and non-tidal rivers meet. It was probably named after a local Saxon ruler, Tudda and in 1887 had a population of 6,500. Here was the first lock on the river. Today's statistics give us an average flow at Teddington of 1,145 million gallons a day (2,000 cubic feet a second). The current flows at anything between half a mile and two and three-quarter miles an hour. In calculating the dispersal of dead bodies, this is important. The Teddington lock was the largest on the Thames, with smaller variants – the coffin, launch and barge locks – alongside. Travellers on the river liked lock-keepers. Like the landlords of hostelries on both banks, they exuded bonhomie, despite the fact that by the 1880s they must have already been kept very busy. In the pre-industrial river scene, the rector of St Mary's church here in the 1670s was the mystic Thomas Traherne. Fascinated by the river's reflections, he wrote:

> By walking Men's reversed Feet
> I chanced another World to meet;
> Tho it did not to View exceed
> A Phantom, 'tis a World indeed,
> Where Skies beneath us shine,
> And Earth by Art divine
> Another face presents below,
> Where People's feet against Ours go.[5]

As the river bends with Twickenham on the north bank, the traveller reaches Twickenham Ait or Eel Pie Island. The various Aits or Eyots along the Thames were used as bridging places earlier in history. The most famous of them was Runnymede, where King John was forced to put his seal to Magna Carta, a list of sixty-three gripes from his barons which today we see as the first faltering steps towards democracy.[6] By 1887, Eel Pie Island was already in decline. It had been, fifteen years earlier, *the* place to be for river-trippers where hundreds of 'Arrys and 'Arriets would arrive by pleasure steamer to munch their way through eels. Trade Union and Benevolent Clubs especially enjoyed these outings. The river itself was shallow here and dredging a constant operation in the 1880s.

For anglers, Twickenham and Richmond were ideal in the ebb tide which lasted for about ten hours. Barbell, dace and gudgeon were in abundance, although this was one of the areas where altercations were not unknown between fishermen and boat owners, each group seeing the river as there for their particular hobby only. Tuicam hom is first mentioned in a charter of 704 and eight centuries later there was a ferry between the town and Richmond. Historically, famous names lived along the banks – the philosopher Francis Bacon; musician Godfrey Kneller; the poets John Donne and Alexander Pope; the artist J M W Turner and the magistrate/novelist Henry Fielding. In *Little Dorrit*, Charles Dickens described the area as 'lonely and placid'.

The river bends again at Richmond, 15½ miles from London. From here, in 1887, it was less than half an hour by train to Waterloo, which accounts in part for its popularity with day trippers. The name was given to it by Henry VII, Earl of Richmond in Yorkshire as he had been before 1485, but there was already a royal residence at nearby Sheen where the first three Edwards had lived. The freshness of the air here saw a vast building programme from the Georgian period 'from the mansion to the cottage'[7] and the views from the Great Park were stunning. The library owned 3,000 books and there was a busy Reading Room at the Quadrant. The 'hideous red brick'[8] church was the burial place of the actor Edmund Keane and, to all intents and purposes, Richmond by 1887 was merely a London suburb. The police station, headquarters of the Metropolitan force's V Division, stood in George Street.

Opposite industrial Isleworth and Brentford, as the river straightened, stood the observatory and gardens at Kew. The Aits here were used to harvest osiers, the willow branches woven into eel-nets where a royal palace stood on the Isleworth bank in the reign of Henry III. In the 1880s the town was renowned for its market gardens, flour mills and cement works. Education was flourishing, with a Green School for girls endowed by the late Duchess of Northumberland and a Blue School which was (at least nominally) coeducational. The most famous inn was the London Apprentice and this area (and no doubt the pub too!) was the domain of the Met's T Division.

John Gay could find little to recommend Brentford in his day:

> Brentford, tedious town,
> For dirty streets and white-legged chickens known.[9]

It had cleaned up its act by the 1880s but it could not disguise its commercial untidiness. Whole fleets of barges operated on the River Brent, linking with the cargo and freight of the Great Western Railway and the result was a little foretaste of the hell that lay below London Bridge.

Against this backdrop, the gardens of Kew looked like a bit of heaven. The village itself was almost buried in urban development and Dickens, like most of the writers on the Thames, looks back with nostalgia to the quiet idylls of 'only twenty years ago'.[10] It was the gardens that drew residents and visitors alike: 'Here are to be seen ... the most beautiful tropical palms, plants, ferns, fern-trees and cacti ... Attached to the gardens is a valuable museum of useful vegetable products.'[11]

All this was free to the public every weekday and even on Sunday afternoons. Maintenance took place on Sunday mornings when the curators and research students could get on with their work unimpeded. The Star and Garter, the Coach and Horses and the Greyhound were the hostelries that provided refreshment after all that hot traipsing through the hollyhocks.

Mortlake had sixteenth-century associations with the philosopher John Dee, magus to Elizabeth and navigation tutor to the explorer Martin Frobisher. By the magician's own account, the angel Uriel appeared to Dee and gave him a magic stone by which he could conjure spirits. All Dickens could think to say about it was that it was the terminus of the 'Oxbridge' boat race, another high-day of the Thames that brought all social classes out to spectate.

Barnes Common was still open ground in the 1880s, but middle-class villas were springing up thick and fast around it. The second railway bridge over the river had been opened here in 1846. Since this stretch of the river was ideal for racing, Barnes and Mortlake amateur regatta in July 1887 saw fierce competition between the various clubs on the Thames. In fact in 1887, the Thames Rowing Club had been the winners for the past two years. There had been a bit of Anglo-American unpleasantness five years earlier when, because the American Hillsdale Crew had been admitted, everybody else refused to compete and the challenge cup, together with its £75 prize, was not awarded.

Chiswick was the 'great garden of London',[12] only five miles west of Hyde Park Corner. The eighteenth-century artist and satirist William Hogarth lived and is buried here and for a while the Radical philosopher Jean-Jacques Rousseau lived over a grocer's shop. Chiswick Ait was a famous landmark in the university boat races and the town had been the centre of a brewing industry since the thirteenth century.

At Hammersmith, the river bends sharply south. When Dickens was writing in 1886–7, the suspension bridge was in the process of being rebuilt. On boat-race days it had had to be closed to the public for several years in the interests of health and safety. Hammersmith had only just acquired status as a parliamentary borough and in 1887 its MP was the Conservative Major-General Goldsworthy. The Phelps family had been boatmen here for generations and in the eighteenth century Phillippe de Loutherbourg used animal magnetism (hypnosis) to cure all sorts of illnesses. The river poet James Thomson wrote in the Dove coffee house in the town and in Dickens's own time, the artist-socialist William Morris based his Kelmscott Press there.

Fulham, the place of the fowls, gets no mention in Dickens's gazetteer at all, even though its market gardens were important as providers for London and it was the permanent out-of-town residence of the Bishop of London. There was a long-standing Viking encampment here in the eighth century and a thousand years later the town was known for its pottery production. At that stage, salmon were caught regularly along the river bank.

It may be that the place was eclipsed by the more flamboyant Putney on the Middlesex shore, at once its 'twin' and rival. In Domesday (1087) it was Putlei and the bridge here replaced an earlier ferry. They made starch, candles, beer and gin nearby, but Dickens records it as a place mostly renowned for its boating crews. The Prince and Princess of Wales had just opened a new bridge on 29 May 1886, probably blissfully unaware that St Mary's church nearby had once been the scene of the Putney debates, when the Leveller John Lilburne had argued the case for crypto-communism when the world was 'turned upside down' in the stormy months after the Civil War. For all he had toppled a king, Oliver Cromwell, who argued against Lilburne, remained a man of the squirearchy and rejected the Leveller's arguments for a brave new world.

Just below the bridge, the Wandle, one of the many tributaries of the Thames, flows into the great river. It has the fastest flow of any of the tributary rivers and the name at least gave rise to the sprawling borough of Wandsworth on the Surrey shore. We shall return to the Wandle again.

The derivation of the name Battersea is wide open to interpretation. It is Patrice-cey in Domesday and there were almost certainly a number of Aits there when the Normans came. Dickens was impressed with the Park, especially in summer, with 'its excellent drives and Rotten Row'.[13] The lake was cluttered with oarsmen, the cricketers played regularly and 'refreshments may be had at nearly all the lodgings'.[14] It was in the river here that the most superb votive offering by the Celts was found – the copper-sheathed shield with its red enamel and swirling La Tene artwork. If Lilburne's Levellers were political extremists in their day, Gerard Winstanley's Diggers were off the scale. They ran a genuine commune on St George's Hill. At a later date Alexander Pope wrote his *Essay on Man* overlooking the river at this point. We shall come back to the haunted waters at Battersea.

Chelsea Old Church had been a religious centre since the eighth century. Near it, centuries later, Henry VIII's Chancellor, Thomas More, lived in a house that fronted the river. He travelled regularly, courtesy of the army of watermen who plied the river in water-borne taxis, to the seats of power – the Bishop of London's Lambeth Palace and Henry's Hampton Court. The river stretch was known as the Cocknies' Sea and sixty years before our trip local young men called 'kiddies' wore tightly curled hair and had coloured ribbons dangling from their breeches in honour of their hero, the highwayman Sixteen String Jack Rann. Chelsea was still, in 1887, a quiet village, but it was growing, especially with a large working-class influx. Its MP was the popular Liberal Sir Charles Dilke, although the promise of high office was denied him after his part in the sordid Crawford divorce case in the year before Dickens wrote.

The suspension bridge, built by the Carron Ironworks in Edinburgh in 1858 cost £80,000 but the true feat of engineering nearby was the Chelsea Embankment. Along with the similar Victoria and Albert Embankments further downstream, this was one of the largest civil engineering projects of the entire nineteenth century and one of the most successful. Its architect was Joseph Bazalgette, who, more than any other individual, changed the appearance of the Thames for ever. Where once there was a clutter of wooden wharves and jetties, where children called mudlarks grubbed in the tidal silt for coal and *anything* that could be cleaned up and sold, there were now clean lines and trim walls. When Aulius Plautius' legions reached the Thames in AD 43, the river was possibly a mile wide at Kew. Bazalgette's work narrowed and deepened it, but it made possible the affluence of streets like Cheyne's Walk, in Dickens's day the home of the celebrated playwright Oscar Wilde. This was the artists' stretch of the river. J M W Turner lived in Chelsea, so did William Etty and most of the Pre-Raphaelite brotherhood – Rossetti, Millais and Burne-Jones – were not far away.

This had been the home, in the eighteenth century, of Ranelagh, one of those pleasure gardens, like Vauxhall and the Cremorne, where it was possible to listen to music in the twilight and watch fireworks sparkling and reflecting on the waters. The diarist Samuel Pepys went to Vauxhall in 1667, when it was still called the New Spring Gardens. He loved 'to hear the nightingale and other birds and here a fiddle and there a harp and here a Jew's trump and here laughing'.[15]

We are now in the last reaches of Dickens's river guide for Oarsmen and Anglers. The whole thing terminates at London Bridge, as though there is no world beyond that. In one sense, this is right. By 1887, the pollution of the City and the Docks meant that fishing was dismal in the extreme and anyone trying to row in and out of the barges, wherries and ocean-going merchantmen was literally taking his life in his hands. Across the river, the skyline of Westminster was unmistakable, with the Houses of Parliament and the exclamation mark at the far end called Big Ben.[16]

Lambeth was the loam-hithe or muddy bank, for centuries the London residence of the Archbishop of Canterbury. It had a reputation for low life and bad health, one of the 'great sinks and common receptacles of all the vice and immorality of London'.[17] Before Bazalgette planned the Albert Embankment, the river's edge marked the beginning of a series of shanty towns, a jungle of wharves, boat houses and rickety stairs rising from the dark brown mud. It became the haunt of magicians in the sixteenth century. Simon Forman lived there; so did Elias Ashmole and John Tradescant. The astrologer Forman once wrote 'this I made the devil write with his own hands in Lambeth Fields, 1569, in June or July as I now remember'.[18]

Even by the 1880s, it was difficult to agree with the poet William Wordsworth's view written from Westminster Bridge as the nineteenth century dawned. Dickens reported that the bridge itself 'was always rather a cardboard-looking affair' that vibrated in high winds because of the lightness of its construction. The site of Edward the Confessor's great abbey was Thorney Island but it was a religious settlement three centuries before Edward. According to legend, St Peter himself had rowed across the river and chosen the site. Freak tides and storms made this part of the river particularly vulnerable. Six years before Dickens wrote, the water height was 17 ft 6ins. Before Bazalgette got to work, it was also prey to drought. The 'Great Stink' of 1858 arose from the appalling pollution in the Thames. The river was not only

the great sewer of London, it was the receptacle of all kinds of chemical waste and rubbish. It was so bad that parliamentary sessions had to be cancelled and it led directly to Bazalgette's embankments.

As the river curves again, we are passing Charing Cross on the north bank. Railway and foot bridges crossed the Thames here, linking with the huge Waterloo Station to the south. The poet Shelley was completely wrong when he prophesied that 'the piers of Waterloo Bridge shall become the nuclei of islets of reeds and osiers'.[19] Industry was here to stay by the time he wrote those lines. The watermen, who numbered in their thousands in his day, were reduced to about 1,500 by the middle of the nineteenth century. Cowper's Gardens had taken the place of Lambeth Marsh at the entrance to the bridge on the south side before the railways changed the shape of the river crossings for ever.

The Temple Pier is on our left, near the stairs on the north bank and we shall return this way later. Ahead of us looms the bridge that marks the end of the Angler's and Oarsman's River – London Bridge. The many-times rebuilt medieval version had so many buttresses to hold it up that the river became rapids under its arches and only the boldest waterman would go there. The playwright and poet Ben Jonson paints a fascinating portrait of the bustle of this part of the river –

> From thence we will put in at Custom-house quay there,
> And see how the factors and prentices play there,
> False with their masters; and geld many a full pack
> To spend it in pies at the Dagger, and Woolsack.
> Nay, boy, I will bring thee to the bawds and roysters
> At Billingsgate, feasting with claret-wine and oysters.
> From thence shoot the Bridge, child, to the Cranes in the Vintry,
> And see there the gimblets, how they make their entry.[20]

The medieval and Tudor bridge was a riot of overhanging shops with market stalls and a chapel. There was even a public convenience, one of the first in the world, at the southern end. In the severe winters of the mini ice age of the fifteenth–seventeenth centuries, the bridge's buttresses slowed the river and the ice covered it 18 inches deep. Frost Fairs were held on the glassy surface, with eel pies and roast ox for sale and jugglers and acrobats to entertain the crowd.

But all that changed with the warmer weather and the bridge itself changed with the coming of the great docks and steam. In January 1815, the London newspapers announced 'the public are informed that the new London steam-boat packet *Margery*, under Captain Cortis, will start precisely 10 o'clock on Monday morning the 23rd inst. from Wapping Old Stairs near London Bridge'.[21] The great architect John Rennie built the new bridge which was opened, with bands playing and flags flying, by George IV in 1827. It had only five arches, the central one being 152 feet long. In 1887 it had policemen stationed along it to keep traffic moving, but even so there was frequent gridlock. Dickens advised staying away from the place in rush hour.

The Thames below London Bridge which Dickens did not describe is now almost unrecognizable, but the ghost of 1887 was captured, fortuitously, by a series of panoramic photographs of both sides of the river taken by the Port of London Authority in 1937. Much of what we see in these astonishing pictures was destroyed by the Luftwaffe in the Second World War, when, at the height of the Blitz, the river seemed like a flow of molten lava and the East End became a rubble-strewn shambles. Dickens dismisses London Docks in a mere fourteen lines, but they were the largest in the world in 1887 and provided work for thousands.

Part of the reason for the lack of awareness about the importance of Dockland is that virtually all the comings and goings of ships went on behind solid walls that were 20 feet high. Unless Londoners worked in the docks, they were an unknown quantity. Virginia Woolf wrote about them in the 1930s, but she could have been describing the Victorian riverscape:

> If we turn and go past the anchored ships towards London, we see surely the most dismal prospect in the world. The banks of the river are lined with dingy, decrepit-looking warehouses. They huddle on land that has become flat and slimy mud ... Behind the masts and funnels lies a sinister dwarf city of workmen's houses. In the foreground cranes and warehouses, scaffolding and gasometers line the banks with a skeleton architecture.[22]

By that time there were 1,700 wharves and warehouses along the Thames from Brentford to Gravesend.

As we glide past London Bridge, the church of St Magnus the Martyr and the Monument are clearly visible beyond the warehouses at Hammond's and Cock's Quay. Both these buildings are reminders of the terrible four nights of fire that destroyed the medieval city, 6,000 of its shops and houses and killed six of its citizens. Such was the heat in the old St Paul's in 1666 that the stones exploded like cannonballs and terrified Londoners swore they saw French and Dutch warships on the river, firing broadsides at them.[23]

On the south side of the Thames, in the congested area which was once the stews of Southwark, stood Shakespeare's Globe and the other Jacobean theatres, jostling with bear-pits and brothels, most of them on land belonging to the Bishop of Winchester. There were granaries and mills here too, prefiguring the industrial river of the nineteenth century. The owners of Hay's Wharf carried out extensive modernization in the 1850s, employing thousands of dockers. Despite the two-week blaze of the warehouses in Tooley Street in 1861, the area survived intact at the time of our river trip.

This is the Upper Pool and already by 1887 most of the little alleyways that led to the river between the legal and sufferance quays had gone.[24] To the east of the Tower, with its familiar turreted keep, its Yeomen warders and its ravens, lay the oldest of the London docks, St Katherine's, a 23½ acre site built originally as Howland Great Dock in the late 1820s. The densely packed streets with their estimated 11,000 inhabitants were demolished as architects Thomas Telford and Philip Hardwick got to work. The Custom House, where Geoffrey Chaucer once worked as Comptroller of the King's Wines and Woollens, regulated the docks from here. Irongate and St Katherine's Wharf dominated the skyline with the grim, high-walled architecture and swinging cranes which now ran all the way to the sea.

Truman's beer was loaded and unloaded at the Black Eagle Wharf and officials of the Dock Company lived in pierhead houses alongside the narrow entrance to Wapping Dock. John Rennie built this in 1805, just along from the Red Cow Inn at Wapping Stairs where, legend has it, the hanging judge, James Jefferies, was caught trying to flee the country in 1688. Oliver's Wharf was still new in 1887, elegant in its Gothic frontage.

The iconic Tower Bridge existed only as a blueprint when Dickens was writing. On the South Bank, Mark Brown's Wharf ran alongside Pickle Herring and St Olave's. Pickle Herring Stairs was the new subterranean crossing point of the river, a subway that carried passengers via cable-drawn trams. Coffee and cocoa were unloaded at Wilson's Wharf and Hay's and Humphrey's Docks were designed by William Snooke and Harry Stock and built by the greatest of all the Victorian building firms, Thomas Cubitt.

On the north bank, Old Aberdeen Wharf replaced the earlier Sun Wharf that lay next to Wapping Police Station at 259 Wapping Stairs. The men stationed here would find themselves very busy in the months of 1887–9.

The river arches once more at Shadwell, flowing on to Limehouse and Poplar. Dickens, anxious to paint an idyllic and quaint picture of the river, glosses over Limehouse Reach in five lines and does not mention Shadwell at all. There was a six hundred-year history of lime kilns in the area, but in Dickens's day the place was still Chinatown with a reputation of oriental skulduggery in opium dens.

Across the river was Bermondsey, the eye or island of Bearmund. A Cluniac abbey stood here in the fourteenth century, but by Shakespeare's time the 'Stink' industries had gathered in its place: the gluemakers and hide workers.

Street names reflect these trades – Leathermarket, Morocco, Tanner – and the hatters of Bermondsey were among those who breathed in the mercury solution said to drive them mad. The place had been torn down by 1887, but Jacob's Island had been the most notorious of the river's rookeries for sixty years, standing on barnacle-encrusted stilts out of the slimy mud and home to thieves real and fictional.

The huge East India Docks ran along the north bank from Orchard Wharf to that loop of the river that skirted the Isle of Dogs. There were still tea-clippers sailing sedately up river in Dickens's day, but the advent of steamships and the opening of the Suez Canal twenty years earlier meant that their death-knell was already sounding. Steamers ran from here to London Bridge every half an hour, at a cost of 6d (forward) or 4d (aft). Horse-drawn omnibuses ran to the Bank of England, fare unknown.

Rotherhithe had been a haven for Saxon sailors and the Pilgrim Fathers sailed from here on the *Mayflower* in 1620 hoping for a better life in the land of the free. The Baltic Docks specialized in timber and grain, but sulphur from Sicily was also unloaded along this river frontage.

Across from the Isle of Dogs where the peninsula – 'the Great Dismal Swamp' as Dickens called it – had been made into a virtual island by the cutting of a canal, stood Deptford, the 'deep ford' of Henry VIII's shipbuilders. The Raven's Bourne enters the Thames here and the water was deep enough for ocean-going ships of the sixteenth century to be built. Martin Frobisher sailed from here in 1576 in search of a North-West Passage to Cathay (China) and his arch-nemesis Francis Drake was knighted on the deck of his own ship by the Queen here after his successful circumnavigation of the globe. The Russian Tsar, Peter the Great, stayed at John Evelyn's house at Sayes Court in the late 1690s before taking back ideas and blueprints for his own extensive harbour and wharves at his new model city at St Petersburg. The Royal Victoria Victualling Yard ran to some 35 acres to the east, a headquarters for all supplies to the largest navy in the world by 1887. Clothing, food, tobacco and rum were all housed here, as well as slaughterhouses, sawmills, biscuit, chocolate and mustard and pepper factories, brewhouses and sail lofts. Smallpox patients were kept in isolation on two ships moored along Greenwich Reach. The distinctive funnels were black and brown to warn foreign shipping to keep away and the windows were of frosted glass.

Greenwich stood out as a shining beacon in a grubby world. The Naval College Hospital and Observatory was built on the site of the old royal palace of Placentia and Daniel Defoe wrote that the water there was 'very sweet and fresh, especially at the ebb of the tide'.[25] The historian Lord Macaulay was hugely impressed by the new building – 'A monument, the most superb that was ever erected to any sovereign'.[26] It was built by William III in memory of his wife, Mary, to a design by Christopher Wren. By the time Dickens wrote, the place was no longer home to naval veterans, but contained a naval museum, in which the coat and vest worn by Nelson on the deck of the *Victory* in October 1805 could be seen by a public admitted free.

Blackwall, on the sharp river bend below Greenwich, was part of the East and West India Docks and, as the Thames straightened, the Victoria and Albert Docks lay side by side to the north. Woolwich, straight ahead, still contained troubled waters in the 1880s, with sudden shallows and unexpected deeps. The water here is salt and in Dickens's day the area was dominated by the huge arsenal and the associated officer training school known as 'The Shop' by generations of artillerymen and engineers. This was a high security area in 1887. Visitors had to have special tickets provided by the War Office and foreigners could only obtain these through their various embassies. Anyone could enjoy the music however, courtesy of the Royal Artillery whose band played on the common or in the Repository Grounds at five in the afternoon between May and October.

Opposite the Plumstead Marshes stood Barking Creek, another tributary river which had a long history. According to Kipling at least, 'Norseman and Negro, Gaul and Greek, drank with the Britons in Barking Creek'. He may have been right, because a sixth-century BC water-pitcher of Greek design was found in the river mud here some years ago. There was a medieval abbey on the site and for centuries the Coe family were watermen in the area.

The village of Rainham is one of the least prepossessing we have seen. The docks have given way here to the start of the flat monotony of the Essex marshes. We steam along Halfway Road and past Frog Island, the little promontory that juts out at the creek. We have no panoramic photograph of the place – those taken by the Port Authority in 1937 end at Woolwich. Modern maps are unhelpful. But on the morning of Wednesday 11 May 1887, the day that we have sailed downstream in our virtual journey, there was a commotion on the north bank, by the river wall at Falls Point, near Mr Hempleman's factory. There was a group of workmen standing at the water's edge and there was a policeman with them, kneeling down, peering at something on the foreshore. It was difficult to tell at this distance what it was. It appeared to be a bundle of sacking, old, saturated.

But inside it was something white, bloodless. It was a human body, but it had no arms. It had no legs. It had no head.

Chapter 2

The River of Death

There are other ways to look at the Thames. Dickens was telling the boating public about the pleasures of the river as part of the growing Victorian leisure industry. The Port of London Authority photographs were taken with the sense of a passing era – the Docks were already in decline by 1937 before the Luftwaffe added immeasurably to the collateral damage.

But there was another side to the Thames – there still is. The body parts floating off the jetty at Rainham were not the first example of violent death that the river had thrown up. The poet Shelley said to Thomas Love Peacock that the Thames 'runs with the blood and bones of a thousand heroes and villains and no doubt the water is sour with tainting'.[1]

Because the river was a natural barrier, it was likely to have been the frontier between the Celtic tribes to the north and south of it. On the upper reaches the Atrebates in what would become Surrey fought with the Catuvellauni of present-day Hertfordshire. Nearer the sea, the Trinovantes of the Essex marshes would have clashed occasionally with the Kent-based Cantiaci and the river would have run red. When the Romans landed in 54 BC, their commander, Julius Caesar, batted aside the Cantiaci and made for the only safe river crossing on the Thames at a time when it was wider and shallower than today. He crossed the river with ten cohorts and 300 cavalry, the equivalent of a legion, and clashed immediately with the able Celtic chief Cassivelaunus, who was almost certainly waiting for him. How many died, and where, we do not know.

The second Roman invasion in AD 43, led by Aulus Plautius, was altogether larger and would mark the beginning of a permanent occupation. Marching west from Thanet, then an island created by the Wantsum river, Plautius' legions crossed the Medway and fought an epic battle there before driving the Celts back to the Thames somewhere in the region of the Higham Marshes opposite Tilbury. The Batavian auxiliaries with the Roman forces were particularly adept at river crossings and the historian Dio Cassius wrote:

some others got over by a bridge a little way upstream after which they assailed the barbarians [Celts] from several sides at once and cut down many of them. But they were incautious in their pursuit of the rest, got themselves entrapped in impossible marshes and lost many men.[2]

London itself was only a village then and the legions made next for Camulodunum (Colchester) as the largest town, which they probably assumed was a capital city on the lines of Rome.

Thirty years later, the Roman grip on Britain was seriously challenged by Boudicca, the warrior queen of the Iceni whose lands lay in Norfolk and Suffolk. Having burned Camulodunum to the ground, her next target was the rapidly expanding 'frontier town' of Londinium, a symbol of the aggressive mercantilism for which the Romans were famous. The traders, metalworkers and spinners who comprised most of Londinium's workforce were put to the sword by Boudicca. Dio Cassius, writing over a century later and with inevitable bias, said:

Those who were taken captive by the Britons were subjected to every known form of outrage ... They hung up naked the noblest and most distinguished women and cut off their breasts and sewed them to their mouths, in order to make the victim appear to be eating them; afterwards they impaled the women on sharp skewers run lengthwise through the bodies.[3]

Almost the only tangible evidence of Boudicca's attack is three skulls, carbon-dated to the period (AD 60) which were found in the Walbrook, a tributary of the Thames. Boudicca's entire campaign was written up years later by the Romans – the Celts had no written language – and the Romans are notorious for exaggeration. The assumption that these skulls are Boudiccan can be challenged. They are of young males and scraping marks on the bone surface indicate that the flesh was deliberately removed. This has an altogether more sinister connotation and may account for thousands of bodies that, at various early times, were dumped into the Thames.

Peter Ackroyd makes the point that 'there is a curious connection between the Thames and severed heads'.[4] Over 300 skulls have been discovered in the river silt, from the Neolithic to the Iron Age period. In 1857, less than twenty years before the first of the torso murders that form the heart of this book, a paper was produced called 'On the discovery of Celtic crania in the vicinity of London'. Battersea Reach, where body parts would be found in September 1873, was referred to in various archaeological journals by Henry Cuming as a 'Celtic Golgotha' (the place of the skull). Kew and Hammersmith have produced heads, as have Mortlake and Richmond. The cult of the severed head was important to the Celts. Warriors decapitated their battlefield enemies and tied their heads to their saddles or chariots. In peacetime, they placed them on poles outside their homes. And the Celts held water to be sacred. A river like the Thames had a persona of its own. It was a god and votive offerings must be made to it. Coins, weapons and above all, human heads, were deliberately placed in the Thames to keep the river safe, to keep the water sweet. What is odd about the eight torso victims is that not one of them had a head.

The novelist Charles Dickens, no stranger to the police or sudden death, wrote of the Thames in *Night Walks* (1860):

The river had an awful look, the buildings on the banks were muffled in black shrouds and the reflected light seemed to originate deep in the water, as if the spectres [of the dead] were holding them to show where they went down. The wild moon and clouds were as restless as an evil conscience in a tumbled bed and the very shadow of the immensity of London seemed to lie oppressively upon the water.[5]

The river claimed a number of souls through sheer accident. Most affected, naturally, were the ferrymen, weir-keepers and locksmen who were at the mercy of the fastest-flowing, most turbulent stretches. The lock at Great Marlow was one of the most lethal, known as Marlow Race for the speed of the current. Sixty people died in 1647 near Goring in Berkshire when the weir dragged their boat down. The most dangerous section of the Thames before the opening of the new one in 1817 was the old London Bridge, but the increase in boating for leisure seventy years later led to more drowning than ever. There were more amateurs, on punts and skiffs, unused to boats or water. Many of them wore unsuitable clothing, especially the women whose heavy dresses held them under the surface. Others were drunk. Sometimes the fog got them, hiding the water's edge until it was too late. 'Fog everywhere,' wrote Charles Dickens in *Bleak House*, 'Fog up the river, where it flows among green aits and meadows; fog down the river, where it rolls defiled among the tiers of shipping and the waterside pollutions of a great and dirty city.'

The worst accident on the Thames took place on 3 September 1878. The *Princess Alice* was a pleasure steamer returning from a day trip to Gravesend. It was evening and she was negotiating the bend by Galleon's Reach, between Crossness and Margaret Ness. when she was hit amidships by a steam-collier, the *Bywell Castle*. There seems to have been confusion over signalling and the *Alice* sank in less than four minutes. 'I can compare the people,' wrote an eyewitness, 'to nothing else than a flock of sheep in the water ... The river seemed full of drowning people.'⁶ A diver sent down into the murky depths the next day found bodies still upright, jammed against the saloon doors where they had tried to get out. An estimated 700 people died, but not all by drowning. Only an hour before the boats collided 75 million gallons of sewage and toxic waste had been pumped out of the Barking and Crossness stations. It was this that the frantically swimming survivors gulped in as they made for the shore. Bodies, alive and dead, were covered in a slime which could not be washed off; the smell was horrendous. Because the corpses bloated so quickly, specially large coffins had to be made for them. They were buried in a mass grave at Woolwich cemetery. Perhaps the most peculiar thing about the *Princess Alice* disaster and one that puts the torso murders into a kind of context, is that 160 of the dead were never claimed.

If war, sacrifice and fate have left corpses in the Thames, so has crime. One of the first recorded pleasure trips on the river took place in October 1555 when an enterprising trader from Abingdon took passengers upriver to Oxford to see the public burning of Bishops Ridley and Latimer in the city square. It was a damp day and the men took an estimated two hours to die. Their 'crime' of course, was belonging to the wrong religious denomination, Protestants in a Catholic land. In some ways, the Abingdon trader was playing the part of Charon, the ferryman of Greek legend, whose role it was to carry the souls of the departed into Hades across the waters of the Styx. For several centuries, it was the custom to place coins in a dead man's hand, on his eyes or even in his mouth to pay the ferryman.

Religion and murder went hand in hand too in the death of Aelfheah, Archbishop of Canterbury, in 1012. A group of drunken Vikings led by a man named Thrym assaulted the Archbishop at their camp at Greenwich and beat him to death on the river bank with ox bones and an axe-head, 'so that with the blow he sank down and his holy blood fell on the earth and sent forth his holy soul to God's kingdom'.⁷ A shrine was built in his memory which is now Nicholas Hawksmoor's seventeenth-century church.

If the river itself did not provide the watery grave of murder victims, it was certainly the way to death. Thomas More was probably the most famous official victim of the Reformation and he entered the Tower, where he was beheaded in 1535, via Traitor's Gate, the river entrance to the castle. In one variant of the legend of the Princes in the same Tower, the bodies of the boys murdered in 1483 were taken from the castle by their assassins and dumped downriver in a place called the 'Black Deepes'.

London Bridge, with its shopping precinct and its rapids, was also a necropolis. As the entrance point to London for most people coming from the south, it was the obvious place to make a statement. 'To encourage the others'⁸ the heads or even other body parts of traitors were skewered on poles and left to rot, a perpetual reminder to behave in a volatile society. William Wallace may have been a nationalist hero to the Scots, but the English hanged, drew and quartered him as a murderer and rebel. His head was spiked for the public's delight on 23 August 1305. The renegade Jack Cade followed a similar fate in 1450. Appalled at the government of the usurper-king Henry IV, Cade led an estimated 40,000 men on London, but they were dispersed and he himself was caught and killed on the Sussex coast. A German visitor in 1598 counted thirty heads on the bridge, along with so many arms and legs that the place looked like a butcher's shambles. Like most of the public demonstrations for deterrent purposes, there is no evidence that the ghastly sights had any effect and the body parts were probably regarded as part of the street furniture.

Witchcraft was linked with the Thames too. In 984 the *Codes Diplomatias Aevi Saxonici* refers to a woman condemned for making a wooden effigy of a man. Such 'poppets' emerge with some frequency by the sixteenth century and are associated with sympathetic magic, the idea of causing harm to a living individual by damaging a likeness of that individual. She was drowned at London Bridge. At Kingston in the summer of 1572, a ducking stool was set up. This was not the traditional 'swimming' test for a witch, but a punishment meted out to scolds, a crime which still exists, but carries no penalty! Two or three thousand people turned out in 1745 to watch the female keeper of the King's Head get her comeuppance.

Places of execution were deliberately built close to the river, as though there was an ancient link between death and the Thames. Both Smithfield and Tyburn were execution sites and they are tributaries of the Thames. Smithfield was the open ground used for tournaments and fairs that straddled the Fleet. Martyrs were burned here for their faith under Mary Tudor. The 'triple tree' at Tyburn marked London's most famous hanging ground, long after the old tree itself had fallen down. The gallows at Dagenham on the Thames itself was still in use in 1780 and gibbets – iron cages in which rotting corpses were suspended – stood at intervals on both sides of the banks. Peter Ackroyd speculates that the 'lost river', one of the Thames's tributaries, known as the Neckinger means the devil's neck-cloth, a euphemism for the rope. The Neckinger ran into the mother-river at Butler's Wharf near Tower Bridge.

Deptford was associated with death for two reasons. Called for a time Deadman's Dock, it was the burial place for the prisoners who died in large numbers aboard the hulks, the ex-warships that served as floating gaols along the river. Over a century earlier, it had been the murder site of the playwright Christopher Marlowe. In May 1593 he visited an 'ordinary', an eating house belonging to Eleanor Bull somewhere on Deptford Strand near the shipyards.

By nightfall he was dead, a dagger thrust into his eyesocket and brain. Most accounts write off the episode as a tavern brawl but, considering Marlowe's lifestyle and that of at least one man in the murder room with him – they were both spies – it seems much more likely that this was a political assassination.[9]

Execution Dock stood at the entrance to what became St Katherine's Dock in 1829. It moved further downstream to Wapping in the sixteenth century and was traditionally the place of execution for sailors or sea-related criminals. The buccaneer Henry Morgan narrowly escaped being sent there in the 1670s. Criminals were hanged by the riverside, then their bodies were covered in pitch or tar and they were lowered by chains shackled to posts into the swirling water. They were left here until three tides had washed over them, although some remained for far longer.

> Take her up tenderly
> Lift her with care;
> Fashion'd so slenderly
> Young, and so fair!
> Look at her garments
> Clinging like cerements;
> Whilst the wave constantly
> Drips from her clothing.
> Take her up instantly,
> Loving, not loathing ...[10]

So wrote Thomas Hood, one of the most sentimental of the Victorian poets. He is describing the removal of a prostitute's body from the Thames – Waterloo Bridge was a favourite spot – and he is talking about suicide. Despite the fact that, in London, the Serpentine and the canals accounted for more suicides in the Victorian period, it was the Thames that had the older tradition. 'Found in the Thames' was a staple conclusion to coroners' reports and inquests as though something drew the poor, the oppressed, the desperate to its embankments, its bridges, its wharves and jetties. 'The Thames', writes Peter Ackroyd, 'is a river of the disappeared ... a great vortex of suffering.'[11] Dead Man's Steps at Wapping was so called because the peculiarities of the tide and current washed up so many corpses there. Dead Man's Island in the river's estuary was the last resting place of cholera victims in the mid-nineteenth century. When they built Tower Bridge in 1894, they included, near the entrance to the Tower itself, Dead Man's Hole, a temporary mortuary for bodies fished out of the water.

The French, always anxious to believe the worst about the British, understood the Thames to be the country's suicide capital. In the late eighteenth century the writer Pierre Grosley suggested that the clutter of wharves and boatyards along the banks was an attempt to deflect would-be suicides from throwing themselves in. In earlier times of course, when the country was still Catholic, suicide was a mortal sin – the soul of a suicide would not find heaven and the body could not be interred in holy ground. Alice de Waynewick nevertheless jumped into the river at Dowgate 'being non compos mentis'.[12] Some suicides no doubt imagined that drowning would be quick and painless, rather like falling asleep. The reality is different. 'Lord, Lord,' Shakespeare's Duke of Clarence says in *Richard III* while awaiting his murder in the Tower, 'methought what pain it was to drown; what dreadful noise of water in mine ears'. Samuel Pepys was told by a waterman in February 1666 of the inn-keeper of the Bear near London Bridge who had suicidal tendencies and eventually succeeded. Twenty years later, the son of Sir William Temple, Secretary for War, leapt into the crashing waters under London Bridge with his pockets full of stones. This was at the point called the maelstrom, where the river is particularly dark and the eddies whirl with a malevolence of their own.

Peter Ackroyd cites a number of nineteenth-century suicides. It was perhaps the speed of that century's growth in London, and the ever-widening gap between rich and poor, which made 'jumpers' more frequent than before. At Henley, a footman whose own brother had died in a drowning accident, drowned himself in a bathing costume. A working man, distraught at the death of his baby, tied his hands and feet so that he could not struggle against the current. Perhaps three or four bodies were recovered each week, although it is difficult to be sure of the cause of death. The 'Bridge of Sighs' of which Thomas Hood wrote was a swing bridge near St Peter's church in the docks. Waterloo Bridge came to be known as Lover's Leap or the Bridge of Sorrow because of the large numbers of such incidents there. Later in the century a boat was moored nearby, specially adapted to haul bodies into it. In 1882 544 bodies were recovered from the Thames. Of these 277 received open verdicts at the coroners' inquests, sometimes because no one came forward to identify them. Saddest of all were the newly born infants found floating in a world that could not afford to keep them.

One of the saddest suicides was that of Montague John Druitt, who has been put forward since the 1960s as a possible suspect for the Whitechapel murders of the 1880s which are bound inextricably with the central theme of this book. The evidence against Druitt is almost non-existent; his name occurs in the infamous Macnaghten Memoranda, random jottings by the Assistant Commissioner at Scotland Yard written in 1894 and naming three innocent men as possible suspects, Druitt among them. His suicide however is beyond doubt. At about one o'clock on the afternoon of Monday 31 December 1888, waterman Henry Winslade found his body floating in the river near Thorneycroft's Wharf, Chiswick. Constable George Moulson, the first policeman on the scene, searched the body and found two cheques drawn on the London and Provincial Bank, two first-class railway tickets, a pair of gloves, a gold watch and £2 17s 2d in cash. Most telling of all were the four large stones in each of the overcoat pockets.

At the inquest held at the Lamb Tap pub in Chiswick three days later, a note was read out which had been found at Druitt's chambers (he was a barrister): 'Since Friday I felt I was going to be like mother and the best thing for me was to die.' In the previous July his mother Ann had been admitted to the Brooke Asylum for Lunatics in Clapton. This pattern, with its inevitable conclusion of suicide 'while the balance of the mind was disturbed', was all too common along the river reaches.

Cashing in on this grisly situation were the dredgermen, whose work Charles Dickens describes in *Our Mutual Friend*. The social commentator Henry Mayhew wrote:

> Dredgers are the men who foul almost all the bodies of persons drowned. If there be a reward offered for the recovery of a body, numbers of dredgers will at once endeavour to obtain it … no body recovered by a dredgerman ever happens to have any money about it, when brought ashore.[13]

Five shillings was paid to anyone collecting bodies from the Surrey side of the river. They were photographed by the 1890s and taken to a variety of mortuaries, like St George's in the East or Whitechapel Infirmary Workhouse in Eagle Place. Members of the public could visit to identify corpses and collect clothing and belongings. After that anyone unclaimed was buried in a pauper's grave.

The men who policed the river, whose job it was to cope with its crime and violence, were traditionally two inches shorter than their counterparts in the Met and their institution, later called Thames Division, was thirty years older. Their motto was *Primus Omnium* (First of All) and they are probably the world's oldest police force.

By the 1790s the Port of London, even before the building of the sprawling docks, was the busiest and richest in the world. Three-quarters of the country's trade goods, estimated to be worth about £75 million a year, passed up the river and the whole area was lawless. Gangs known as 'light horsemen' robbed unarmed vessels of their goods before they could be unloaded. Others connived with corrupt revenue officers to cream off a portion of the cargo, aided by unscrupulous watermen and 'lumpers' (dockers). An estimated £500,000 was lost in revenue to the government each year. By day, 'heavy horsemen', with special pockets sewn inside their trouser legs, wobbled precariously on the decks of their barges and wherries, weighed down with sugar, tea and coffee which were still luxury commodities with a huge tax on them.

The goods were usually passed to receivers in the pubs and brothels along the shore and the savagery of the 'bloody code' by which men and women could be hanged for even minor offences meant that, in the rare event of a court case, juries would usually fail to convict.

Into this chaos stepped two men whose unlikely partnership drew a line in the sand as far as river crime was concerned. Patrick Colquhoun had had a full and varied career as a businessman trading with the American colonies before settling first in Glasgow as one of the city's leading commercial lights and then in London as a stipendiary magistrate. John Harriott had been both a naval and an army officer before a musket ball smashed his thigh on service with the East India Company. He then settled in Essex as Surveyor of Roads. Both men became caught up in various defence roles during the war against Revolutionary France, but in 1795 Colquhoun published *A Treatise on the Police of the Metropolis* recommending the creation of a river police. Living at Wapping, he had ample opportunity to see at first hand the 'depredations which have been heretofore experienced' but 'improving the morals of the maritime labourers'[14] was probably a pious hope.

Three years later Colquhoun and Harriott were effectively given the task of cleaning up the Port of London. Their headquarters was 259 Wapping High Street, the back of which overlooked the river. Funding for their work was provided partly by the government and partly by the shipping companies who had been losing so much profit by the vast scale of theft.

The original River Police was made up of surveyors, land officers, constables and quay guards, together with the more reliable watermen and lumpers. They were armed with cudgels, cutlasses and firearms which must only be used in self-defence. At the top of the institutional tree the six surveyors received between £75 and £100 a year each, considerably better pay relatively than the detectives of other divisions who would work on the torso cases seventy years later. At the bottom, the watermen received £1 3s a week plus 10 percent of the contraband recovered. The great pressures on police forces – succumbing to drunkenness and bribe taking – would be met with dismissal. Ship's captains could request the presence of constables on board their vessels while moored anywhere along the river, working alongside customs officers to reduce smuggling and outright theft. Lanterns in the ship's rigging showed the presence of a constable at night to deter would-be thieves.

The River Police were still essentially a private security force. Attempts at creating a fully organized, government-funded body of men to replace the wholly inadequate system of parish constables ('charlies')[15] had always foundered, not only on the cost but on the average Englishman's belief that such a force would be used as a private army by the government of the day. Despite this opposition, however, an Act of Parliament created the Thames Marine Police in July 1800. By the time Robert Peel at the Home Office created the Met (1829) the still separate River Police had three stations along the Thames. The original Middle Station was at Wapping; the Upper Station was on board the *Port Mahon*, moored off Somerset House; and the Lower Station was in a small building at Blackwall. Fifteen rowing galleys, each carrying a four-man unit, plied the river day and night between London Bridge and Deptford.

Ten years later in the increased centralization that was a marked characteristic of nineteenth-century government, the Marine Police disappeared into the expanding Met, to be called simply Thames Division. In some respects however, the River Police retained an air of individuality. They wore straw hats in the summer and reefer jackets with white shirts. Photographs taken as late as the 1890s appear to show men in police galleys in fancy dress, but it is actually official uniform.

A new Wapping police station was opened in 1872, with a yard alongside for the maintenance of the galleys. The *Investigator* replaced the *Mahon* in 1836 and after 1864 the *Royalist* (referred to in press reports on the torso murders) was moored off Blackwall. In the decade in which the torso murders began, Thames Division was divided into four watches, each six hours long, so that in effect the river was constantly patrolled. Plainclothesmen arrived in the form of one detective sergeant and three detective constables three years before the creation of Howard Vincent's Criminal Investigation Department in 1878.

Like his more famous father, Dickens had definite views on the detective police on the Thames. He noted that arrests fell from 107 in 1875 to 88 the next year and 73 in 1877. At the beginning of the Ripper's year (1888) Superintendent Skeats of Thames Division believed that this was the result of declining crime of all types because of the deterrent effect of his men. What is interesting is that Scotland Yard itself began to doubt the need for specialist river detectives. In fact when it was suggested in April 1884 that Thames Division's jurisdiction be extended upriver to include patrols between Battersea Bridge and Teddington, the Commissioner asked for volunteers from T and V Divisions to row there on their rest days! The arrival of the torso killer should have made them all reconsider.

In May 1888, the force numbered 200 men led by a chief inspector. Under him were seven inspectors, forty sub-inspectors, 147 constables and five detectives. Two steam launches had been added to the fleet of twenty oar-driven galleys, one for use by a visiting superintendent (Skeats in 1888) and the other, called *The Alert*, to watch the bridges. An article in the *Illustrated London News* for that month noted grimly that the Waterloo police station had the largest share of suicides. The boat permanently moored there, as we have seen, had a special roller fitted to the stern to make hauling bodies out of the water easier. According to this account, there were twenty-five suicides in 1887 and Thames Division was able to prevent a further fifteen.

These people were charged – attempted or actual suicide was a crime until 1961 – and received what today we would call counselling from a prison chaplain. 'If once they are rescued,' said the police spokesman, 'they seldom try the river again' – although of course there is no way of tracing what other means they tried.

The Waterloo police station is described as 'very cosy'. An inspector and his wife had private rooms there and there was a charge room and office. The reserve room was where the constables hung their oil skins and a special room, fitted with a bed and a bath with hot and cold water, was available for attempted suicides.

At Wapping, the Division's headquarters, a collection of photographs was kept permanently of the bodies of those found drowned to aid identification.

Half a century later, Molly Lefebure was secretary to Dr Keith Simpson, the Home Office pathologist during the Second World War and found herself attending more crime scenes than any woman had done before. One routine day went:

> Three cases at Hackney, one a suspected food poisoning, two at Walthamstow, one an old woman fell out of bed, the other an infanticide. A suicide at Wandsworth cut throat. Two straight cases and a drowner at Southwark.[16]

One unusual, river-related suicide she reported took place at Battersea in 1942. Among the gruesome souvenirs that 'CKS' collected was a heavy metal weight and a note which read 'I expect you will find me over Battersea bridge – if you are interested.' The note's writer had fastened one end of the rope to the weight and the other around his neck. Police found his hanged body the next day.

But we are not concerned with suicides or accidental drowning or ancient votive offerings. We are concerned with murder and one series of murders in particular. In 1568 George Napier, a Jesuit priest operating clandestinely in what was now essentially a Protestant country, was hanged, drawn and quartered at Oxford. His severed body was thrown without ceremony into the Thames but by the time it reached Sandford, three miles to the south, it had, according to certain eyewitnesses, become whole again.

This would not happen to the torso killer's victims – their bodies remained separate for ever.

Chapter 3

'Found Dead': Rainham, May 1887

It was a little after dawn on Wednesday 11 May 1887 that lighterman Edward Hughes saw something floating in the water. In common with thousands of men along the Thames, his job was to transfer goods aboard the flat-bottomed barges called lighters, from ship to shore. In the May of 1887, Hughes was working in the Victoria Dock that ran from Bugsby's Reach where the Greenwich Marshes jutted north and made the river bend to Albert Docks lying alongside.

That morning, Hughes was on his barge lying alongside the jetty at Hempleman's Factory. The ebb tide was flowing fast by then and he hauled the floating bundle up on deck. Any experienced lighterman would not have found this odd. As we have seen, half London used the Thames as a dumping ground and it was not that unusual to find 'floaters' in the water. Writing a few years later, R Austin Freeman travelled through dockland in a steamer and noticed a rowing boat with three uniformed men in it.

> Suddenly, the man in the stern stands up and all three stare fixedly at what appears to be a submerged basket floating down in mid-stream … As they reach it the coxswain takes a length of thin rope and seizes the floating object and for an instant a human head appears above the surface. Then the boat starts off again and we see that the line has been made fast to the derelict, now towed astern and rolling over and over at the end of the cord with a horrid semblance to life. We realize that the mysterious boat belongs to the Thames police and that presently another poster bearing the words 'Found Dead' will appear among the collection of bills which decorate the door of the riverside mortuary.[1]

Rainham appears as a small village in Domesday in 1087 and by the time of its 'mystery' in 1887 had a population of 1,669. The church of St Helen and St Giles was the only building standing from its medieval past. The wharf had been developed since the 1720s to carry farm produce upriver to London and a new one, with a retaining flood wall, had been built in 1872. The marshes here are only 5 feet above sea level, a situation made even wetter by the existence of the Ingrebourne Tributary at the western end of the parish. Frederick Hempleman & Co was one of several manufacturers clustered around the ferry area that produced artificial manure.

Hughes took the bundle ashore. It was a coarse canvas sack and in it was the pallid, waterlogged torso of a female. The arms, legs and head had gone and a section of both breasts had been hacked away. Horrified, Hughes sent a colleague for a policeman. He found Constable Stock of the Essex constabulary and they carried the remains to the ferry building. Unusually thorough for a provincial 'copper', Stock noted that the cord around the sack had been wound round several times and he got a message through to his superior, Inspector Allen. A number of officers were detailed to search the area, knocking on doors, wading about in the shallow water, checking anywhere where other body parts could have lodged.

It was fairly obvious to the authorities that Rainham itself was a red herring. For all the press dubbed the finding of the woman's remains the 'Rainham Mystery', the true source of that mystery probably lay much further upstream. But the law said that all corpses found in an area were that area's responsibility and, as Rainham had no mortuary or coroner's court, the torso was placed in a shed next to the Phoenix Hotel in readiness for the inquest which would open in the hotel on Saturday 14 May.

The coroner was C C Lewis, covering the South Essex district and once the jury were sworn, he explained the circumstances surrounding the finding of the torso. His first witness was Dr Edward Galloway, the police surgeon from nearby Barking (the Met's R Division), who had carried out a post-mortem on the remains. In accordance with the medical practice of the time, he reported on what he saw and made various extrapolations later. The legs and thighs had been removed with a perfectly straight cut made with a very sharp saw, leaving the last two bones of the lumbar vertebrae, the tendons and muscle tissue around this having been cut by a keen-edged knife. The same blade had passed through and separated the abdominal wall. The upper portion of the breasts, the head, arms and legs had all been removed, the lower limbs taken cleanly out of their pelvic sockets by means of cutting obliquely from the inside to the out. All cuts were clean, with no signs of jadedness and the work, in Galloway's opinion, was that of an expert. The fact that there was no sign of external violence – no extraneous cuts or bruising – meant that it was impossible to say exactly how the victim died.

Galloway believed that the body had been dead for about two weeks. That took the likely date of the murder, which this clearly was, to the beginning of

May. He estimated the victim's probable height as 5ft 3ins or 5ft 4ins, making her infuriatingly average and estimated that her hair was brown (although without pubic or armpit hair, this had to be conjecture). He believed her to have been in her late twenties, but she could have been as old as 35. He told the court:

> The general appearances led me to believe that the body had never been used as a hospital subject and it would be quite contrary to the Anatomical Act[2] for a body to be parted with without the knowledge of the hospital authorities.[3]

Pressed by the coroner, Galloway reluctantly admitted that he believed whoever had dismembered the corpse had 'a thorough knowledge of surgery'. His reasoning was sound enough:

> not only has the cutting-up been performed in an exceedingly skilful manner, but the operation had been carried out on that part of the spine offering the least resistance to separating and that would only be done by a person having a very intimate knowledge of anatomy.

What Galloway was doing, of course, and he must have been aware of this, was pointing the finger at a doctor, more specifically a surgeon and it was this, as much as the gruesomeness of the remains, that led to the press coverage. It was not yet front-page news simply because it appeared to be an isolated case.

The rest of this first day saw the testimony of Edward Hughes and his colleagues who reported their finding of the corpse. At that point, to give the police more time for their investigations, Lewis adjourned proceedings.

The problem, for the Thames River Police, the Essex constabulary and R Division was that the body could have floated from anywhere upstream, even, quite possibly, west of London. One obvious line of enquiry was to ask anyone with a female missing from their family to come forward. A North London man reported his wife missing. A Mrs Carter had disappeared from her address in Vauxhall Street, Lambeth, and Mrs Cross of Albany Terrace told police that her 'daughter of weak intelligence and fond of going on the barges on the river'[4] had also disappeared. None of these proved to be the half-body at Rainham.

When the inquest reopened on Friday 3 June, Inspector Allen gave testimony as did Superintendent Dobson of Brentwood. Neither the police nor Galloway, recalled, could give a definite cause of death. Without it, the jury had no choice but to deliver the wholly inadequate verdict of 'found dead'.

Two days later, the horror returned. As the *Essex Times* reported it on 8 June:

> On Sunday morning [5 June] great excitement was caused on the Victoria embankment on its being made known that a portion of the mutilated remains of a female had been picked up near the Temple Pier.

The pier lay halfway between Blackfriars and Waterloo Bridges along a very different part of the river from Rainham with its marshes, new road layout and burgeoning chemical works. At the landward end of the pier stood the elegant chambers of the Temple Law Courts, where future Ripper suspect M J Druitt had his office. The huge, imposing facade of Somerset House and King's College lay to the west and the Temple gardens, heavy with spring blossom, to the east. The pier itself was very busy, as a focal point for passengers taking pleasure steamers up and down the river.

Whoever saw the 'large parcel' first reported it to the pierman, J Morris, at ten o'clock. Morris fished it out of the water just below the pier and discovered that it was a human thigh, wrapped in sacking and tied with cord.

Later that day, another piece of sacking was found floating in the Thames, this time further upstream and on the south bank by Battersea Park pier along Chelsea Reach. Once again, a busy part of the river. Once again, a body part wrapped in coarse canvas. The current here is odd, with the eddies described in Chapter 1 potentially slowing the progress of anything floating. While researching this stretch I noticed however that a piece of wood, some four feet long and perhaps five inches wide was travelling downstream past the pier site in a direct line and at some speed. The River Police, who knew these currents better than anyone, conjectured that this latest find was dumped into the river off one of the bridges upstream but close by. Logically, that made it Albert or Battersea, half a mile and three-quarters of a mile away respectively, near the point at which the Wandle enters the Thames. This latest bundle was the 'upper portion of a human body'.

The first medical man to inspect the Temple Stairs find was Dr Hamerton, assistant police surgeon. He noted that the thigh had been taken cleanly out of the socket of the pelvis. The first thought from the River Police was that this was a new murder, with no connection to Rainham, but once Dr Galloway could investigate, he was of the opinion that the parts came from the same body. Once again, Galloway affirmed the apparent surgical skill required to remove the thigh and made a fascinating observation: 'These body parts have been removed with skill, not simply torn off to hide a murder.'[5]

What was certain to police and doctors was that the finds were not all placed upstream simultaneously and allowed to float downstream at the river's whim.

The Temple and Battersea finds had not been in the water that long (the skin was not wrinkled or waterlogged) and that meant that someone was placing random body parts in the river at different times and at different places.

River of death the Thames may have been, but these finds were bizarre and unprecedented. On the afternoon of Saturday 11 June a high-level conference was held at Battersea. Galloway was there, along with a colleague, another divisional police surgeon Dr Kempster and the area's coroner A Braxton Hicks. Two officers of Scotland Yard were also present – Arthur Hare and Superintendent John Shore. The seriousness of the situation was made evident by Shore's seniority – he was deputy to the Chief Constable, Adolphus ('Dolly') Williamson. Braxton Hicks was the son of a famous obstetrician and had been in post as coroner for the South West District of London for only two years at this point. Four years later, he would preside over the inquest into Matilda Clover, one of the victims of the Lambeth poisoner, Dr Neill Cream.

Another coroner, S F Langham, who would preside a year later at the inquest on Ripper victim Katherine Eddowes, had already muddied the waters of *this* murder by allowing the thigh section found at Temple Stairs to be placed in a pauper's pine coffin and sent for burial at Ilford Cemetery. With any bizarre murder, especially when the culprit is never found, there is the temptation to point the finger of conspiracy. Langham presumably had nothing to hide and could no doubt plead lack of staff and resources, but his decision was at best a dereliction of duty and sums up the general attitude about the Torso murders. An inquest on a single body part would be pointless and a waste of time. The result: the killer of at least eight women walked free.

It may be that Langham was given a suitable dressing down in private, because the Home Secretary, Henry Matthews, ordered an exhumation of the torso at Rainham, which had been buried in the local churchyard. The Ilford thigh was dug up too. Braxton Hicks ordered the preservation of the parts in spirits of wine, the conventional preservation technique of the day and the parts sealed hermetically in case other parts should turn up.

They did, days later. *The Times* reported that a 'parcel containing a portion of the remains of a human body was picked up near the spot where part of a woman's body was discovered some time since'. Unfortunately, the reporter did not record whether this was Rainham or Battersea, but the likelihood is that it was off Waterloo Pier, close to the bridge and upstream from Temple Stairs.

The final act of the Rainham tragedy was played out exactly a week later, when labourer William Gate saw a bundle floating in the waters of Regent's Canal, near the St Pancras Lock. This was a slight departure for the Torso killer. So far the Rainham body parts had all been found in the Thames itself, but the canal was an artificial waterway that ran into it and some distance from the river itself. The canal was 9 miles long and had been designed by the architect John Nash. It began in Paddington's Little Venice and flowed to the Regent's Canal Dock at Limehouse, just upriver from the West India Dock and below Shadwell. The canal itself, although popular today as a leisure area, was built too late to be commercially successful. By the 1820s when it was complete, the transport revolution was about to switch to railways.

Gate found a sack containing two human legs and reported the find at the nearest police station. The limbs had been in the water for some time (there is of course no tidal movement in a canal) and the wrinkling of the skin suggested an older woman. When Dr Galloway assembled the various parts, however, he could add yet more to the Rainham torso. On Tuesday 19 July he spoke to various reporters and *The Times* of the 21st was able to confirm that 'the entire body excepting the head and upper part of the chest, are now in the possession of the police authorities'.[6] Galloway was quoted at length.

> The thigh found in the Thames corresponded with the trunk. The chest also corresponded exactly with the trunk and had been sawn through. The collarbone and the breasts had been taken off. I have formed the opinion that the trunk had been in the water about a fortnight and that the death of the woman took place in May. I have seen the remains found at St Pancras [Regent's Canal] and I am of the opinion that they belonged to the same body.

The canvas in which the parts were wrapped was also the same, except for the thigh.

The police continued to ask for reports of missing persons to be verified by families and friends, but nothing positive came of that.

On 13 August, the Rainham drama came to a close. Dr G Danford Thomas was one of the great London coroners of his day. As coroner for Central Middlesex some of the most infamous cases came before him as a matter of routine. Now he presided over the Rainham Mystery at Crowndale Hall in Camden Town. Inevitably, as the man most concerned with the post-mortem work, Dr Galloway was there, but so too was Dr Thomas Bond, A Division's police surgeon who fifteen months later would feature prominently in the Ripper investigation.

Bond had wide experience. He graduated from King's College Hospital in 1864 and served with the Prussian army as it swept to victory over the Austrians in the war of 1866. He had been police surgeon to A Division for twenty years by the time of the Rainham case, as well as assistant chief surgeon at Westminster Hospital. He had been brought in by the Assistant Commissioner of the CID, James Munro, probably as a second opinion for the less experienced Galloway.

Bond told the inquest that the Rainham victim was a young woman between 25 and 40, between 5ft 2ins and 5ft 4ins in height and she had never given birth. 'The different parts had been divided by some persons having a knowledge of anatomy.' Galloway's testimony seemed to have shifted a little by mid-August: 'The body had been divided by someone who knew the structure of the human frame, but not necessarily a skilled anatomist.'[7] What we have here is a sense of squirming in the spotlight and a certain professional unease. It was to dog the Ripper case a year later too. If the Torso killer had sufficient anatomical skill, the likelihood was that he was a surgeon, or at least a physician. The medical profession is notorious for closing ranks when one of their own falls under suspicion.[8] 'The removal [of the head]', Bond wrote later, 'was not for the study of anatomy, but was done for the purpose of covering up a murder.'[9]

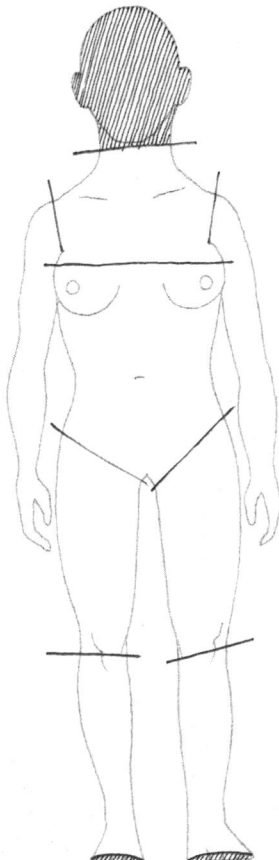

The thick black lines represent the cuts made to dissect the body. The shaded areas are the parts that were never found.

Inspector Hare told the inquest that, despite extensive enquiries all over London, no further progress had been made since the original finding of the Rainham torso. In short, the police had drawn a blank. Once again, the only possible conclusion was 'found dead'. Clearly a murder had been committed, but there were no marks on the body to indicate how. Without the remotest chance of identification, it was not possible either to know why.

Most bizarrely of all, no one, either among the police or the press seems to have thought of making links with the macabre events of fourteen years earlier ...

On 1 July, Bond was officially called in to examine the eleven separate body parts of the Rainham corpse. He was assisted by Dr Charles Hebbert although it is likely that he merely took notes rather than performed any kind of autopsy himself. Interestingly, the report begins with the sex organs and because this was a medical article written by a doctor for doctors, it is highly technical. The ovaries were small and the *rugae* (internal ridges) of the vagina prominent, indicating that this was a woman who had never given birth. The pubic hair was black, and an incision had been made in the vaginal wall's cartilage. There was no sign of bruising near any of the incisions on the body, proving that dismemberment was done quickly and soon after death. Allowing for the water's action on the body parts, Bond believed the skin to be fair.

The arms had been removed by oblique cuts downwards and outwards from the tip of the shoulder and the humeri (upper arm bones) had been cleanly disarticulated. Despite the fact that water-logging had led to some of the skin peeling away – it was especially thick and white on the palms of the hands – it was possible to tell that there was no ring indentation on either hand. The corpse was probably unmarried.

Similar disarticulation had occurred on the thighs, the right patella attached but separated from the lower leg at the knee joint. The left thigh (found in Regent's Canal) showed more signs of decomposition, the head of the femur riddled with water-worm holes. The lower legs were well shaped and muscular, the feet small and undeformed. Presumably, Bond and Hebbert noted this because, among the poor especially, cheap ill-fitting footwear led to frequent deformities. There were circular depressed marks, almost half an inch deep below both knees. Because of water action, the skin on the thighs was peeling off and the toe nails and phalanges (small bones) had gone.

What did the dismembered body tell the doctors? The Rainham corpse was clearly female and, because of the state of the bones, over 25 years old. The skin implied Caucasian origin, but the hair and complexion were dark. Hebbert wrote at length on the various methods for estimating height and, whichever way it was done, the dead woman had been about 5ft 3ins tall, which made her depressingly average for the time from the point of view of the police officers trying to identify her.

There was a glimmer of hope – and certainly a narrowing of the field – in Bond's/Hebbert's discussion of the victim's condition of life. Decomposition of the hands meant that it was impossible to say whether she had been used to hard manual work. The uterus implied virgin, but the vagina was too badly decomposed to make this certain. It was possible that the small uterus meant that conception was unlikely. She had recently menstruated and the tell-tale grooves below the knees showed 'that garters were worn ... a custom, I believe, more common among the lower orders than the upper classes, who either wear garters above the knee or suspenders'.[10]

It was in their discussion of the method of dismemberment that Bond and Hebbert become most interesting. In keeping with similar judgements made by medical men on the Ripper victims who would litter the streets of Whitechapel and Spitalfields the following year, they were anxious to distance doctors from such appalling barbarity. A saw and a very sharp knife were used, which were clearly the tools of a surgeon's trade, but Hebbert's argument is rather weak:

> I do not think that any surgeon or anatomist could have done the work as well, as they are not *constantly* operating, while a butcher is almost daily cutting up carcases.[11]
> It may be argued that such skill would be gained by a hunter, as either are in the habit of rapidly and skilfully separating limbs and of cutting up a trunk into several parts.[12]

Hebbert reasoned that the method of disarticulation used, cutting round the flexure of the joint and then twisting to cut the sinews, fits with either profession very neatly.

In terms of the date of the murder the doctors were less helpful. Decomposition had set in to the extent that 'some months' had elapsed since death, perhaps raising doubt on Galloway's likely May murder. And there, in the absence of any further information, the matter was quietly shelved. Before the Thames torso murderer struck again, the most infamous serial killer of them all made his entrance.

Chapter 4

Jack

Ann Rule wrote, in her excellent book on the Green River killer:

> It was 1988, and the centennial anniversary of the most infamous serial killer of them all. Jack the Ripper had stalked unfortunate ladies of the night in London exactly a hundred years before ... Old Jack was a piker compared to the GRK's toll; he had claimed less than half a dozen victims, but his fame had magnified exponentially over the years because he was never caught.[1]

And in the only full book written to date on the Thames torso killings, author R Michael Gordon writes:

> The Whitehall Torso Murder would soon become lost in the shadow of Jack the Ripper. And this vitally important point explains why so little work has been done on the torso killings. It may even partially explain why the world's first serial killer literally got away with murder.[2]

To understand how this happened, we have to evaluate the Whitechapel murders and the impact that the man who was Jack the Ripper had on London at the time and the world ever since. I have written two books on the Ripper, a drop in the constant deluge of research that has gone on since 1888, the year of the majority of Jack's killings. Since that 'Autumn of Terror' there have been thousands of books, both fact and fiction, movies, articles, television documentaries, video games, even an opera. There is an excellent website – Jack the Ripper Casebook – which provides chat-rooms, regular updates and the most minute discussions about the crimes and times of the Whitechapel murderer. Ripperologists all over the world have their own pet theories, are usually quick to rubbish anyone else's, often claim they are bored by endless speculation, yet keep coming back for more. The Thames torso killer lost himself in this obsession and eludes us still.

The jury is still out on the number of murders committed by Jack. Melville Macnaghten, head of the Met's CID from 1891, claimed there were five. At the time, the media postulated as many as eleven, although this included one of the torso killer's victims, found under railway arches in Pinchin Street.[3] My own view[4] is that Jack killed seven times, all but one of his crimes being perpetrated in the adjacent parishes of Whitechapel and Spitalfields in the East End.

The killing zone was unique in London: a desperately poor tangle of dingy streets, courts and alleyways, where drunkenness, chronic poverty and violence were a way of life. In 1888 it had a 90 per cent immigrant population, composed of recently arrived Jews, mostly from Russia and Poland so that it became known as the ghetto. Journalists were fascinated by it, writing articles and even poetry on the dilapidated buildings and wrecks of lives who occupied them. Jack London, in 1902, described it as The Abyss. He stayed there for some weeks, with ex-Detective Sergeant William Thick of H Division, known to the underworld as 'Johnny Upright'. London checked himself into the casual ward of the workhouse – 'The Spike' – and mixed with the dossers who scrounged their 'tommy' (food) as best they could. The experience affected London profoundly and one friend said he was never the same again. For him, Spitalfields and Whitechapel were the mouth of hell. An estimated half a million people lived there in varying degrees of poverty and desperation, alleviated by drink and, in some cases, paid for by prostitution.

Martha Tabram was born Martha White in Southwark, south of the river, in May 1849. She married twenty years later and had two children, but her constant drunkenness led to a marital breakdown. For about two years she lived with William Turner and used both this and her married name on the streets of Whitechapel where she was working by 1888. By this time, she was 39, but looked older. She had something of a reputation as a cadger, causing a nuisance by pestering family members for cash.

Late on the night of Monday 6 August 1888 she was in the company of another prostitute, Mary Ann Connolly, known as Pearly Poll, and two off-duty soldiers of the Coldstream Guards, based at Wellington Barracks. The four had drunk in various pubs (the area was littered with them) before Poll had gone off with her Guardsman up Angel Alley off Whitechapel High Street and Martha had gone up parallel George Yard with hers.

At 4.45 the next morning, John Reeves, a dock labourer, stumbled over Martha Tabram's body on his way to work. It was lying on the first-floor landing of the tenement block at 37 George Yard Buildings. The subsequent inquest showed that the woman had been partially strangled and stabbed thirty-eight times in the abdomen and groin. The thirty-ninth stab wound was probably delivered first and was the most likely cause of death. It had been made by a long, strong blade, possibly a bayonet, rammed into her chest. The finding of the inquest, delivered on 23 August, was one that would become depressingly familiar in the weeks ahead – 'murder by some person or persons unknown'.

The Whitechapel murderer had struck for what I believe was the first time. But the Thames torso killer had already beaten him by fifteen years.

Polly Nichols met Jack as she walked along Buck's Row, today's Durward Street. She had left the Frying Pan pub on the corner of Thrawl Street and Brick Lane at half past twelve in the morning of Friday 31 August. Fifty minutes later she staggered drunk into the doss house at 18 Thrawl Street. Single beds in these houses cost 4d and many 'ladies of the night' went out on the streets to earn the cost of a place to sleep. Polly did not have 4d, but she told the doss house deputy, 'I'll soon get my doss money. See what a jolly bonnet I've got now.'

An hour and ten minutes later, another prostitute, Ellen Holland, met Polly at the corner of Brick Lane and Osborn Street. The East End was literally alight that night. Huge crowds thronged the roads to the docks to watch a huge blaze that threatened Shadwell Dry Dock. It had started in the warehouses of Gibbs & Company and quickly spread, even after an unusually wet summer, to the adjacent Gowlands's Coal Wharf. It would be morning before it was put out and by then Polly Nichols was dead. She'd told Ellen Holland she'd earned her doss money three times over, but had spent it and she wandered off in the direction of 'Flowery Dean' (Flower and Dean Street, today's Lolesworth Close).

Mary Ann Nichols was 45 at the time of her death. She was 5ft 2ins and was married with five children. By 1880, the marriage had broken down, partly because of her husband William's infidelities and partly because of her drinking. She moved from doss house to doss house and in and out of various workhouses. At the end of 1887 she was living rough – 'carrying the banner' as it was euphemistically called – and sleeping in Trafalgar Square. Her one chance to get out of a downward spiral of poverty and drink had come earlier in that month of August 1888 when she got a job as a maid to a respectable and religious family in Wandsworth. She stole clothes worth £3 10s from them and left.

Carman Charles Cross found Polly's mutilated body lying at the entrance to the locked gates of Brown's Stable Yard. The subsequent post-mortem carried out by Dr Rees Llewellyn of the Whitechapel Road revealed that she had been strangled with what police and police surgeons today call a 'blitz' attack and her throat had been cut right back to the vertebrae. There were jagged, deep cuts to her abdomen and genitals, less tentative than the attack on Martha Tabram. Some Ripperologists today see this as the work of two different men, but they could also be the same killer growing in confidence and getting into his stride.

The murder of Martha Tabram caused little more than a ripple in the press. After all, brutality of this kind was endemic on the streets of Whitechapel. Much of it was drink-related and prostitutes, inevitably, were the usual and easy targets. Frederick Charrington was heir to a fortune by virtue of his father's brewery company but the sights he saw in the Abyss saw him walk away from that fortune and become a lifelong teetotaller, doing what he could to ban the demon drink. Outside the Rising Sun, he saw a man beating his wife to a pulp.

> I looked up and saw my own name in high gilt letters ... and it suddenly flashed into my mind that that was only one case of dreadful misery and fiendish brutality in one of the several hundred public houses that our firm possessed.

The murder of Polly Nichols however drew more press interest. Tabloid newspapers were making their presence felt at the time. Cheap paper manufacture coupled with an increasingly literate public meant that sales were on the increase *if* the right stories could be found. Then, as now, sex and slaughter sold; except that Victorian middle-class sensibilities would not accept titillation over the breakfast table – so ''orrible murder' reigned instead. There was a political, anti-establishment dimension to this too, the radical *Star* in particular having it in for Sir Charles Warren, Commissioner of the Met, for his rough handling of the working class in the Trafalgar Square riots of Bloody Sunday in November 1887. Local papers like the *East London Advertiser* and the *Eastern Argus* saw a chance to challenge the nationals, *The Times* and the *Telegraph*. The Whitechapel murderer was their pin-up boy, although of course they railed about the monstrosity of it all. It was in all their interests to keep lurid crime on the front page and in moments of quiet (for instance there were no Ripper murders during October 1888) a need to drag in any and every salacious detail to keep readership up.

And the readership drooled over the details concerning 'Dark Annie' Chapman on 9 September. Late on Friday the 7th, Annie was admitted to the kitchen of Crossingham's doss by the deputy, Timothy Donovan. She had had a fight days before, was still bruised as a result and was taking tablets she had almost certainly got from Whitechapel Infirmary. She couldn't afford her bed for the night and left Crossingham's at a little after half past one on Saturday morning.

Four hours later, she was seen by fellow prostitute Elizabeth Long talking to a man outside 29 Hanbury Street. He was a little taller than her (she was only 5ft) and Elizabeth heard him say, 'Will you?' And Annie said, 'Yes.'

What probably happened minutes later is that the couple went through the door that led to an alleyway. This in turn opened onto a small yard at the back of number 29, with a 6ft wooden fence around it, a privy and three steps down to ground level. At a little before six, carman John Davis, who worked in the market in Leadenhall Street and lodged at number 29, went into the yard, probably to use the privy before he went to work. He saw Annie Chapman lying at the bottom of the steps. Her skirts had been pulled up, her body ripped and her intestines were lying over her shoulder. Horrified, he ran for help.

'The abdomen had been entirely laid open' was The *Lancet's* précis of Dr George Bagster Phillips's post-mortem.

> The intestines, severed from their mesenteric attachments, had been lifted out of the body and placed on the shoulder of the corpse; whilst the pelvis, the uterus and its appendages with the upper portion of the vagina and the posterior two-thirds of the bladder, had been entirely removed. No trace of these parts could be found …

In common with many serial killers the world over, Jack was taking trophies, body parts which would remind him of the thrill he had experienced during the murder, except that the phrase 'serial killer' had not been coined yet and there was no one who had experience of such a phenomenon. To all concerned, from coroners to police surgeons to hard-bitten detectives and certainly to the public, the Whitechapel murderer had to be a maniac and that meant a slavering lunatic with terrifying strength and hideous features then appearing nightly on the London stage in an adaptation of Robert Louis Stevenson's *Jekyll and Hyde*.

The *Star* encapsulates the sensation perfectly:

> London lies today under the spell of a great terror. A nameless reprobate – half-beast, half-man – is at large, who is daily gratifying his murderous instincts on the most miserable and defenceless classes of the community … Hideous malice, deadly cunning, insatiable thirst for blood – all these are the marks of the mad homicide. The ghoul-like creature who stalks through the streets of London … is simply drunk with blood and he will have more …

He had two more on the same night. The 'double event' took place on Saturday 29/Sunday 30 September. The torso killer was also back at work by this time, as we shall see, but so far the only find had been the arm near the sluice along Chelsea Reach, below Grosvenor Road. That had taken place three days after the murder of Annie Chapman and, if it caused any ripple of interest, that disappeared by the morning of 30 September as Londoners awoke to appalling atrocities.

The body of Elizabeth Stride had been found in the narrow entrance to Dutfield's Yard along Berner Street. Her throat had been cut, but there were no tell-tale mutilations, Jack's 'signature' carved in blood. That was because he had almost certainly been interrupted by travelling salesman Louis Diemschutz who drove his pony and trap into the yard a little after one o'clock on that Sunday morning. The animal had shied at the unexpected bundle in its path and Diemschutz had got down and lit a match. Seeing the blood trickling in the gutter, he ran for help up the nearest stairs to the International Working Men's Club, of which he was a member. While he was doing this, Jack was almost certainly crouching behind the open gate and saw his chance to escape.

Lust-murderers like the Ripper have an overwhelming compulsion not just to kill but to mutilate in their own unique way. Frustrated and with the blood of Liz Stride on the blade in his pocket, he went west in search of another victim. Such was the furore in the press and the demands on the Met that police patrols had been stepped up. Perhaps this was why, with so many 'cusses of coppers' around, Jack went out of his comfort-killing zone into the territory of the City Police. Here he met Kate Eddowes.

Those who raged in the press against prostitution would have said that this meeting was fate, a kind of divinely orchestrated vengeance from God for a wicked lifestyle (witness the 'Moab and Midian' letter written to the Central News Agency which we will discuss later). In fact none of Jack's victims began a life of vice. They were not the children of prostitutes, merely the daughters of poverty. Kate hailed from Wolverhampton and the family moved to Bermondsey when she was a child. In the 1860s she lived with an ex-army man, Thomas Conway, who wrote chapbooks which the pair sold in Birmingham and elsewhere. By 1880 the relationship had collapsed, despite producing three children, and Kate was drinking heavily. She moved in with a market porter, John Kelly, the following year and the pair seemed to be happy. Even so, work was irregular and they slept more often than not in doss houses. From time to time Kate went into the workhouse.

The last day of her life is well chronicled. She was arrested, dead drunk, in Aldgate High Street and locked up at Bishopsgate Police Station to sober up. At one in the morning, Constable George Hutt released her on the improbable grounds that it was 'too late for you to get any more drink' (improbable because the pubs rarely closed) and she wandered away with a cheery 'Good night, old cock'. Half an hour later she was seen talking to a man who was probably her murderer at the entrance to Church Passage which led to Mitre Square.

It was here, in the darkest corner and ironically outside a policeman's house, that nightwatchman George Morris of the nearby warehouses of Kearley & Tonge found her butchered body. What had alerted him was the arrival, on his nightly rounds, of Constable Edward Watkins. Within twenty minutes, the square was full of policemen and two doctors. One of these, Police Surgeon Frederick Brown, noted the appalling savagery and made a detailed sketch of what he saw. Kate Eddowes had been ripped upwards from the pubis to the breastbone. Her liver had been slit, her colon dumped feet from the body and her uterus and one kidney had been removed. It was the worst attack yet but it followed the pattern of Annie Chapman. What was new was the mutilation to the face. The earlobes had been cut, the eyelids nicked, and there was a deep gash across the nose and cheek. Most oddly of all there were two triangular cuts, like inverted vs, one on each cheek.

Police combing the area in the next hour found a torn piece of Kate's apron lying in a drain by a stand pipe in Goulston Street, some three minutes away to the east. What they did not find was her killer. If the timings of the police patrols have been logged accurately, Jack had partially strangled Kate, cut her throat, carried out the dreadful mutilations and gone, wiping his bloodied hands on the apron section, in a space of fifteen minutes.

The most enigmatic of Jack's victims was Mary Jane Kelly and she most resembles the torso victims in that she was 25 (all the others were in their forties). By 9 November when Mary died, the torso-related murder known as the Whitehall Mystery had been and gone, from the finding of the trunk in the Scotland Yard foundations to the second part of the inquest on 22 October. Despite press attempts to link all these murders, Jack did not strike at all during October, so there is a gap of nearly six weeks in his killing spree after the frenzy of the 'double event'.

Mary told so many different stories about herself that it is difficult to know what to believe. She probably came from County Limerick in Ireland and may or may not have lived with a collier in Wales until he was killed in a pit accident in 1881 or 1882. She came to London in 1884 and, almost certainly living by her wits and prostitution, moved about considerably, latterly with Billingsgate porter Joseph Barnett. Alone of Jack's victims, Mary rented a room, 13 Miller's Court off Dorset Street, and owed several weeks back rent by the time she died.

It was in this context that her body was found. 'Indian Harry' Thomas Bowyer went to Mary's room to demand the rent on the morning of Friday 9 November. It was Lord Mayor's Day but for a rent collector it was business as usual. The door was locked, but a window pane was broken and Bowyer could peer into the dingy, 12ft by 12ft room. What was left of Mary Kelly lay on the bed, her legs open, her face unrecognizable and her body hacked to pieces. Doctors Thomas Bond and Bagster Phillips carried out the subsequent post-mortem and both men saw the corpse in situ where at least two photographs were taken.

The face was gashed in all directions, building on the more systematic work on Kate Eddowes and the throat had been cut right back to the vertebrae, the fifth and sixth being notched by the blade. Both breasts had been removed with circular cuts, one placed under the dead woman's body. The stomach had been ripped open and the skin removed. Both legs had been hacked so that the right thigh bone is clearly revealed in one of the photographs. Flesh from the body had been placed on the table next to the bed. Mary's heart was missing – another trophy for a serial killer. Bond estimated that Jack had taken perhaps two hours to carry out the mutilations and this, of course, was the only time that he killed indoors.

According to Melville Macnaghten – and most theorists since – Mary Kelly was the last of the victims of Jack the Ripper. So appalling were the mutilations and so sated was the murderer, that his mind gave way altogether and … Thereafter, various official views, usually offered years later in unreliable memoirs and always with a certain smugness on the part of their authors, range from vague stories of suicide (such as Montague Druitt in the Thames) to incarceration in asylums. None of these is very satisfactory and they were almost certainly intended to show Macnaghten and his predecessor Robert Anderson in a better light. We shall meet this arrogant 'I know who it is but I can't tell you' attitude at least twice more in this book.

My own view is that Jack did kill again. He was indeed sated after Mary Kelly and it was thirty-three weeks before he took to the streets again. The torso killer had struck again by this time too, but it was the summer of 1889 and the hypertension caused by the Ripper seems to have waned. Nobody, it appears, was ready for what happened to 'Clay Pipe' Alice McKenzie on Wednesday 17 July.

Constable Walter Andrews found her body lying between two costers' carts along Castle Alley, a narrow, dark thoroughfare that ran between Whitechapel High Street and Wentworth Street. Her throat had been cut and her skirts were pulled up to reveal Ripper-style mutilations. It was nearly one o'clock in the morning and the body was still warm, the throat wound still trickling blood. In all likelihood, Andrews's arrival had disturbed Jack at his work because the cuts were not as deep and determined as in earlier examples of the Ripper's handiwork and the subsequent post-mortem would reveal that no organs were missing. All this led Bagster Phillips, who had presided over all the Ripper's victims' post-mortems, to doubt whether this was a Ripper crime at all, but merely a copycat killing, designed to deflect the authorities from someone who knew Alice personally. Thomas Bond however was sure that the Castle Alley murder was a Ripper crime and I am personally inclined to accept his views.[5]

In a sense, the number of victims belonging to the man who was Jack is irrelevant. The only other full book on the torso murders attempts to tie them in with these – in other words, using Macnaghten's 'canonical five' for the Ripper plus the four the author attributes to the torso cases,[6] Jack's tally should be nine. I personally believe that Jack killed seven times, although his first attack, on Martha Tabram, may have been carried out on a woman already dead.

What is certain is that the torso killer was not the Whitechapel murderer. Whoever he was, he must have been eternally grateful to Jack, who not only hid his crime at the time, but has left him in a river fog of obscurity ever since.

Chapter 5

The Whitehall Mystery: Scotland Yard, September 1888

Scotland Yard was full. Since the Police Act of June 1829, the headquarters of the Metropolitan Police had been housed at 4 Whitehall Place. The building's back door opened onto Scotland Yard, the area in Westminster where Scottish visitors attending the court of James I had stayed in the early seventeenth century. As the headquarters staff grew and policing became more complex, additional buildings were annexed by the Force and the whole place was bursting at the seams.

There was a need to find somewhere new and larger and the idea was to utilize the site being developed further south along the Embankment, reclaimed from the river by Joseph Bazalgette in 1863. Originally the property had been bought from the Crown to become an opera house whose architect was Norman Shaw. In 1885, with opera house plans already drawn up and the foundations in place, the police took over instead and Shaw modified his drawings. The result was red and white brick Gothic, with circular turrets, small offices and labyrinthine corridors. Until 1967 this building was the symbol of the lantern-jawed detective in trilby hat and trenchcoat, smoking his pipe and driving out through its gates in a gleaming black Wolseley, sirens clanging. Two and a half thousand tons of granite were quarried by the convicts on Dartmoor and shipped to the site.

Work had already begun on New Scotland Yard – a project that would not be completed until 1891 – when a labourer, Frederick Moore, saw something lying in the river mud at low tide. It was 11 September 1888 and the whole of London was buzzing with the murders of Annie Chapman in Whitechapel three days earlier and of Polly Nichols the previous week. Perhaps men like Moore were more alert than usual to gruesome discoveries; it had not yet been established that the Ripper's killing zone was firmly fixed in the East End.

Moore was working that day at Deal Wharf near Grosvenor Road and saw a pale object lying near the sluice off Ebury Bridge Road. Grosvenor Road ran parallel to the river and what Moore found was lying only a couple of hundred yards away from where a section of the Rainham torso had been discovered the previous year. Speaking at the later inquest, Moore told the coroner, 'I went over and picked it up. I found that it was a woman's arm, with a string attached to the part nearest the shoulder.' In fact, Moore's attention was drawn to the macabre find by other workmen; only he, it seemed, had the nerve to handle it.

This stretch of the river linking Pimlico and Chelsea was the patch policed by B Division and Constable 127 William James was the first on the scene. Constable 634A T Ralph passed the offended limb to Dr Nevill who examined it in the local mortuary. He believed the arm had been recently amputated and that it had been removed from the body with great skill.

On 16 September the arm was re-examined by Dr Thomas Bond and Dr Charles Hebbert, both of whom were about to become embroiled in the Ripper case. The pair carefully measured the limb, a right arm, and found that it had been removed cleanly using seven separate cuts. The lack of pronounced muscles, the condition of the nails and the long, tapering fingers led them to conclude that this was a woman's arm and that in life she was Caucasian, about 20 years old with a dark complexion. She would probably have been about 5ft 9ins tall.

The arm had been removed after death by 'a person with some knowledge of anatomy',[1] and a ligature had been used to prevent the draining of blood from the cut end. Hebbert seems to have believed that a newspaper was at some time wrapped around the stump, but does not say why. By the time he examined the arm, decomposition was under way.

It was two and a half weeks after that that more of the body was found. Carpenter Frederick Windborn was one of the huge gang of skilled and unskilled men employed by J Grove & Sons to convert Norman Shaw's opera house into Scotland Yard. The foundations were already in place, a series of gloomy catacombs between the busy thoroughfare of Parliament Street with its solid government buildings and the embankment that skirted the river. The maps produced by G W Bacon for the Ordnance Survey in that year merely show a blank space alongside Westminster Pier, which gives a totally false impression. In reality, it was a series of vaults below ground level with wooden fences, scaffolding and cranes all over the place; a busy site in a city that is constantly being rebuilt.

At six o'clock in the morning of Monday 1 October (it was barely light by then) Windborn with his mate George Bodden collected his tools from his usual hiding place behind some boards. This was standard practice for workmen. Carrying heavy chisels and hammers around was awkward and leaving them in plain sight at the workplace was inviting theft. Presumably, there were little caches of equipment all over the catacombs of Scotland Yard. In reaching for his gear, Windborn felt something and struck a Lucifer to see what it was. It was a parcel, but he thought no more about it and started work on the floors above. It was still there the next day when he collected his tools again and at one o'clock, probably during Windborn's lunch break, his foreman, Mr William Brown joined him and the conversation turned to the parcel. Brown ordered it to be opened. The parcel was some 2½ feet long and perhaps 2 feet wide. It was paper wrapped in string and inside was the maggot-infested torso of a woman.

At the subsequent inquest, Windborn and Bodden explained the significance of the dumping site. Windborn was in the habit of leaving his tools there over the weekend and believed that the particular vault was difficult to locate. Even in broad daylight, it required the use of a match to find your way about. Bodden had fetched the parcel on the instructions of Brown and realized that it was cloth wrapped around what he took to be 'old bacon'. The string that held it all together was of different types.

Brown himself went to King Street police station at 3.30 that day to report the gruesome find. Detective Constable Hawkins of A Division returned with two uniformed men and gave his version of events to the coroner:

> I saw lying in the vaults of the new police buildings an open parcel in dress material, which had been tied round and a body of a woman in it. I looked further along the recess where it had been and saw a piece of more dress material. I saw the place where it had stood. The wall was very black and the place full of maggots. I left the body in charge of a constable and sent for the medical officer, Mr Bond.[2]

Bond arrived shortly after four and noted everything that Hawkins had seen.

> I thought the body must have been there several days from the state of the wall; but I could form no definite opinion as to how long it had been there. The lower part of the large bowel and all the contents of the pelvis were absent. The decomposition was very far advanced and the body was absolutely full of maggots.[3]

The luckless A Division constables had the task of loading up the remains onto an ambulance (actually a handcart) and wheeling it round to the mortuary in Millbank Street. In keeping with many of London's mortuaries at the time, Millbank was in the yards attached to a dwelling house and shop and it is almost devoid of proper modern appliances. A few wooden partitions have been run up, but there is neither antecedent room to conduct post-mortem examinations, nor means for ensuring the most ordinary sanitation and assisting in the ready and safe identifications of the dead.[4]

Whoever murdered the woman found in the basement of Scotland Yard had luck on his side. In 1888, fingerprinting was still, in practical use, three years away; genetic fingerprinting, DNA, still a century in the future. By the 1920s, forensics experts had a relatively tight grasp on the time it takes for a body to putrefy, but Bond was still having to make educated guesses.

Aitchison Robertson in 1921 broke down the decomposition pattern as follows. The first evidence of putrefaction is of a sweet, sickly smell that pervades a room in which a body is lying. That neither Windborn nor Bodden was aware of a smell may be due to the fact that the vault was too airy or because of the general pervading smell of the river. It is also possible that the dress material effectively kept the odour in. It all depends on the weather. Early October in London can be mild, but if it was cold, it may be six or seven days after death that the smell becomes obvious.

Between the first and third day after death, the skin over the abdomen turns greenish yellow and this spreads to the genitals, trunk, limbs, chest and neck, which turn green or brown. Gases in the intestine cause the body to swell. The degree of larval infestation also gives a clue as to the length of time a body has been left exposed. The common blowfly lays first, usually in the mucous membranes of the eyes, nose and mouth. The eggs take three weeks to develop. The problem is that other insects lay later – green and grey flies three or four days post-mortem, Lepidoptera and Colcoptera three or four months. After eight months, Picophila and Anthomyia arrive along with Necrobia. Because Bond was probably unaware of this egg-laying cycle, he could not be sure how long the woman had been dead.

At the inquest, labourer Ernest Hodge swore that the parcel was not there on Saturday 29 September, but of course in the near darkness he may have missed it.

On the night of the find, the trunk was immersed in an alcohol solution in Westminster mortuary (one of the better equipped morgues in London) to kill the maggots and aid in the post-mortem of the next day. Once again, Bond and Hebbert were called upon to piece together what had once been a life. The body was female; unlike the Rainham torso, the breasts were present. The head had been severed at the sixth cervical vertebra and the pelvis and lower abdomen at the fourth lumbar vertebra. The bones at each end of the remaining spine had been cut through, not disarticulated. The body's length was 17ins, the chest

35½ins and the waist 28½ins. The skin was not badly decomposed, the breasts large and prominent and the nipples small and well-shaped. There were no visible scars or other marks which might have aided identification, except the tell-tale marks of the string which held the parcel together. The lineae albae (nerve-carrying tendons) were no longer present with the abdomen. As with the Rainham corpse, the cuts were clean and the limbs disarticulated.

The neck was decomposed but the head had been removed by two clean lateral cuts joined with jagged incisions in front and behind. The heart and lungs were healthy, indicating as did the Rainham body that this woman did not suffer from any of the endemic chest conditions like tuberculosis which dogged the working class. The stomach contained partly digested food, but perhaps because of the passage of time that had elapsed, it was not possible to say what it was. Such forensics were possible. For instance, in the Ripper murders of the same year, where the bodies were all found within hours and sometimes minutes of death, stomach contents were easily identified. The liver, spleen and kidneys in the Whitehall case were normal, so this was not, like so many working-class women, an alcoholic. The armpit hairs were dark; like the Rainham corpse, another brunette.

The most fascinating piece of evidence of course was the reuniting of the Pimlico right arm to this trunk. The claim that hairs from the arm and armpit were identical may have been guesswork, but there was no doubt at all that the arm was a perfect fit.

What could Bond and Hebbert tell the coroner at the forthcoming inquest? The Whitehall body was that of a well-nourished woman and the breasts indicated that she had never suckled a baby. Death, they believed, had occurred two months previously, which would take the murder to early August. The dismemberment all happened post-mortem and, tellingly, decomposition had happened in the open. The presence of maggots were testimony to this.

What does not appear in the Hebbert article is the fact that the newspaper Windborn mentioned as part of the wrapping of the parcel was the *Echo* dated 24 August 1888; if the doctors were right, some weeks after the murder.

Chief Superintendent Joseph Henry Dunlap was placed in charge of the case and his eyes and ears on the ground was Chief Inspector Wren of A Division. This unit, covering Whitehall, had 38 inspectors in 1888, 60 sergeants and 835 constables, giving a total strength of 935 men. As many as possible were combing the area, checking buildings old and new, knocking on doors, asking questions. By the beginning of October, the Whitechapel murderer, now dubbed Jack the Ripper by a slavering press had claimed at least four victims,[5] including, only three days before the Whitehall discovery, two women on the same night. Questions were being asked of the police of the Metropolis and they were all under a huge spotlight.

Such was the influence of the Ripper crimes that the Whitehall discovery chimed with one of the more bizarre elements of it. Shortly before or after Windborn made his find and certainly on the same day, Robert James Lees, from Peckham, visited the police with theories from the 'Other Side'. Lees was one of a large number of what the Victorians called sensitives, mediums who claimed to have links with the spirit world. Today, desperate police forces, especially in the United States, occasionally consult psychics to find some kind of solution to ongoing cases. Just as often, psychics attach themselves unbidden to task forces and scenes of crime officers, firmly believing that they can help. What they usually do is to muddy operational waters and often compromise crime scenes.

Such a one was Robert Lees, but he got short shrift in 1888. He wrote in his diary for 2 October, 'Offered services to the police to follow up East End murders – called a fool and a lunatic.' The next day he 'got trace of a man from the spot in Berner Street [Dutfield's Yard, the murder site of Elizabeth Stride]'. This time he went to the City police, who were investigating the second murder on the night of the 'double event', that of Katherine Eddowes – 'called a madman and a fool'. On the Thursday (4 October) he went to Scotland Yard itself – 'same result but promised to write to me'.[6] There is in fact no independent evidence that Lees went to the police at all – only his diary quoted above. Presumably, however, if he got the response he claims, an incredulous or bored desk sergeant would not even have bothered to enter the details of his visit. Lees is not known to have had any telepathic flashes of insight into the torso killer.

Bloodhounds were brought in to assist A Division in the search for more body parts. A trunk and an arm had been found, but what about the other arm and legs? Above all, what about the head? The dogs appear to have been used to no effect, although without the farce associated with Barnaby and Burgho, the Scarborough-based pair bred by Mr Edwin Brough and brought in at the insistence of Sir Charles Warren, Commissioner of Police, to help with the Ripper murders. In embarrassing trials held in Hyde Park on 9 October, the dogs lost their own handlers in the fog.

The dump site itself (no murder site was ever identified in any of the torso murders) was described by *The Times*. Steps led down from the Embankment and a slope led further into the bowels of the building. The ground was rough here and should have produced at least possible results of boot-prints which could have been used in eliminating the workmen on the site. Given the darkness of the place however, this must have been problematic. Because of the difficulty in reaching the exact spot where the torso was found, *The Times* reporter surmised that the body must have been left there in the day (when light was minimal instead of non-existent) and must have been left by someone familiar with the building's layout. The conventional way into the site was via gates on

Cannon Row and as these were locked, high and difficult to negotiate, this was not likely to have been the way the torso was delivered. Access from the river was much more likely, either via one of the innumerable carts of builders' materials coming and going, or from the Westminster Pier where timber was unloaded.

A bizarre coincidence was reported on 20 October, but it came from the pages of the *Illustrated Police News*, one of the most salacious scandal sheets of the day and having no actual connection with the police at all. The 'First Evidence' referred to in its banner headline concerned a resident of Llanelly, South Wales, who found himself in Cannon Row the Saturday before the body was found (29 September) – a day when Ernest Hodge said there was no parcel there. The unnamed witness saw three men outside the Scotland Yard site, two of them with a barrow containing a bundle. A third man climbed over a hoarding into the ground, presumably with said bundle. The Welshman reported all this to the police who duly apprehended a workman who admitted to having been there. 'Beyond this the police, it is said, succeed in obtaining no clue.'[7]

None of this makes sense. If these three men were really dumping a body part, would they choose the most difficult way in full view of a nosy bystander? And if the police *did* interview someone in this context, why is there no record of it anywhere? This seems to be an example either of the man from Llanelly building up his part for his fifteen minutes of fame or the *Illustrated Police News* indulging in a little fiction for the sake of good copy.

Since 24 September, a number of letters and postcards had been steadily arriving at the Central News Agency, individual newspaper officers or police stations. The most famous of those, on the 27th, purported to come from 'Jack the Ripper' and the most brilliant pen-name in modern history caught on. One that was received by the Central News Agency at their New Bridge Street premises on 5 October was forwarded to Chief Constable Adolphus Williamson at the Yard. It was not written by the Whitechapel murderer, but it did throw a lurid spotlight on the torso murders.

Dear Friend,
In the name of God hear me I swear I did not kill the female whose body was found at Whitehall. If she was an honest woman I will hunt down and destroy her murderer. If she was a whore God will bless the hand that slew her, for the women of Moab and Midian shall die and their blood shall mingle with the dust.

The rest of the letter descends into bloodthirsty ramblings that would not be out of place in a Tod Slaughter screenplay from the 1930s. Ironically, it was forwarded to the police by Thomas Bulling who many experts believe today was the sender of the original 'Dear Boss' letter and creator of the infamous sobriquet to boost newspaper sales. The mindset of the 'Jack' who wrote the 5 October letter will be discussed later, because it tells us a good deal about the torso murders.

From various reports, it is clear that torso mania was spreading almost as widely as the work of 'Saucy Jacky' but of course it was in the interests of the press to maintain the fiction that *all* these victims, the dismembered and the left-in-the-street, were the work of the same man. On 24 August, a right foot and part of a left leg had been found near Guildford Station in Surrey, lying on railway tracks and probably tossed from a train. On 5 October, a grim-faced Inspector Marshall from A Division brought the remains back to London to be examined by Bond and Hebbert. They examined them at Millbank the next day and were in no doubt all that the boiled specimens had no connection with the Whitehall case. They were the bones of a bear!

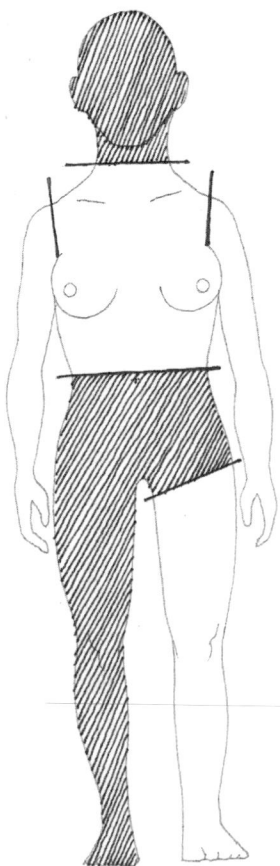

The thick black lines represent the cuts made to dissect the body. The shaded areas are the parts that were never found.

The mortuary of St George's in the East as it is today. Bodies recovered from the Thames as well as the Pinchin Street torso were brought here for dissection. Photo: Carol Trow

The headquarters of the River Police (Thames Division) at 259 Wapping High St. The building was originally the home of the magistrate Robert Colquhoun who founded the unit in 1795. The insert shows a typical police galley of the 1880s which could be fitted with sail for work nearer the Estuary.

Accident survivors and rescued suicides were given a bath and a bed in this room in Waterloo police station. The highest number of suicides took place off Waterloo Bridge.

One of the most unpleasant duties of Thames Division was pulling suicides out of the Thames.

The rest room at Waterloo police station of the Thames Division. Note the oilskins hanging on the back wall.

The railings outside 33 Fitzroy square. A package containing body parts was found here by a patrolling policeman in 1884. Photo credit: Eloise Campbell

The Thames as the Victorians would have liked it to be. These girls are punting somewhere near Oxford.

The ground-level window of New Scotland Yard. A ramp led down below this point into the basement, where a torso and separated legs were found during the building process in 1888. Photo credit: Eloise Campbell

Norman Shaw's opera house became the headquarters of the metropolitan Police at New Scotland Yard in 1893. Body parts were found in its basement three years earlier. Photo credit: Eloise Campbell

The ornamental gardens in Mornington Crescent where body parts were found in 1884. There was controversy over whether these belonged to other remains in neighbouring squares or not. Photo credit: Eloise Campbell

A Thames Division galley upriver along Chelsea Reach where body parts were found in the 1870s and 1880s. An inspector and three constables patrol the river.

Thames Division police galleys patrolled the river night and day on the alert for crime of all sorts.

The peculiar eddying current along Chelsea Reach was responsible for carrying body parts both up and down the river. Photo credit: Eloise Campbell

The Drill Hall and Armoury at 33 Fitzroy Square. Body parts were placed behind the railings at the bottom left of the picture in 1884. Photo credit: Eloise Campbell

The foreshore along Chelsea Reach showing the skeleton outline of the old wharves before the Embankment development by Joseph Bazalgette. Photo credit: Carol Trow

Dr Thomas Bond was the brilliant police surgeon of A Division Metropolitan Police who worked on both the torso victims and those of Jack the Ripper.

Battersea Park from Battersea Bridge. Harrison Barber's slaughterhouse lay a quarter of a mile away. Photo credit: Eloise Campbell

The lodge entrance to Battersea Park. To the right of this position and straight ahead in the undergrowth were scattered the body parts of the prostitute Elizabeth Jackson. Photo credit: Eloise Campbell

Nothing of the Victorian Alfred Mews remains, but somewhere along this street near a rubbish bin were found parts of a human body which were taken for disposal at King's Cross station. Photo credit: Eloise Campbell

The inquest on the Whitehall torso was held on Monday 8 October, the start of a month of unusually bad fogs that shrouded the river and crept all the way down to the Sessions House in Broad-Sanctuary Street in Westminster. The jury had already been to view the remains in Millbank mortuary and settled down to listen to a string of witnesses who trooped before the coroner John Troutbeck. Frederick Windborn explained his finding of the parcel with the aid of a building plan drawn up by the police which was probably a blueprint of Norman Shaw's. George Bodden followed with the information that he had carried the parcel to a better-lit part of the foundations at the request of William Brown, the foreman. Slightly against the run of events, Troutbeck then called Frederick Moore who had found the arm off Chelsea embankment at Pimlico, then Brown himself. Brown believed that only someone who knew the site personally or had it minutely described to him could find the vault where the parcel had been left. The hoarding around the site was 8 or 9ft high and, as there was no sign of damage to this, it had to be conjectured that someone capable of climbing this while carrying a dead weight like a human trunk would have to be exceptionally strong. There were signs everywhere to the effect that there was no public access to the site, but there was no nightwatchman to enforce this. One of the three gates was left unlocked, but it could only be opened by a complicated string mechanism, which was understood by only a few.

After lunch, Dr Bond was called. He gave his address as the Sanctuary, Westminster Abbey, and discussed his findings both at the site and in the mortuary. Although Hebbert's subsequent report does not mention it, Bond stated at the inquest that the adhesions to one lung indicated severe pleurisy at some stage. He could categorically say that neither suffocation nor drowning was the cause of death. Pressed by Troutbeck on this point, Bond ventured that the cause might be haemorrhage, presumably to the missing head. He thought this because the heart was pale and free from clots.

Dr Hebbert followed with details of the right arm and the coroner asked him if the separation of the arm might have been carried out by a surgeon for anatomical purposes. Hebbert doubted that, but offered the information that the newspaper sections wrapped around the trunk carried animal blood stains, which were not those of a bird or reptile. Hebbert was guessing here. Birds and reptiles have nuclei in their red blood cells which explains his findings, but no one could tell animal from human blood before the researches of Dr Paul Hulenhuth in 1901. Perhaps this is another example of the medical profession trying to put a butcher in the frame!

Inspector Marshall was quizzed by Troutbeck as to how he thought the killer had got into the site with his macabre package. He said the complex latch could be managed by anyone with a bit of persistence and that it was possible to climb the hoarding on the Cannon Row side. In the event of no further evidence, the coroner adjourned the inquest for two weeks.

It is difficult to understand quite how a London journalist, Jasper Waring, was able to persuade the police to let him onto the New Scotland Yard site, but in their presence, on Wednesday 17 October, he turned up, complete with a Russian Terrier dog. The animal immediately began digging excitedly and pulled out from the earth a left leg with foot attached. The inevitable Thomas Bond was sent for and had the limb removed to Millbank mortuary. After dark on the same day, the police returned with the dog. *The Times* reported: 'The scene is described as a very weird one, for the only illumination of the dismal place was by candles and the dog did not seem in the best form, this possibly arising from the strange surroundings.'[8] Nevertheless, the animal found the missing left arm buried below where it had found the leg and foot.

These new finds were at once alarming and embarrassing. The police, after all, had already searched the entire premises and allegedly used bloodhounds. Effectively, it was a member of the public who did their job for them and, as a journalist, one who could do them a great deal of harm in the negative publicity stakes. The alarming aspect was the fact that the limbs had been buried and had almost certainly been there for longer than the torso. In other words, the killer had visited the site at least twice and had had the leisure to bury part of his victim. He had also *not* buried the trunk. Why? Was he disturbed by the arrival of a work-team? Or was this some kind of statement, the significance of which was as yet not understood? As in so many aspects of the Thames torso murders far more questions were raised than answers.

Then as now in the case of missing persons, the police had any number of leads to follow. London was the biggest city in the world in 1888 and unknown numbers trickled into its streets every week, looking for the gold pavements and the bright lights. None of the once-promising leads threw up anything. The Whitehall torso remained for ever 'the woman in the vault'.

The inquest resumed on 22 October and coroner Troutbeck's first witness was once again William Brown, the foreman. He had been in the vault where the body was found on Friday 28 September, measuring up for surveyors and had a light with him. He conceded that the parcel might have been there as he did not delve into the recess as Windborn had to get his tools. Since some suspicion had now attached to the work crew because of the relative difficulty in accessing the site, George Evans, the clerk of works, was called next. He had been on the site on Saturday 29th and had seen no one carrying a parcel of any description.

Labourer Richard Lawrence of Stendale Road, Battersea, was less than helpful when he admitted to leaving his tools in the same recess as Windborn on Saturday 29 September. He retrieved them again on Monday 2 October (the day the body was found) and saw nothing. Since he had no light with him, this was hardly surprising. Lawrence's testimony is typical of the non-evidence that clutters all police enquiries. Clearly the parcel and body parts were in place that Monday, but many of us, Richard Lawrence included, make woeful witnesses and we often miss what is literally under our noses.

Jasper Waring explained to the inquest the finding of the leg through the good nose of his dog. It was in the same recess as the trunk, but on the opposite side and about a foot below ground level. It appeared to have been there undisturbed for some time. His colleague, Mr Angle, who had been with him, believed the depth to have been no more than four or five inches and the ground hard and trodden down.

As usual, Dr Bond's evidence was perhaps the most useful. The appearance of the earth led him to believe that the leg had been there for some weeks. He also poured scorn on the various witnesses who were implying that the torso had not been there before the weekend of 29/30 September. In his opinion, it had been there much longer and decomposition had occurred at the spot. Two weeks of course had passed between the first and second inquests and it is unlikely that the 'crime scene' had been taped off as is de rigueur in modern murder investigations, so the area was by now hopelessly compromised. The earth, which might have yielded the boot-prints of the killer, had been trampled on by Windborn, Hodge, Brown, Lawrence, Waring, Angle, unknown policemen and a dog!

Bond's purely medical testimony on the leg was written up later by Dr Hebbert for his paper. Again, dismemberment had been done cleanly and efficiently at the knee joint and the limbs were carefully measured. There was a small amount of bruising, the size of a shilling, on the inside and outside of the leg. The date of death was estimated at between six to eight weeks, which would take us back to a murder committed in late August or early September.

The trunk, the arm and the leg clearly belonged to the same person, but three different methods of dispersal had been used. The trunk, in its dark vault and badly tied parcel, had been exposed to air. The arm, lying on the Thames mud, had been immersed in water. The leg, between 4 and 12ins under Scotland Yard's lowest foundations, had been buried. This was a riddle, certainly, for forensic experts, but what does it tell us about the killer?

Such were the limits of the law in 1888 (and I suspect today) that Troutbeck could only advise the jury that their choice was either 'wilful murder' or 'found dead'; the victim remained anonymous. Despite the best efforts of Dr Bond, he could find no actual cause of death. Even so, *someone* had cut up a woman's body and had gone to considerable lengths to scatter the various parts. It defies belief then that the jury opted for 'found dead'.

Chapter 6

The Frankenstein Connection: Horsleydown, June 1889

Even by the time the Port of London Authority took its photographs of the Thames Docklands in the 1930s, St George's Stairs had all but disappeared. They ran down to the river in Bermondsey between Butler's Wharf warehouse and the much larger Cole's Wharf, both of them built in the mid-nineteenth century. Ironically, the Old Stairs still stood in the 1930s, running through Courage's Granary to the river mud. It was at one or other of these stairs that John Ryan, a riverside labourer, was standing on the morning of 4 June 1889 when he saw some boys throwing stones at something in the water. One of them hooked the floating object, which appeared to be an apron, onto the mud of the shore and found part of a woman's body.

The nearest policeman was on a galley patrol boat within yards of the stairs and Ryan shouted to him. Constable 63 Freshwater of Thames Division stated at the later inquest that he was handed a parcel containing what he believed to be human remains and took it to the station at Wapping. In what was now a well-established routine, Freshwater contacted the Assistant Divisional Surgeon, Dr McCoy, who carried out preliminary investigations.

Half a mile away, 15-year-old Isaac Brett, a woodcutter of 7 Laurence Street, Chelsea, was walking on the Battersea foreshore under Albert Bridge and decided to take a dip on what must have been a warm summer's day. He had not been in the water long when he saw a parcel tied with a bootlace floating nearby. Pulling it ashore he was advised by a passing stranger to take it to the police. There had been no known torso activity since the Whitehall Mystery inquest had closed eight months earlier and now two parts of the same body had turned up on the same day.

When Brett took his parcel to the nearest police station, Sergeant William Briggs of V Division examined it. It contained a thigh, but, for the first time, this was wrapped in clothing which could aid identification. Part of a ladies'

Ulster (overcoat) was there and the right leg of a pair of drawers (underwear). These had a name – L E Fisher – written in black ink on the waistband. This was the only name ever linked in black and white to the torso killings and it seemed full of possibilities. If this was the leg as well as the knickers of L E Fisher, what were those possibilities? A name on underwear implies laundry usage or some kind of communal living such as a college or school, probably of the boarding variety. L E Fisher would surely be found quickly or, even if this was her leg, links could be made to find her killer.

Dr Felix Kempster who had worked on the Rainham case two years earlier was called in as was the by now inevitable Thomas Bond. The thigh was officially the responsibility of Inspector John Ryan (no relation to the Thameside labourer) of Thames Division and Inspector Tunbridge of Scotland Yard.

For the rest of that day and the next, officers of the Thames and other divisions searched the shorelines in Horsleydown and Battersea and began to drag the river near Vauxhall Bridge. There was no underwater unit in the Met until 1962, largely because diving was extremely hazardous and the river so murky and polluted that little would be found anyway. In a typical year since its formation as part of Thames Division, the unit has undertaken some 200 searches, recovering approximately 20 bodies, 12 firearms, ten knives or swords, 15 cars and a dozen motorbikes! In any case, the torso killer was not weighing his body parts down; he was placing them in packages he knew would float. This was an important clue, whether the police at the time recognized it or not. Dismemberment was not to conceal and 'lose' body parts – it was to taunt and terrify.

Dr Kempster's findings on the thigh were that it had not been in the water long and that death had occurred only twenty-four hours earlier, which gave a murder date, if murder it was, of 3 June. There were four bruises on the thigh, almost certainly caused by a firm finger grip and these were caused while the victim was still alive. *The Times* of 5 June reported that the Horsleydown and Battersea finds came from the same body and an inquest was held the following day.

The coroner here was the redoubtable Wynne E Baxter of Middlesex's South-East Division who had already grabbed considerable headline space in the Ripper case, presiding over the inquests of Polly Nichols, Annie Chapman and Liz Stride. He was also in the chair in the inquest on non-Ripper victim Rose Mylett, a prostitute who almost certainly met her death at the hands of a one-off client in Clark's Yard, Poplar, on 20 December 1888. Baxter was not impressed by the Met and was contemptuous of Dr Bond's assertion that Rose was a murder victim, ranting that she died by accident due to the tightness of her bodice and her state of drunkenness. Since his background was legal rather than medical, he was sticking his neck out to challenge a man of Bond's probity. A very arrogant and political animal, Baxter was accused of electoral impropriety in 1887 and used 'Inquest, London' as his telegraphic address. He was famous for his lengthy inquests, leaving no stone unturned, but he was proved wrong on more occasions than was seemly in such an important office.

The inquest into the Horsleydown remains was notoriously short, however, to give police time to investigate. The evidence as it stood could not decisively establish whether a murder had actually been committed. It was the next day when more evidence came to light, not quite in the river but in the general vicinity, not only of the thigh found by Isaac Brett, but the body found along Battersea Reach sixteen years earlier.

Dickens wrote:

Battersea Park, one of the youngest of the London parks ... is certainly one of the prettiest. No park ... in London can compare with the sub-tropical garden. It is emphatically one of the sights which no visitor should fail to see, especially in the latter part of the summer.[1]

One of the sights they would not have liked to see was the one that greeted gardener Joseph Davis on the afternoon of 6 June. He was working in the shrubbery near the wrought iron fence that divided the park from the river, about 200 yards from the nearest gates at Albert Bridge when he came across a bundle. On opening it, Davis dropped the thing in shock as he recognized parts of a human body. The package had been tied with white Venetian blind cord. The gardener dashed to find a patrolling park policeman, Constable 502 Ainger of V Division, and the pair agreed that this was the upper part of a woman. As with the thigh, it was wrapped in clothing, a burgundy coloured skirt.

In Battersea Mortuary, the Divisional Police Surgeon examined the find the same day. He wrote later:

The chest cavity was empty, but many internal organs, including the spleen, both kidneys and a portion of the stomach intestines were present. The lower six dorsal vertebrae were in their place, but the lower five ribs were missing. A portion of the midriff above the breasts and the integumentary covering to the chest bone were cut down the centre as though by a saw. The ribs were also sawn through. Decomposition had set in, but had proceeded no further than was consistent with the assumption that the remains formed part of a living body not more than four or at most five days previously.

If the doctor was correct about that, then the murder may have occurred as early as 2 June.

6 June was a red-letter day for the torso killer. Shortly before Joseph Davis made his grisly find in the rhododendron bushes, barge-builder Charles Martowe, of Wye Street, Battersea, was working at Copington's Wharf when he spotted what looked like part of a body bobbing in the water. The find was reported to the police and Inspector William Law of Thames Division took possession of it at Waterloo Pier. This station was of course little more than a stone's throw from Temple Pier where part of the Rainham body had been found two years earlier. Law surmised that if this segment had been dumped in the river on the flood tide it would have had time to reach the spot where it was found, assuming it was placed there at Battersea. Yet more body parts were located by engineer David Keen near Palace Wharf. By the next day *The Times* reported that all the sections belonged to the same body, but there was more to come.

The Thames had its own community of gypsies who migrated along the whole of the tidal river's banks, camping on the open shore in summer or dossing in the rookeries before their demolition for Joseph Bazalgette's Embankment. Some of them worked irregularly in the docks, but many eked out a meagre existence by fishing, still using sticks and spears thrown from rough willow-wood canoes. They were in some ways an archaic throwback and were trusted and loved by no one. One of them was Solomon Hearne who camped on the open ground at Lammas Hard along the Town Meadows in Fulham, just east of Wandsworth Bridge. He found a woman's leg lying on the foreshore wrapped in the collar of a chequered Ulster, identical to the one found days earlier near Albert Bridge.

At Battersea Mortuary, Dr Felix Kempster preserved the limb in spirits of wine which was now his routine procedure. He confirmed that the leg belonged to the other body parts and had been cut off just below the knee.

Two more sections would be found on 7 June. David Goodman, a nitric acid maker of 15 Prairie Street, Queen's Road, Battersea, found a piece of flesh on the mud at Palace Wharf, Nine Elms, slightly downriver from the leg. Much further downstream, near the West India Docks at Limehouse, lighterman Edward Stanton saw a dark bundle floating in the water. It was tied with string. The material was the ulster's sleeve and the parcel was passed to Inspector Hodson of Thames Division who was already on the river supervising a search for body parts. Kempster confirmed that the sleeve contained a right leg and foot, all belonging to the same body.

But the grisly discoveries went on. Saturday 8 June saw rain driving over the city, threatening a return of the dismal summer of the previous year. William

Chidley, lighterman, was already at work at Bankside in Southwark by eight o'clock and he hauled a floating package to the shore. It was wrapped in plain brown paper and contained a woman's left arm. Kempster reported that the

> limb was well moulded and the hand small and shaped with every appearance of having been well cared for. The arm had been severed from the body in a very skilled manner and the person who cut it off must have had a very considerable knowledge of anatomy.

The police themselves found the next body part later that day. At about half past twelve, an object was noticed in midstream between Battersea Park Pier and Albert Suspension Bridge. There was no wrapping this time, possibly because it had become detached, but the body section was the lower back, pelvis and buttocks. Sub-inspector Joseph Churcher took the find to Battersea mortuary.

It must have been manna from heaven for Claude Mellor when he made the next discovery of 8 June. He was a journalist who had been assigned to the torso story and he was walking along Chelsea Embankment at mid-day. He was passing a line of evergreens that skirted the railings that edged the gardens of a private estate when he noticed something hidden in the undergrowth. He found patrolling Constable 182B Jones and took him back to the site. It was clear by the broken bush-tops that the object had been thrown over into the garden. It also became clear to whom the property belonged as detectives made their enquiries; this was the home of Sir Percy Shelley, whose ancestor Mary had created one of the most terrifying of all horror monsters, the 'Prometheus unbound' that we know today as Frankenstein's Monster. A freak of unnature sewn together from body parts.

And that, metaphorically, was what Drs Bond, Kempster and Hebbert were doing at Battersea mortuary on 10 June. In his report presented as a medical paper later in the year, Hebbert refers to this murder as the Thames case, which rather downgrades the others and by the time he was lecturing he could afford to be smug because the victim, alone of the torsos, had been identified. First, he lists the parts found – 'two large flaps of skin, the uterus and placenta; both arms and hands; both thighs; both legs and feet; the trunk divided into three parts'. In other words, all that was missing, as in nearly all the other cases, was the all-important head. The top portion of the trunk had been removed from the head at the sixth vertebra by a series of clean, confident cuts. The chest had been opened in front by the midline, the sternum cut through and the contents of the chest (lungs and heart) had been removed. The arms had been removed by three or four long, sweeping cuts, the joints neatly disarticulated. The skin was peeling off in places from the sodden flesh, but the portion had not been in the water that long.

The second section of the trunk contained both breasts and fitted exactly with the first, including the vertical cut through the sternum. The ribs were present and, although the intestines had gone, the kidneys, spleen, pancreas and liver were still in place, along with the duodenum and part of the stomach. Despite decomposition of the liver, all the internal organs were healthy.

The final part of the trunk showed that the thighs had been removed by long sweeping incisions and the same skilful disarticulation of the joints. The pelvis contained the lower part of the vagina and rectum and the front part of the bladder, including the urethra. Hebbert was able to say that the vagina itself showed no damage, either from violent rape or childbirth and this is important in terms of explaining the killer's motivation which we will examine later. The flaps of skin to which Hebbert referred came from the abdominal walls and right buttock. The skin was fair and the pubic hair a light sandy colour. The uterus had been cut, but the existence of placenta and the organ's dilation made it clear that the woman had been pregnant and the foetus removed by her killer. The dead woman would have been between six and seven months pregnant.

It was the arms that would confirm the corpse's identity days later. Indentations on a finger of the left hand implied a wedding ring, but a number of circular scars on the upper left arm indicated vaccination. It was the inch long scar on the lower forearm that would provide the vital clue. The leg sections fitted perfectly and were well shaped with no deformity to the feet.

What conclusions could the doctors draw? The dead woman, they knew, was over 24 years old and probably under 35. Her hair and complexion were fair. As usual, Hebbert wrestled with the problem of height, but his best calculations gave a measurement of 5ft 4¾ins. A fine-tooth saw had cut through bone and a very sharp knife through skin. All joints except the left knee had been very neatly disarticulated. There appeared to be no sign of hard manual work by the condition of the hands and no marks of a garter on either leg. All parts belonged to the same body and death probably took place about twenty-four hours before the discovery of the first two portions, i.e. 1 or 2 June. There was no evidence of the cause of death, but again, the medical men were quick to distance their profession from such foul deeds; 'the skill not showing the anatomical knowledge of a surgeon, but rather the aptitude learnt by a butcher, horse-knacker or other person used to deal with dead animals and to readily separate limbs at the joints'.[2]

The doctors of course were concerned with the purely medical. The police took their findings and added their own, talking to reporters in an attempt to identify the corpse. *The Times* of 13 June reported that the body was accompanied by 'an old brown linsey [woollen] dress, red selvedge, two flounces round bottom, waistband made of small blue-and-white check material similar to duster cloth, a piece of canvas roughly sewn on end of band, a large brass pin in skirt and a black dress button (about the size of a threepenny piece) with lines across in pocket'. The torn ulster was grey with a black cross-hatching pattern forming a check design. The material was good quality, but old. The drawers were old too, with square patches on both knees with the tell-tale 'L E Fisher' written in black ink. The various parcels had been tied with black mohair bootlaces, pieces of Venetian blind cord and string. All these articles could be viewed by anxious (or of course morbidly curious) friends or family of missing persons.

The problem was that, the name apart, the clothes were ten a penny with nothing unique about them. Any of them could have been picked up for a song

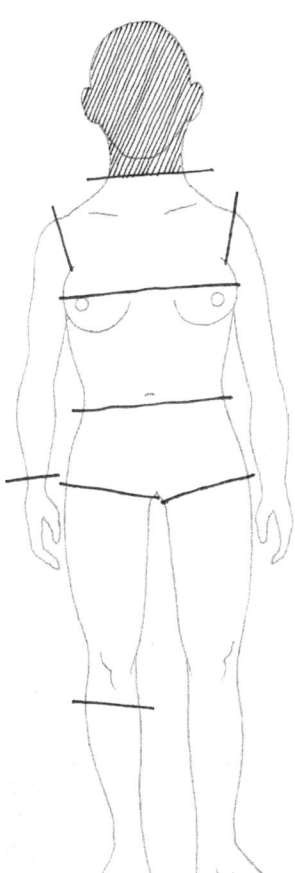

The thick black lines represent the cuts made to dissect the body. The shaded areas are the parts that were never found.

in, for example, the Rag Fair in Whitechapel and there was no guarantee that they had belonged to the deceased anyway. But surely, *somebody* out there, the police hoped, must have missed a sandy-haired girl in her mid-twenties, seven months gone, who chewed her nails to the quick.

Red herrings dogged the police enquiries at every turn. On 9 June a 'small liver' was found floating in the river at Wapping. It was taken as a matter of course to Battersea, but it did not belong to the dead woman. In fact, Dr Kempster was not even sure it was human. Early the next day, lighterman Joseph Squires had found the dead woman's right arm, folded double with string near Southwark Bridge. The pickle jar found on 13th however had no connection with the Thames mystery. It did contain the body of a foetus, but in Kempster's opinion, had not come from the murdered woman. Infanticide was not uncommon in Victorian England, where poor women, at a time of non-existent birth control, often felt they had no choice but to visit the highly dangerous abortionists who haunted London's back streets.

Missing persons enquiries were also, at first, leading nowhere. Constable Fisher of the Hertfordshire police let the Met know that his sister was missing. Although technically Mrs Wren by 1889, her maiden name was L E Fisher and she was 25 years old. She had labelled many of her clothes and had abandoned her husband and child on 18 May 1888 to live with another man. Whether she was the same L E Fisher as the barmaid at the Old Dock Tavern along the Thames the police never discovered. *That* L E Fisher was missing too.

There are three L Fishers listed in the census of 1881; the only L E Fisher would have been 9 at the time of the Horsleydown Mystery. The L E Fisher who was the missing barmaid was found to be alive and well and living in Ramsgate, Kent.

By the time of the resumed Inquest on Saturday 16 June, the police had been carrying out extensive searches for the dead woman's missing head, including the use of dogs. The fiasco of bloodhounds in the Ripper case nine months earlier was not forgotten and the *Weekly Herald* was one of several newspapers openly critical of police efforts:

> The advisability of employing bloodhounds to trace the perpetrator of the crime has been eagerly discussed by the inhabitants of the district. It is considered, however, by experts that the time has gone by for such an experiment [the murder was assumed to have happened some six weeks previously] and it is pointed out that in the case of the Blackburn murderer who was discovered by such means, the circumstances were different and that the present case does not admit of that.[3]

The Blackburn case was the murder of 7-year-old Emily Holland in 1876. She was abducted shortly after four o'clock as she walked Bisley Street in Blackburn on 27 March. She was on her way to a local shop to buy tobacco. The dogs were called in to aid in the search for her and discovered her dismembered body in a trunk (some accounts say chimney) wrapped in a copy of the *Preston Herald*. She had been raped and her throat had been cut prior to dismemberment. Emily's killer was local barber, 26-year-old William Fish, a father of three who ran a shop in nearby Moss Street. He was hanged at Liverpool Gaol on 14 August.

Jasper Waring's excellent dog Smoker was called in again, after his triumph in the foundations of Scotland Yard ten months earlier. Since most of the body parts had been found in water and the Shelley section clearly thrown from the riverside walkway, Battersea Park was the only area where any kind of scent might remain. It was too tall an order for Smoker however and the police came to the conclusion that the head had either been burnt or buried.

Wynne Baxter had had only one portion of a torso to work on. Braxton Hicks had an entire body without a head. The regulations were very clear; inquests were held on bodies in the area where they were found and since most of the body parts had been located on the river's south bank, the jurisdiction fell to the coroner for mid-Surrey who held court at the Star and Garter pub in Battersea on Saturday 16 June.

Dr Thomas Bond was the first witness and revealed that he had been called in by Sir Robert Anderson, Assistant Commissioner at Scotland Yard. R Michael Gordon, anxious to lay the torso murders at Jack's door, believes this had a connection with the Ripper, but Anderson's role covered all crime in London. Having explained the medical findings, Bond asserted that, in his opinion, the same man was responsible for the dismemberment at Rainham and in Whitehall. When Hicks asked him if the heads, thrown into the river, would sink, Bond answered 'Yes'. It was the correct answer to an obvious question, but neither coroner nor police surgeon fully understood the workings of a serial killer's dark mind.

The fact that the dead woman had been pregnant led the coroner to follow a line of enquiry that included abortion. Could this have been carried out 'by means of drugs'? Without the brain, throat or stomach, Bond could not comment. And if the killer was skilled at dismemberment, did he also have the medical knowledge to know that these body parts must never be found, or they might lead directly to him?

The various riverside witnesses whose testimony we have heard already followed Bond into the make-shift witness box and Hicks, assured by Inspector Tunbridge that enquiries were still ongoing, adjourned the inquest until 1 July.

It was now that a breakthrough happened, the first meaningful one in the entire case. Catherine Jackson came forward to identify the dead woman, not as the elusive L E Fisher, but as her daughter, Elizabeth; and she recognized her corpse, lying in Battersea mortuary, in an ever-increasing state of decomposition, by the scars on her left forearm.

The police could now put, literally, flesh on the bones of their investigation. Elizabeth had been 24 years old, 5ft 5ins tall, plump and well formed. She had reddish gold hair with lovely teeth and nicely shaped hands. The Ulster was indeed hers, given to her not long before she disappeared by a family friend, Mary Minter. And the police also discovered that Elizabeth had bought old clothes labelled L E Fisher; the apparent red herring had been netted after all.

Elizabeth Jackson was the youngest of three daughters – the others were Annie and May – born to Mr and Mrs Jackson in Chelsea in 1865. In common with many young girls throughout the country, she began work as a servant in 1881 and was of 'excellent character' until November 1888 when she suddenly left both home and job. The last link with her family was in Turk's Row, Chelsea, when Annie met her in the street. The sisters rowed about Elizabeth 'picking up men for immoral purposes' and the younger girl left. The next time Annie saw her, she was lying headless and in pieces on a mortuary table.

Chapter 7

The Women of Moab and Midian

Turk's Row lies off fashionable Sloane Square, but it is only a stone's throw from the river and the various body parts found in and near Battersea Park. Elizabeth Jackson had travelled some three hundred yards from her place of work to her death.

The police uncovered the fact that Elizabeth was living with a 'protector' (pimp) called Charlie and during November she took up with John Faircloth, a miller and Cambridgeshire man who was 37 and had served in the Grenadier Guards. Edward Cardwell's army reforms of 1870–1 had altered the enlistment period for Other Ranks. Such men served six years with the colours and six with the Reserve. It is likely that Faircloth had already 'done his time' and the pair seem to have gone to Ipswich for four months, although exactly why is unclear. It was here that Elizabeth bought the L E Fisher clothing. They were in Colchester on 30 March 1889 and unable to find work, returned to London. Elizabeth was some five months pregnant by this time and they moved into the lodging house of Mrs Paine in Manilla Street, Millwall, on 18 April. This was very near the river, next to the West India Dock pier. At Elizabeth's last inquest, Mrs Paine reported that Faircloth was violent towards the woman who appeared to be his common law wife. They parted on 28 April, perhaps four days before she died, Faircloth going south to try his luck in Croydon.

Elizabeth told him she was going home to her mother, but Catherine Jackson was in the workhouse by then, so it is likely that her father was dead and there was nothing that passed for a family home. On 29 April Elizabeth left Mrs Paine's owing a week's rent. She was sleeping rough on the Thames Embankment, along with a lot of other down-and-outs. Journalist George R Sims wrote a few years later:

> ... soon after 1 a.m. the sleepers-out have settled down into their al fresco slumbers and so the Embankment presents a picture of the mingled magnificence and despair that is perhaps without parallel in the world. Here

the lost souls wander gloomily. Here the homeless vagabond and the prowler in search of prey herd together. Men, old and young, grey-haired women and girls just come to womanhood crowd together in sheltered corners ... there are some desperate men among the Embankment 'dossers' – men who would not hesitate to fling their stunned and despoiled victims into the Thames if the opportunity were given them ... But not all these children of the night are criminals or roughs. Some are the sons and daughters of despair.[1]

From this hard, cold bed, Elizabeth made her way back to her old Chelsea haunts. Her mother's friend, Mrs Minter of Cheyne Road, met her and gave her 3d for a meal and the old Ulster her body parts would later be found wrapped in. Elizabeth was coping but could not go into the workhouse because she knew her mother was there. Mrs Minter saw her again the next day in the same place, still soliciting, no doubt. Later that day, another witness, Annie Dwyer, from Turk's Row, saw Elizabeth with a man wearing a dark coat, light moleskin trousers and a rough cap. Like all the eyewitness accounts of men seen talking to the Ripper's victims shortly before their deaths, this is almost useless. Annie believed the man might have been a sailor, but there is nothing overtly in his dress to indicate this. He was probably simply a client.

On 31 May, with only days to go before her daughter's murder, Catherine Jackson saw Elizabeth in the Queen's Road, Chelsea. The girl's first instinct was to run, but she stayed put and told her mother all her woes. Exactly what Catherine was doing out of the workhouse is not clear, but she may have been trying to find work. Elizabeth told her mother that John Faircloth was the father of her child and that he had left her. At that last meeting, Elizabeth was wearing a cheap brass ring on her wedding finger.

John Faircloth probably was the father. But if Elizabeth was seven months pregnant in early June 1889, she conceived the previous November, which meant that the shadowy 'Charlie' could have been responsible or even Elizabeth's former employer which would explain why she left Chelsea so precipitately.

'If she was a whore God will bless the hand that slew her,' wrote the anonymous crank to the Central News Agency back in October in connection with the Whitehall Mystery, 'for the women of Moab and Midian shall die'.[2] Moab and Midian were biblical cities of the Old Testament, steeped in the kind of licentiousness we associate with Sodom and Gomorrah. And there were powerful elements in Victorian society that had a pious, high-and-mighty attitude towards prostitution. So all-prevailing was this, especially among the literate middle class, that the subject could not be discussed openly, still less written about. Out of this came the euphemism 'the oldest profession'.

One of the very few who dared to be open about the subject was 'General' William Booth of the Salvation Army. Booth operated originally from the Mile End Waste in the East End in 1865, bringing comfort and the promise of salvation to the hopeless. He wrote *In Darkest England and the Way Out* in 1891, two years after the torso killings stopped. In the business of saving lives and souls, Booth's 'Sally Army' girls worked from Angel Alley off the Whitechapel Road and had hundreds of cases of prostitution on their register. The cases do not make pleasant reading but they paint a picture of working-class life very different from anything we know today. The twenty-first century's bogeyman is the paedophile and frightened, ignorant parents demand lists of these people and their addresses 'so they can keep their children safe'. Most examples of sexual abuse of children are actually committed by family members or neighbours. Incest was not even regarded as a crime until 1908. 'E C', Booth's records tell us, was 'aged 18, a soldier's child, born on the sea. Her father died and her mother, a thoroughly depraved woman, assisted to secure her daughter's prostitution.' 'E A' was '17 ... left an orphan very early in life and adopted by her godfather, who himself was the means of her ruin at the age of 10'. Another orphan, 'E' married a soldier who left her pregnant. 'Being on the verge of starvation, she entered a lodging house in Westminster and "did as other girls".'

The 'Great Social Evil', as prostitution was called by the 1870s, had a fascination for the Victorians. Prostitutes were 'unfortunates', 'ladies of the night', 'scarlet sisters', rather as they are 'workers in the sex industry' today and there was a hierarchy among them as in many other professions. Henry Mayhew, publishing his brilliant *London Labour and the London Poor* eleven years before the first torso murder, divides prostitutes into eight categories, although his dividing lines were of necessity blurred and he may not have been quite accurate. He was after all a forty-something middle-class sociologist (the term had not been invented in his day) and he seemed to want just to *talk* to the girls. Many of them called him 'a funny old party'.

At the top of the tree came the prima donnas, the kept mistresses. The best known of these was Catherine Walters, known as Skittles, who wore ridiculously tight riding habits to encourage aristocratic suitors on Rotten Row of a morning. Those ladies were beautiful, educated, often talented musicians and actresses and cost a fortune to maintain. Their houses are still there in James Street and Duke Street and some of them were friends of royalty. Next came the convives, still 'an ornament to their sex' but less expensive. Many of them seemed to have been happy to have their rent paid, their wardrobes provided and the odd present, like a sewing machine, given to them. Below those groups came 2a, b and c, operating at the same level, but organized in different ways. The independents worked alone, street walkers, but elegant and refined. They could be found centred on the Haymarket and its environs in the mid-century, but increasingly along the Strand and some of the fashionable London squares. The Rose Tattoo murder of October 1884 has a link here.

Mayhew divided 2b in half. The board lodgers were given board (i.e. food and a bed); the dress lodgers were given board and dress. In both cases, they worked under a woman who ran a brothel. Since Paris was regarded as the centre of sin by most Englishmen, European terms were often used. The brothel was the bordello; the mistress was the madame. In the West End, there were 'poses plastiques' and 'tableaux vivantes', the equivalent of pole-dancing but without the pole. Gentlemen out on the town could spend an evening or all night at the bordellos – in Mayhew's day Kate Hamilton's in the Haymarket was the best known – dinner and champagne were on offer too. *The Man of Pleasure's Pocket Book* written in the 1850s and regularly updated, carried advertisements for girls. Mrs Merton's 'sister hills' were 'prominent, firm and elastic'. Mrs Woodford's breasts were 'rather small, but as plump and hard as an untouched virgin's'.

Some of these women were street walkers, usually venturing out at four in the afternoon and letting men take them to dinner, the theatre or a dance before 'earning her supper'. Such women were noticeable when drunk in their hired finery, but otherwise they blended with 'respectable' ladies and that sometimes posed a problem for the police.

Commentators at the time – and historians, since – have focused on this 'gay' life (the term meant female prostitution) because it is exciting, exotic and involves famous names. Edward, Prince of Wales and his circle, the Duke of Brunswick and the Marquis of Waterford mixed with social reformers like Mayhew, Charles Booth, William Booth and even the leader of the Liberal Party, William Gladstone. We are concerned with groups 3 to 6 on Mayhew's list. The low lodging women and the sailors' and soldiers' women are the whores lit by the spotlight of the Ripper. Of interest too, potentially, are Mayhew's lowest of the low, the park women and the thieves' women.

So much research has been carried out on Jack's victims that we almost expect East End prostitutes to be middle-aged. Martha Tabram was 39, but looked much older. Polly Nichols was 45; Annie Chapman two years older; Liz Stride was 45; the woman who died on the same night, Kate Eddowes, was 46; Clay Pipe Alice McKenzie was probably 45. Only Mary Kelly was in her twenties. Yet *all* the torso killer's victims were probably between 23 and 35 and if we are trying to home in on the sort of women who were his targets, we should concentrate on the younger 'motts'[3] of London. In this category of course comes Mary Kelly herself, but the Ripper case has highlighted other prostitutes' names who were her age or younger.

Lizzie Albrook was about 20 in 1888. She lived in Miller's Court, Dorset Street, in the same enclave as Mary, whom she visited on the night of her murder on 8/9 November. Lizzie worked in a lodging house in Dorset Street and may not yet have been on the game. Mary frequently warned the girl 'whatever you do don't you do wrong and turn out as I have'.[4] Elizabeth Burns, known as One-Armed Liz, was 18. She was attacked on 18 September 1888 by the deranged and dangerous Charles Ludwig, who threatened her with a knife in Aldgate. She was rescued by the timely arrival of a patrolling policeman. Frances Coles was known as Carrotty Nell, a good-looking blonde 26 years old at the time of her murder on St Valentine's Day 1891. Wounds to her throat when she was found lying in Swallow Gardens under the railway arches near Chambers Street, Whitechapel led the press and for a while the police to speculate that this was another Ripper killing. She was probably killed in a 'domestic' by her current 'bully', a violent ship's fireman called James Sadler, but there was insufficient evidence against him.

Mary Jones would have been called a madame in the West End. She was about 24, the same age as Elizabeth Jackson and was charged with brothel-keeping by Inspector Arthur Ferrett of H Division on 7 December 1888. Her 'colleague' Gertrude Smith was much older (57) and was sentenced to a £10 fine with 5 guineas costs. It is likely that this was the result of a routine clampdown, irrespective of the Ripper murders, as the police from time to time were pressured by do-gooders and the Christian lobby to clean up London.

Rose Mylett was another victim attributed to the Ripper. Also known by her street names of Drunken Lizzie Davis and Fair Alice Downey, she lived at a variety of East End addresses before 20 December 1888 when her body was found in Clarke's Yard near Poplar High Street. She had not been robbed (there was still ½d in her pocket) and the body was still warm when Constable Robert Goulding found her at quarter past four in the morning. The medical opinion, via the ubiquitous Dr Thomas Bond, was that she had died of natural causes as a result of accidental strangulation due to her tight-necked bodice. As there was no alcohol in her stomach and she had been seen arguing with a couple of sailors the previous evening, the ever-irascible coroner, Wynne Baxter, begged to differ and instructed the jury to return a verdict of 'Murder by person or persons unknown'. It is possible (although unlikely) that Bond was genuinely at a loss to explain this one and bowed to Metropolitan pressure from Robert Anderson himself. Rose Mylett was 26.

With the exception of Mary Kelly, it seems from what we know that the rest of Jack's victims began as respectable women, married and often with children, but that drink and bad luck drove them to the streets. Taking a random 100 cases of women who had turned up in General Booth's Salvation Army Rescue

Homes, his analysis was as follows. In 1890, 14 per cent had 'fallen' because of drink (compare a tentative figure of 85 per cent of Jack's victims); 33 per cent had been seduced, and saw themselves as 'ruined'; 24 per cent had become prostitutes because of the bad company they kept – perhaps 'Charlie' and John Faircloth fitted this role in the case of Elizabeth Jackson. Only 2 per cent were driven by poverty and 24 per cent accosted men through 'wilful choice'. These figures came from the statements of the girls themselves and cast doubt on the usual line that the appalling poverty of the East End was a direct cause of prostitution. That said, of the 100 women under Booth's spotlight, only 48 of them were decently dressed; 52 were either destitute or in rags.

'The profession of a prostitute', wrote General Booth, 'is the only career in which the maximum income is paid to the newest apprentice.'[5] And they started young, often with the connivance of their parents in order to bolster the weekly income. Children were a commodity in Victorian England, to be stuffed up chimneys or sent down mines. Do-gooders like Lord Shaftesbury worked long and hard to end the abuse of child labour, but Acts of Parliament only went as far as factory owners and children's parents were prepared to let them go. Small outlets like sweat shops in which girls worked for long hours making clothes were exempt from such legislation and the 'climbing boys' act had only recently been passed when the torso murders began. So if children were routinely exploited by adults in the workplace, why not sexually?

Superintendent Joseph Dunlap of C Division, who would become involved in the latest of the torso murders, gave evidence before a committee of the House of Lords at the behest of the London Society for the Protection of Young Females in 1881. He admitted there was a great deal of juvenile prostitution in his Division, focusing on one brothel in particular, where girls as young as 12 were available. Until 1885 the age of consent was 12 and a change of the law in that year only raised it to 13. Pornographic photographs offered for sale in London were of 7 and 10 year olds whose 'secret charms are completely devoid of hair as nature has not yet given them these revolting tokens of puberty. Like grown up ladies these little girls indulge in all debauchery.'[6]

Dunlap's recent raid on the brothel had uncovered 'elderly gentlemen' in bed with two girls who regarded the whole thing as a joke. The cost was 6 shillings for two girls; 4 shillings for one. No charge was made against the children or the client. The brothel-keeper was committed for trial. The superintendent's view was that teenagers become prostitutes because it was a better option than the drudgery of the 'tweeny' or downstairs maid. The hands of the torso victims were well-manicured (except Elizabeth Jackson who apparently bit her nails) because in all probability they were prostitutes. A serving girl's hands would be red from the washing and scrubbing, her nails broken and chipped from black-leading the grate and making the fire.

In the year of the Ripper, Beatrice Potter Webb wrote an article for the *Nineteenth Century* magazine called 'Pages from a Workgirl's Diary'. Like other (usually male) journalists who went underground to record the life of the poor, she took various menial jobs in the sweated trades and mixed with girls who took to the streets when times were hard. There were no trade unions yet for these girls and much of the work was tough and dangerous. Flower and chestnut sellers standing all day in the pouring rain; match sellers freezing on street corners; match-makers whose bones were rotten with the effects of phosphorus – who could blame any of them for selling herself for a larger profit? One of the girls told Beatrice Webb about a brothel run by 'Mother' Willit in Gerrard Street, near Shaftesbury Avenue, in the heart of the West End:

> So help her kidnies, she al'us turned her gals out with a clean arse and good tog [clothes] and as she turned 'em out, she didn't care who turned 'em up, cause 'em was clean as a smelt and as fresh as a daisy.[7]

Unlike European cities where red light districts were beginning to develop (the Parisian police kept a register of brothels and they were sanctioned by law) London's Unfortunates could be found almost anywhere. In the East End, Spitalfields and Whitechapel – the Abyss – were legendary, but the docks had their centres of sin too. The Ratcliffe Highway was once considered the most dangerous street in the country, crammed with pubs and brothels to entertain the vast number of foreign sailors constantly in port in the biggest dock system in the world. Shadwell High Street, Brunswick Street, Frederick Street, these and others like them were places where a cheap, willing girl could be found at any time of the day or night. Henry Mayhew recorded some of them – Cocoa Bet, Salmony-faced Mary Anne, Black Sarah. They plied their trade out of the Duke of York and the Ship and Shears, the Half Moon and the Seven Stars. And if anyone objected to the fact that several of these ladies were coloured, a poem of the time put everything in context –

> The night when her sable o'ershades us,
> Will veil all the pomp of the day,
> Then Sall[8] is as good as my lady,
> And cats are all equally grey.[9]

Back in the West End, where Elizabeth Jackson and probably the other torso victims earned their living on the streets, one brothel, run by Madame Audray in Church Street, Soho, had a rather revolting sales pitch in the guide books available for men-about-town. It compared itself with an abbatoir.

> This abbess [Audray] has just put the kipehook [kibosh] on all other purveyors of the French flesh market. She does not keep her meat too long on the hooks, though she will have her price; but nothing is allowed to get stale here. You may have your meat dressed to your own liking and there is no need of cutting twice from one joint; and if it suits your taste, you may kill your own lamb or mutton for her flock is in prime condition and always ready for sticking.[10]

One man who took her literally was the torso killer.

Chapter 8

The Pinchin Street Torso: Whitechapel, 10 September 1889

On 4 September 1889, while police numbers began to be cut back again in the once-more quiet wake of the Ripper murder of Alice McKenzie, a letter was sent to the City Police. It was postmarked SE5, the area around Camberwell and Denmark Hill, and was unsigned. On the face of it, it was a typical 'nosey neighbour' letter, similar in vein to dozens that had been received over the past eleven months. This one, though was very detailed and almost apologetic.

> I think a murder was committed last night at 65 Gt. Prescott St. It may have been the young servant who I was told had been made [maid] to one of the daughters in the day. I heard another was to be killed to day if <u>some one</u> told. The mistress told me in the afternoon if the young servants did not please her she sent them away. Some in the house wanted me to be killed but the eldest daughter would not allow it. I think some one was brought in and his [illegible] of one night before. I am very sorry to say this and am sorry that the family should be Jewish. I would ask if it would not be possible for a detective from London not known here to take the furnished bedroom and by God's help put a stop to what I fear is a practice of young women brought in and then murdered. I am very sorry to have to give information but I must please God … If I did not tell it would seem as if I connived at the shedding of blood.

The unsigned letter was passed to Leman Street police station and found its way into the hands of Inspector Edmund Reid, in charge of H Division's CID. Reid was one of the most colourful policemen involved in hunting the Ripper, the *Weekly Despatch* going so far as to call him 'one of the most remarkable men of the century'. He was an amateur actor, singer, conjuror and balloonist who would eventually figure as Detective Dier in the thrillers of the novelist Charles

Gibbon. Reid's later memoirs prove that he was woefully wide of the mark in his analysis of the Whitechapel murders and he dismissed this letter as he knew the woman who wrote it and she was insane.

Even so, *someone* was bringing young women in somewhere and murdering them and the next one would take place only a few hundred yards from Great Prescott Street.

John Cleary visited the offices of the *New York Herald* to report a killing. A policeman, he told the newsdesk, had found a body at about 11.20pm on Saturday 7 September in Back Church Lane, some 300 yards from the Berner Street site of the killing of Long Liz Stride. Cleary had learned this from a personal friend, a police inspector he had met by chance in Whitechapel High Street. Two reporters, anxious to capitalize on what may well have been another Ripper killing, asked Cleary to go to the site with them, but he refused. He also now modified the story to the effect that his informant was an ex-officer, no longer serving with the Met. Back Church Lane was deserted and at Leman Street police station, the reporters learned that no murder had taken place there. With so many bogus letters being sent to the police and journalists, the whole incident was written off as a hoax.

Constable 239H William Pennett was a sergeant by the time he appeared in a group photograph of his Division. He is sitting on the floor in front of senior officers, with his ankles crossed and his helmet in his lap. He looks grim and determined, probably much as he did about five in the morning of Tuesday 10 September when he discovered a mutilated torso under a railway arch in Pinchin Street. The line was owned by the Tilbury & Southend Railway Company. This was just yards from Cleary's claimed murder site in Back Church Lane; in fact Pennett had just walked along it. There were four arches that led to the Whitechapel Vestry stone yard and all except the first were boarded off. At first, as he shone his bull's eye lantern, Pennett saw nothing, but then a sense of horror gripped him. A headless, almost naked, female torso lay on its front about one foot from the right-hand wall of the arch and about eighteen feet from the Pinchin Street pavement. The right arm lay under the body, the left alongside the trunk and a bloody, torn chemise was draped over the neck and right shoulder. Pennett rolled the body over, despite the appalling smell and saw the bowels protruded through a deep gash in the abdomen.

The procedure for any London policeman was to remain with a corpse. Pennett told a passing street cleaner to find the nearest constable, but decided he could not wait for that and blew his whistle. Two colleagues arrived, Constables 205H and 115H, one of them running off to the King David Lane police station for reinforcements while the other stayed with Pennett and they inspected the archway. There was no discernible blood on either the ground or the wall and the body itself was already starting to decompose.

Pennett wrongly believed that the killer was still nearby and on this premise the machinery of the overstretched H Division swung into motion, with Reid and his colleague Inspector Charles Pinhorn in charge of the investigation on the ground. Pinhorn had already worked on the Liz Stride case and knew this patch like the back of his hand. Both men reported to Superintendent Thomas Arnold as head of H Division, another experienced officer who had been involved in the Israel Lipski case two years earlier.[1] Under Pinhorn a search of the immediate area uncovered two men asleep in the archway next to the body. Richard Hawke was a sailor, sleeping off a night of drink alongside fellow tippler Michael Keating, who lived at 1 Osborne Street, Whitechapel, but had clearly been too drunk to make it home the previous night. At Leman Street these two were sure there was no body there when they arrived, which meant that the murderer had taken a huge risk by placing it feet from the sleeping men. In the pitch blackness under the arch of course he may have been totally unaware of their presence.

The first medical man on the scene was Dr Percy Clark who arrived about six o'clock. He was assistant to the police surgeon, George Bagster Phillips, who had presided over most of the Ripper's victims. Phillips was on holiday so Clark supervised the removal of the remains to the mortuary of St George's in the East (the shell of which still stands) – and examined it further.

Hebbert's *Exercise in Forensic Medicine* makes it clear that he was present at the Pinchin Street victim's post-mortem. The trunk was plump and well formed, the breasts full and there was dark hair in the armpits and on the pubes. The hands were small and the nails were well kept. Rigor mortis had come and gone, the flesh already turning green. The cut surfaces at the hips were dry and black, that at the neck moist and red. The various organs were weighed (there is no mention of this in Hebbert's earlier reports) and all were confirmed as being 'fairly healthy'. The stomach appeared to contain plums and there was no abnormality of the intestines. The uterus was weighed and measured and the ovaries were found to be cystic and already degenerating. Hebbert estimated the woman's height to have been 5ft 3½ins and she would have been between 25 and 40 years old. She had never borne children, nor had she suckled one. The vagina was distended so she was not a virgin. The hands gave no indication of hard manual work but intriguingly, the right little finger had a small circular hardening which might have been caused by writing. There was no mark of a wedding ring. The cause of death was blood loss. All the dismemberment cuts were made after death with a very sharp knife. Once again, as with earlier victims, Hebbert judged that the killer was skilled in anatomy in the sense that a butcher or slaughterer would be. The cuts 'do not indicate a special anatomical knowledge of the human body'.[2]

What does not appear in Hebbert's report is the odd description issued by the police to the press: '... both elbows discoloured as from habitually leaning on them. Post-mortem marks apparently of a rope having been tied around the waist.'

Once again, there was hysteria in the East End, Pinchin Street being clogged with the ghouls who had had a field day in similar dingy thoroughfares in Whitechapel over the previous eighteen months.

On 11 September, the day after the torso was discovered, the Commissioner of the Met, James Monro, wrote a detailed report to J S Sanders, private secretary to Henry Matthews, the Home Secretary. In it, he explained that Pinchin Street was one of the quieter areas of the East End. Most of the

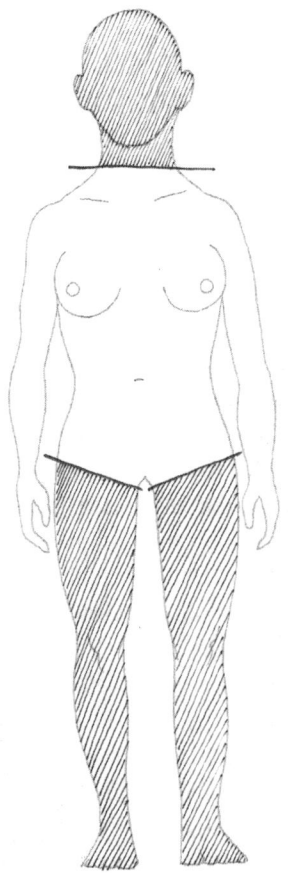

The thick black lines represent the cuts made to dissect the body. The shaded areas are the parts that were never found.

buildings along it were warehouses, the south side formed by the railway and its arches, so that it was not a street that would be busy with locals day and night, unlike most of Whitechapel. Monro was at pains to point out that the officer who found the body passed the place and checked it every half an hour, despite the huge pressure the Division was under. Monro believed that the torso had been placed in the archway between five and five thirty on the morning of 10 September. This is almost the only occasion in all the eight torso murders when such precise timings are possible. And yet the police still missed their man.

From the forensic evidence, Monro worked on the basis that the woman died on the night of Sunday 8 September. This was exactly a year after the murder of Ripper victim Annie Chapman and that dark – and irrelevant – fact probably led all sorts of people to all sorts of speculation. Monro's next conjecture was very sound and leads us closer to our man:

> The body must have been concealed, where the murder was committed during Sunday night, Monday and Tuesday up till dawn. This leads to the inference that it was so concealed in some place to which the murderer had access, over which he had control, and from which he was anxious to remove the corpse.

Monro conjectured that this took place in a house or lodging and that the body had to be removed before the smell began to arouse suspicions of neighbours.

The dump site was important and Monro allowed himself some rhetorical questions. Was this Jack's handiwork? If it was, it represented a new departure, because of the very different MO involved. Of the Ripper's victims, only Mary Kelly died indoors. And all of them were the work of a disorganized killer who selected his victims by place, carried out a frenzied 'blitz' attack and left them where they lay. Monro did not use this terminology but even so he doubted whether the Pinchin Street victims came under this category. There was no sign of the Ripper's frenzy, no focus on the reproductive organs; rather, there was an almost leisurely skilled dismemberment of the body and no definite cause of death. If the body had not been found in Whitechapel no one would have made any connection with the Ripper at all.

Monro had clearly seen the corpse himself and makes the interesting point that the wound leading to the vagina may have been made to *simulate* the widely reported Ripper crimes. Monro's conclusion was that this was not Jack's work, but that it bore a closer link with murders 'known as the Rainham mystery, the new Police building case and the recent case in which portions of a female body (afterwards identified) [i.e. Elizabeth Jackson] were found in the Thames'.[3]

What evidence had the police on the ground uncovered? Detailed searches in the area revealed nothing. Waste ground, carts and the railway line were scoured. Thames Division rowed up and down the stretch of river around Wapping known as the Lower Pool, looking in vain for other body parts to complete the Pinchin Street torso. Blood-stained clothing was found in Batty Street, not far to the north-east, but it proved to be menstrual blood and completely irrelevant.

In the days ahead, the *New York Herald* remembered the story of John Cleary. Chief Inspector Donald Swanson, who had headed up the Ripper investigation between September and October of the previous year, interviewed the paper's night editor, Mr Cowen and Mr Fletcher, one of the reporters who had gone to Back Church Lane days earlier on a wild goose chase. Cleary had given his address as 21 White Horse Yard, clearly a lodging house. The deputy there, Mr Yates, knew no one of that name, but a John Leary had stayed there for three weeks and left, owing rent. When this man was eventually found, he was not the informant who had gone to the *Herald*. As a result of police enquiries, John Arnold, a newspaper seller, came forward to say that it was he who had gone to the *Herald* although he gave no explanation of why he gave a false name and address. He had been approached on the evening of Saturday 7 September, having left the King Lud pub at Ludgate Street and was walking up Fleet Street. A man in a uniform had said to him, 'Hurry up with your papers; another horrible murder'. When Arnold asked where, he was told, 'In Back Church Lane.'

Arnold's description of the man was detailed. He was 35 or 36 years old, about 5ft 6 or 7ins, with a fair complexion and moustache. He wore a cheese-cutter cap (a working man's flat cloth version) and a black tunic with black shoulder cords and lightish coloured buttons. He also carried a parcel about 6 to 8 inches long. The uniform details are odd. They do not sound military, but may be connected with the railways or even the docks. Above all, the mention of a parcel smacks of similar descriptions of men seen talking to Ripper victims on the various nights in question. As was apparent at the time, most people expected Jack to be carrying his murder weapon with him, either in a parcel or a Gladstone bag.

I believe there is more to Mr Arnold than meets the eye but in the event, the police had no luck tracing 'uniform man'.

At Leman Street, Superintendent Arnold briefed Dr George Bagster Phillips, back from holiday and Colonel Bolton Monsell, the Chief Constable of the Met. They were joined by Monro and a decision was made to transfer one hundred extra men from other divisions into Whitechapel. Detectives Godley and Thick were dispatched to make house-to-house enquiries, focusing on butchers' premises and to sift the usual batch of missing person reports. Thick may have annoyed more than a few residents in this context because H T Hazelwood of High Road, Tottenham, wrote to the Home Office suggesting that he, Thick, was probably the Ripper and should be watched.

The inquest opened in the Vestry Hall, Cable Street, St George's in the East, with the ever-flamboyant Wynne Baxter in the chair. Reid was there along with Henry Moore from the Yard. We have already in effect heard Constable Pennett's testimony. Inspector Pinhorn explained that the arches in Pinchin Street were regularly used by down-and-outs who were turned out night after night. He could not explain how the torso had got there. It would have had to be carried on a coster cart or similar vehicle and at that time of the morning, such carts would be travelling in the opposite direction, those bound for Spitalfields Market not leaving until six o'clock. There was no sign of wheeltracks or footprints in the dust and debris near the body. In all this, Pinhorn seems to have had a touching faith in the mindset of a murderer, as though someone who had recently killed and cut up a woman would not be using his cart before the accustomed hour!

The medical evidence would have to wait because Dr Clark was busy with another case at the Old Bailey and Phillips was still making his own investigation on the Pinchin Street corpse. Accordingly, Wynne Baxter adjourned until 24 September.

Until then, likely suspects were rounded up by the police and odd characters were reported to them. They all had to be investigated. *The New York Herald* felt a certain proprietary interest in all this because of the 'John Cleary' link and somehow came up with a possible identity of the Pinchin Street corpse – Lydia Hart, an East End prostitute. She was however found alive, if not too well due to drink, in an infirmary by one of her sons.

By the time the inquest was resumed, Drs Clark and Phillips were available and gave their findings to a packed courtroom. Clark believed the murder had taken place about twenty-four hours before he saw it, which would take us to the early morning of Sunday, 9 September. The body seemed to have been recently washed and there were bruises on the back which were caused in life. The pale mark around the waist was caused, he believed, not by a rope but by ordinary clothing. The backs of both hands and forearms were badly bruised. This would have been caused by a tight grip. There was an old injury to the right index finger and a vaccination mark on the left upper arm. 'Both elbows were hardened and discoloured, as if they had been leant upon.'

Bagster Phillips gave his evidence next, explaining that Dr Gordon Brown, the newly appointed City Police surgeon, had attended the post-mortem too. He had also officiated in the case of the Ripper victim Kate Eddowes, butchered in Mitre Square, and had produced the most detailed of all the Whitechapel murder reports. Phillips assured Wynne Baxter's jury that there was no sign of poison and this evidence may have been given in relation to the later Ripper cases in which it was rumoured poison was used. He believed the disarticulation weapon to be at least 8 inches long and that the wounds had been carried out by someone 'accustomed to cut up animals'. He also believed that the actual murder might have been committed by a cut to the throat which had been hidden by subsequent decapitation.

The two down-and-outs under the arches with the body gave their evidence. Michael Keating, licensed shoe-black from Osborn Street, said he could not afford his doss money for the night and so was 'carrying the banner', the all-too frequent necessity of the East End's desperately poor. 'I was not sober' he hardly had any need to tell the jury. The first thing he had been aware of that morning was the police waking him up and the inspector (Pinhorn) covering the body with a piece of sacking in which Keating kept his blacking box. This was not a regular sleeping spot for the shoe-black and he was not aware of other sleepers at the time. Richard Hawke, from St Ives in Cornwall, had been paid off his ship seven or eight weeks before and had been staying at Greenwich Hospital. He had left there two weeks before and gave no account of himself until he reached the Pinchin Street arches at about twenty past four on the morning of 10 September. He had drunk about three pints and 'was not exactly sober'. With him was another seaman from the Sailors' Home and they both lay down in the next arch to the one where the body was found. Neither of them saw or heard anything.

Next came cabman Jeremiah Hurley, of 10 Annibal Place, who worked for John Smithers of Well Street. He was knocked up by a policeman at five o'clock (this was an unofficial service local beat 'bobbies' often did) and was entering Pinchin Street from Phillips Street at five thirty when he saw a man 'who had the appearance of a tailor'. Author R Michael Gordon says that this man was located and he had no knowledge of the murder, although what it was about his appearance that led Hurley to assume he was a tailor it is difficult to say.

Inspector Henry Moore showed the jury a plan of the crime scene as drawn by Inspector Charles Ledger of G Division. It still survives and is a very accurate drawing, showing the boarded up arches and two lamp brackets fitted to the wall.

When Dr Phillips was recalled, the coroner asked if there was any similarity between the Pinchin Street victim and 'the woman in Dorset Street' (Mary Kelly). The reply was that Kelly's injuries showed wanton savagery, whereas the Pinchin Street corpse bore the hallmarks of careful dismemberment for the sake of disposal.

That was as far as the inquest could go and Wynne Baxter was no doubt less than happy when he told the jury to consider their verdict. It could only be 'wilful murder against some person or persons unknown'.

Sergeant Godley's missing persons angle was still throwing up possibilities however. The *Morning Advertiser* of 30 September carried the story that the Pinchin Street torso could have been that of Emily Barker from Northampton. Her mother claimed that she had made the chemise wrapped around the remains (which would explain why it had no manufacturer's label) and that she recognized the mark on her finger. Emily had last been seen alive by a missionary 'carrying the banner' in a doorway two days before the Pinchin Street discovery. She had not been fully clothed then and was clearly living a 'wild life'. In fact, Emily was too short and too young to be the Pinchin Street victim and the *Advertiser* reported on 1 October that Scotland Yard were satisfied that the remains were not those of Emily Barker, whom presumably they had found alive and well.

Four days after that, the Pinchin Street victim was preserved in alcohol and laid to rest. Inspector Moore reported on 5 October:

I attended at the cemetery at time specified and witnessed the interment. It was placed in grave number 16185 and upon the metal on box was the following:

> This case contains
> body of a woman (unknown)
> found in Pinchin Street
> St Georges-in-the-East
> 10th Septr./89.

Do clues still lie in that specially sealed box in the East London Cemetery, Plaistow, waiting for a more technologically advanced age ... like ours?

Chapter 9

'Dealers in Horror': Battersea, 5 September 1873, and Putney, June 1874

The torso killings did not begin with Rainham in 1887, although they did end with Pinchin Street two years later. To find the start of this particular trail of terror, we have to go back fourteen years.

1873 was a year for deaths. In December, the first of the 'London peculiars', the thick fogs that enveloped the capital with sulphurous gloom, struck, killing an estimated 1,150 people in three days. On 1 May in the native village of Chitambo in what is Zambia today, the explorer and missionary David Livingstone was found dead in his hut, kneeling as if in prayer. A week later, in Avignon, France, the political campaigner and philosopher John Stuart Mill died of tuberculosis. His autobiography, published later in the year, heaped praise on his late wife, Harriet: 'A real majestic intellect, not to say moral nature like yours, I can only look up to and admire.'

Not everybody was as eulogistic on womankind. At Durham, on 24 March, a dozen pressmen, a couple of medical students and a ghoul named Crooks who specialized in attending hangings, stood in the execution shed at the gaol to say a sorrowless farewell to the mass poisoner, Mary Ann Cotton. The hangmen were William Calcraft and Robert Evans, neither of them particularly efficient at their task and Mary Ann did not go quietly. According to her biographer, she was

> swinging round, her chest heaving and her clasped hands jumping up and down. Then she began to twist about and to sway from side to side … Her body, unlike her mind, was loathe to give up life; it waged its desperate, frightful, hopeless fight. Shocked, hurt, in pain, it writhed, threw itself, jerked, the jumping hands frustrated by the pinioned arms from easing the agony of the cap and the rope, strangling mercilessly, inefficiently.[1]

And in September, another woman died. We still have no idea who she was.

With a rich irony, *The Times* featured a series on the Thames and its Embankment, a proud look at the extraordinary achievements of Joseph Bazalgette and the difference his engineering feat had made to London's inhabitants. But right next to it, in the edition of 8 September, was a whole column and a half headed 'Suspected Murder'. Three days earlier a Thames Police galley rowing routinely near Battersea saw an object floating in the river. It turned out to be the left quarter of a female torso. On 7 September two more portions were found, the right thigh floating off Woolwich and the right shoulder, with part of the arm attached, off Greenwich. The police noticed and subsequent medical reports confirmed that the arm was smeared in tar which probably occurred as the limb bobbed downstream, colliding with mooring ropes and other debris. *The Times* commented that the Woolwich find was the only one to be located below the various canals and each piece was found on an ebb tide, lower and lower down the river.

The consensus of opinion was that the body parts had entered the Thames not far from the point where the Wandle enters it and had been washed downstream. This is an important fixing point as we shall see. The Wandle runs north to meet the Thames just west of Wandsworth Bridge, so the assumption was made that the body parts were placed in the river from the south shore and not from a bridge.

The Times reported that death was caused by a blow to the right temple which crushed the skull, except that the skull was missing and that the first body part at any rate had been dumped in the river within hours of death. This meant that the first torso murder along the Thames had possibly taken place on Friday 5 September. 'Such', said the reporter, 'are the bare outlines of this evidently atrocious crime.' The *Lancet*, the medical journal founded by Thomas Wakley fifty years earlier, postulated that the body was drained of blood via a section of the carotid artery in the neck, since there were no clots elsewhere in the body's veins.

The inquest which followed shed more light. Constable Richard Frame of Thames Division had been on duty the previous Friday, rowing up to Chelsea Bridge from Somerset House. At half past six the galley was at low water opposite the Battersea Waterworks. The body part was lying on the foreshore, three or four feet from the water's edge. Frame's colleague checked and discovered that it was a 'portion of a woman's body, being the left breast entire'. The find was taken to the police station ship *Royalist* moored on the Thames Embankment. This vessel remained in use until 1898 and was known by Thames Division as 'The Abode of Bliss' ('Daddy' Bliss was the inspector in charge who lived on board with six constables). From there, the torso section passed to Battersea police station where it was examined by Dr Kempster, the divisional police surgeon.

On that same day, South-Western Railway Company policeman Henry Locke was on duty at the company's premises at Brunswick Wharf, Nine Elms. The trees themselves had long gone and this stretch of the river was heavily industrialized. The body part found here was nearly two miles downstream of the torso, a little upstream from Vauxhall Bridge. At half past ten Locke saw something floating in the water and, believing it to be a dead sheep, threw stones at it (!). He asked a bargee nearby to fish it out and discovered that it was the right breast of a woman. Locke passed it to a Met officer.

That officer was Constable 349W Henry Turner who took the torso part to Inspector Starkey of the Thames Police. Since the item had been found in the river, it naturally came within his jurisdiction. From there, it was passed to Dr Kempster.

Any crowd of people on the foreshore merited investigation and John Parker of the Thames Division saw just such a group at a quarter to seven the next morning, Sunday 7 September. This was Duke's Shore at Limehouse and Parker was passing in his galley. To the immediate east lay the huge West India Docks behind their granite walls and on the mud of the water's edge lay what was perhaps the most ghastly of all the torso killer's handiwork. It was 'the head of a woman with the bone out. It was the face and scalp of the head and had the ears, eyelashes but no eyes, the nose partly cut off, and the upper lip partly cut through, as was the cheek.' It appeared to have drifted down with the tide and although *The Times* report of Parker's evidence is confused, it seems that the face was shown to Inspector Marler of the Thames Division at Wapping police station before being taken to Scotland Yard.

At this point in the inquest proceedings held on the afternoon of 8 September in the boardroom of the Clapham and Wandsworth Union Workhouse, the coroner, W Carter, had had enough. He rounded on the police present, including Superintendent Butt of W Division and the Yard men Inspector Sayer and Sergeant Lansdowne, complaining that the face had been handled by too many people, as had the other body parts.

Inspector Marler probably did not have a pleasant time in the witness box. He was part of the overlong evidence chain himself and had also taken possession of what he believed to be the dead woman's lungs, which turned out to be those of a sheep. He was the first to notice a wound to the right temple.

Dr William Henry Kempster of Bridge Road, Battersea, was surgeon to V Division. He talked the coroner's court through his inspection of the various body parts and without the benefit of a second opinion, as we have with Dr Hebbert's analysis of the 1880s torsos, we have to hope that Kempster got it right. The right thorax, he said, was of a woman of about 40 years old, who was 'very stout'. Only part of the diaphragm remained of the internal organs and the breast had been separated between the second and third cervical vertebrae. There was also a higher cut where an attempt had been made to separate the body diagonally. A knife and a very fine saw had been used to remove the arm socket neatly from the trunk – exactly the same tools used in the later dismemberment cases. The retraction of the muscles led Kempster to believe that the cutting had been carried out very soon after death.

Four hours later he received the other side of the torso and they fitted exactly. This was more useful forensically. There was a coloured wart or mole near the right nipple, another mole on the neck and there was an old scar near the breastbone which was probably caused by a burn and probably done in childhood.

The next day Kempster took possession of the 'integuments of the head'. The chin was missing and so was half the mouth. The doctor believed that the scalp had been cut and the face pulled off the skull within thirty-six hours of Kempster first seeing it. The cut was clean, but had removed the nose and split the mouth. The hair and eyebrows were dark and the skin olive. 'There was a little moustache – the feminine moustache, as we call it', Kempster told the horrified jury. The hair on the head was 'very dark, very thin and somewhat short'. It may be that this was a piece of sloppy reporting by *The Times* because later editions gave the hair as long. In the meantime it led to speculation that the woman was a recently released convict, still sporting her prison haircut. Presumably there was enough of the nose left for Kempster to speculate that it was round, fat and short. The ears were too and had some time been pierced for earrings. The dead woman had been pregnant at some time and the extensive bruising on the right temple, three or four inches in diameter, was delivered in life. He did not speculate that this was the likely cause of death. There were three cuts to the head – one, obviously, to remove scalp and face, the others probably the result of an attack from a blunt instrument.

At this point Carter adjourned proceedings to give the police time to continue their enquiries. One obvious line of investigation was missing persons and a steady stream of people visited the remains at the Wandsworth and Clapham Workhouse mortuary to attempt to identify the body. This was a revolting experience, causing several of them to faint and gave rise to the real fear that 'dealers in horrors' were simply coming forward in ghoulish fascination. Ever since the Ratcliffe Highway murders[2] in 1811 – and probably earlier – the public had held a remarkable fascination for bloody killing. Portions of the Red Barn where Maria Marten had been buried in 1828 were physically ripped up and taken away as souvenirs. The skin of her killer,

William Corder, was made into a cover for a prayer-book. Freak shows up and down the country exhibited tableaux of grisly murder and in the year of the first torso murder, the wax effigy of poisoner Mary Ann Cotton was shown at Madame Tussaud's premises in Baker Street. The exhibition catalogue read: 'The child she rocked on her knee today was poisoned tomorrow. Most of her murders were committed for petty gains; and she killed off husbands and children with the unconcern of a farm-girl killing poultry.'[3]

One visitor to the mortuary who appeared to be genuine was a man from Bermondsey convinced that the dead woman was his daughter. Since she had had smallpox and no such scarring could be found on the Thames corpse, this seemed unlikely, but the stricken old man refused to be shaken in his certainty. Mr Hayden, the workhouse medical officer quizzed him further. The 60-year-old man, not named by *The Times,* lived in Britannia Place, Hoxton, and his

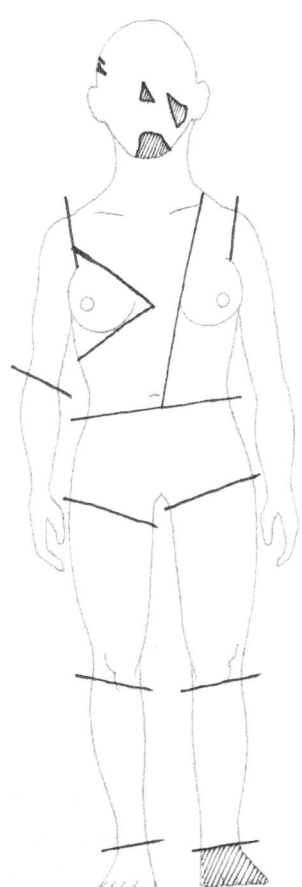

The thick black lines represent the cuts made to dissect the body. The shaded areas are the parts that were never found.

39-year-old married daughter had been missing for three weeks. His son-in-law had gone 'into the country' to bury his mother and his daughter 'went away in drink'. She had borne a child fifteen years ago. Kempster was of the opinion from the state of the breasts that the woman had indeed suckled a child at some time. The pair had lived in the City Road, so if it was her, she was a long way from home.

> If morbid curiosity had led the old man to travel this distance, he had all the horrors he could have desired. He was taken to the dead-house where the severed breasts were taken from a shell [coffin] and put together and the ghastly face having the scarred nose with the scalp, thinly covered with hair, was taken from a jar of spirits and laid before him.

But he could not remember any mole or wart, nor could he recall a burn wound to the chest. His daughter had a mole on her cheek, but that part of the cheek was missing.

The whole thing was inconclusive, but what emerges from *The Times* account is that the police considered seriously at this stage that the crime might have been committed on a barge and were particularly interested in the canals that led to Limehouse where the face was found. How much of this was the result of clues of which we now know nothing and how much of it was the natural xenophobia of the river is difficult to say. Bargees were often gypsies and assumed to be involved in all sorts of crime.

But there were more body parts to come. On 11 September a dock labourer named Gerrard found a foot floating in the river off Hammersmith Docks. This of course was important in that Hammersmith is some way *up* river from the earlier finds. Did the tide carry the foot upstream or was it placed there later as part of a continuing process? *The Times* now doubted the Wandle estuary as the dump point of the previous body parts. The police believed that the various sections were 'dropped' at high tide, about two o'clock on the previous Friday morning. The Thames Division, with their long experience of tides and currents, were of the view that three of the eleven body parts ended up 'below bridge'. The earliest found portions were carried from the Middlesex to the Surrey shore, one ending up on the mud, the other carrying on the stream further down. A piece as light as a foot would easily get caught in a 'lay-by' and be carried upstream again by the next incoming tide.

A full count of the eleven parts found by 11 September meant that what were still missing were: the skull, both hands, both legs, the left shoulder joint and the internal organs. What was curious was the absence of clothing; the Thames torso was totally naked. The dredgers of whom Charles Dickens senior wrote regularly sold clothing from corpses in the Thames, but no one had yet come forward to offer any of these to the police.

In the meantime, as was inevitable with a crime as repellent as this, the police were inundated with false alarms. On 10 September intestines taken aboard the *Royalist* proved to belong to two sheep – the bargemen were blamed for that too. Another set of enquiries also involved bargemen. On the day before the likely murder date, a bargee and his wife were heard quarrelling. This was a typical 'domestic' of the type the police met with regularly, but barges, by definition, were on the move all the time. This one was traced by detectives to Higham, near Rochester, and one plainclothesman kept watch throughout the night. When the barge moved off to Crawford and then Gravesend, he followed, only to be confronted – and abused – by the woman whose 'disappearance' he had been investigating.

The Times of 12 September reported that the old man who was convinced that the victim was his daughter had been overjoyed to find her very much alive in the Waterloo Road.

An altogether more likely lead involved a Mrs Cailey, who until recently had lodged in Battersea, only yards from the river. Analysis of the newspaper accounts of the time allow us to piece together this one line of enquiry and it is a reminder of how painstaking police investigation was and how time-consuming.[4] On 12 September, a week after the murder, an informant of South Street, Battersea Fields, reported to Inspector Hewlitt of the local division that her lodger had been missing since 2 September. She had been abandoned by her husband and assaulted by four men on Victoria Bridge in the days before her disappearance. She kept late hours and was continually boasting of being about to come into a large inheritance. The case of Mrs Cailey was explained at the resumption of the inquest on the fifteenth.

Carter again presided and Inspectors Sayer and Brady were there from the Yard. The first witness called was Richard Stratford 'a seeker of what I can find' who lived at East Greenwich. He was dredging on 8 September at Blackwall Point on the Kent side of the river when he found the tar-smeared thigh portion which he took to Greenwich police station. On the same day, Thomas Evans, waterman and lighterman of Nelson Street, Woolwich, found another thigh in the water near Woolwich Dockyard wall. He turned it over several times with his boat hook before taking it to Woolwich police station.

The next day, William Bennett, a platelayer from Plumstead, Essex, who worked at the Royal Arsenal in Woolwich, saw something on the bank. He was laying down a light-gauge railway at the time and broke off to investigate. This was the pelvis, although Bennett assumed it was a thigh. Coroner Carter intervened to ask Bennett to point to his own thigh and the platelayer pointed to his 'lower side' (presumably hip). Later that day, John Prince, waterman and lighterman of Manor Street, Chelsea, was in midstream at the Albert Bridge works, ready to 'pick up anything' which might fall from the works, such as timber, and he saw a handless arm. He noticed two bruises just above the wrist before he handed the limb in to Battersea police station.

On the same day William Prince (John's brother), apprentice to a waterman, was in his boat off Wandsworth Distillery about a quarter of an hour after high tide when he noticed a leg floating by and he thought it looked as if it had been 'pressed down' as though by weights.

The second arm was found on Wednesday by carman Edward Patterson of the Parade, Lambeth. He was on a barge (he does not explain why) at White Hart Docks, near Vauxhall, when he saw the bruised limb. He fished it out, wrapped it in straw and took it to Kennington Lane police station. It was the next day that Joseph Gerrard, waterman and lighterman of Queen's Street, Hammersmith, found the right foot floating near his barge.

Throughout these tense days, of course, the Thames Division galleys were on particular alert and it came as no surprise when Inspector Edmund Walker found a badly decomposed leg off Eastern's Wharf, Commercial Road, Lambeth. The coroner and jury then had the grisly task of viewing the assembled body parts.

Dr Kempster now had more of the body to report on and was able to say that the existence of one ovary and a portion of uterus with the pelvis proved that the victim had never given birth but she may at one time have miscarried. There were old scars on one arm and on one thigh, near the knee. The peculiar blistering on some of the skin surfaces he put down to the sun's rays on the exposed area bobbing above the river surface. Some of the bruising described by various finders was in fact decomposition. He believed there had been two very violent blows to the head, delivered in rapid succession, which would have resulted in immediate loss of consciousness and probably death. There was no sign of any stab wound and it was just feasible that the separation of body parts could have begun while the victim was still alive. Dr Edmund Hayden MRCS concurred with Kempster's findings, agreeing that the body was probably cut up while still warm.

Sergeant Lansdowne had clearly been following up another lead. Was it possible that this was some sort of medical school prank, that a cadaver available for legitimate dissection under the terms of the Anatomy Act could have ended up in the river as some sort of hideous joke? Since the medical schools were all closed until 1 October and no London hospital reported a body missing, this seemed unlikely. *The Lancet* leapt to the defence of medical students:

The public has, happily, in the course of thirty years, learnt to dissociate the medical student from the Burker[5] who may now be fairly said to be extinct. But, as recent events seem to show, there is still a tendency to make the student the scapegoat of any horrid murder or frightful mutilations. This is to be regretted for more reasons than one but chiefly because it interferes with the course of justice by leading it off the proper track.[6]

When the inquest turned its attention to a possible identification of the dead woman, the spotlight fell on Mrs Cailey. Mary Christian was the wife of Benjamin Fisher Christian and they took in lodgers at their house at 15 South Street, Battersea Fields. Since he is described as a traveller, it is likely that it was Mrs Christian who effectively ran the lodging house. Mary Ann Cailey had arrived with a Mr Beer at the beginning of August, from Dorsetshire, saying she needed rooms until 'her affairs were settled'. She claimed to be 33, but Mrs Christian had her doubts, putting her nearer to 40. The lodger needed to deal with a solicitor named Thompson of Lincoln's Inn in connection with her finances. Mrs Christian assumed this to be property or inheritance or both. Mary Cailey was currently the Christians' only lodger so had a room to herself. She was tall, a little under 5ft 9ins, and stout. Mrs Christian had last seen her on Thursday 2 September, when Mary Cailey left about ten in the morning, saying she was getting her things out of pledge and to receive money from her solicitor.

It was clear to Mrs Christian, who seems to have been sensibly nosy, that Mary Cailey was not all she seemed. She kept late hours and when Mrs Christian felt obliged to mention this, she merely laughed. About a week before she left she had been attacked by four men near Victoria Bridge. They had knocked her to the ground and hit her, probably with fists, on her temple just under the hair line. What struck the landlady as odd is that the lodger did not mention the attack on the night she claimed it happened, but a few days later. When Mrs Christian asked Mary Cailey where she went all day and until so late an hour, she claimed she went to see an old lady in Paulton's Square, Chelsea. There was no mention of Lincoln's Inn, the solicitor, or Mr Beer, who left as soon as Mrs Cailey was ensconced at the Christians'.

Mary Christian's description of the lodger's clothes, though very detailed, was almost pointless in that the Thames torso had been naked and no clothes were forthcoming. Her hair was thin and black however and Mary Christian had the dreadful job of examining the corpse. She could not be certain: 'I fully believe that is the face of Mrs Cayley, but I should not like to swear to it.' Doctors Kempster and Hayden both said that the bruise described by Mrs Christian could not possibly be the one visible on the temple of the corpse. At that point, coroner Carter gave his conclusion that a murder had been committed and suggested the government might like to offer a reward to further the case. The jury duly returned 'Wilful murder by person or persons unknown', although Kempster was sure that the dismemberment at least was carried out by one person alone.

It must have been soon after the inquest formally closed that Abel Beer visited the workhouse mortuary and told the police that the corpse was that of his sister, Mary Ann Cailey – he even remembered the scald mark on the stomach she had suffered as a child. For some reason, detectives working the case doubted it; perhaps they had seen ghouls like Abel Beer before and he apparently was beginning to have second thoughts too.

The Times editorial on 16 September, though accurate in other respects, got it hopelessly wrong on the dismemberment. This was done 'evidently without the guidance of even the most rudimentary knowledge of anatomy; for bones had been sawn through with considerable labour when the same kind of dismemberment might have been accomplished easily by means of the knife alone …' The paper retracted this later. Whoever dismembered the torso victims – all of them – was very adept at joint disarticulation and did it well. *The Times* speculated that the actual murder took place on Thursday 4 September and summed up the ongoing problem for anyone involved in working – or researching (!) – the torso killings:

> The facts point to a murder of a character more than usually atrocious; but the remains have not hitherto been identified and there is absolutely nothing to guide suspicion to the place where the murder was perpetrated. Not a particle of the dead woman's clothing has been found; and although it is conjectured that a barge may have been the scene of the tragedy, it is at least equally possible that it occurred at some distance from the river and that the pieces were carried thither after the commission of the crime.[7]

Four days later the police produced the elusive Mrs Cailey. Various newspaper descriptions had brought her out of the woodwork and had also alerted her siblings. Mary Ann was the daughter of William and Mary Beer of Uplyme, Dorset, and they had not heard of her for three years. One brother *thought* the body in the mortuary was his sister, a second brother was certain, so was her sister and a friend confirmed it. All the more bizarre then that Inspector Sayer's men found Mary Anne very much alive in the West End late on Wednesday and took her immediately to the mortuary when 'she was confronted with her own portrait'.

Her story was that she had 'been to Scotland with a gentleman' and had been so horrified by mention of the Thames murder that she refused to read or hear about it. She was reunited with Mrs Christian and this must have been a doubly interesting meeting as she owed the woman several weeks' rent. There is little doubt that Mary Ann Cailey was a prostitute. Her staying out late, her unverified links with a square in Chelsea, her sudden 'flit' to Scotland and the rough treatment she received at the hands of the men near Victoria Bridge, all lead in that direction. Mrs Christian's seems to have been a respectable house and Mary Ann Cailey should have counted herself lucky on two counts – one, that the police did not charge her with wasting their time and, two, that she did not, after all, meet the torso killer.

Police enquiries of course continued. Leads were followed wherever they led. Missing women were located where possible; 'domestic' rows were checked. One man eventually found in Brighton had deserted his wife and left her on the charge of the parish. This was an indictable offence, but she was not dead and he was not the torso killer.

Hayden and Kempster had carried out a bizarre piece of reconstruction. They had not only sewn the body together again, but had pulled the skin of the face over a butcher's block and taken a photograph of the result. 'The features are so characteristic,' said *The Times* on 20 September, 'and pronounced that any one who knew the woman could hardly fail to recognize her.' This seems unlikely. The photograph does not appear to have survived, but bearing in mind the nose and lips had been cut and it had been in the water for several hours at least, identification must have been almost impossible. A knife had clearly been used to remove the skin from the tissue underneath and this had left a 'buttonholed' effect. *The Lancet* believed that this was accidental and not an attempt to render the face unrecognizable. The police were keeping the photograph to themselves and only those with a genuine reason for viewing it would be allowed to see it – the dealers in horror were never far away.

The police were clearly desperately short of clues. Earlier Thames tragedies had usually produced a plethora of solutions from members of the public. This one did not. In the case of the Waterloo tragedy, the murder of prostitute Eliza Grimwood on 26 May 1838, her remains, badly mutilated and with an attempt at decapitation, were found in a carpet bag which could be traced. In the Great Coram Street murder at Christmas 1872 the victim was Harriet Buswell aka Clara Barton, a 27-year-old prostitute, and her quarrel with a German client overheard. 'In this case,' said *The Times*, as a sort of built-in obituary for the whole torso series, 'there are only pieces of flesh.' On 20 September the ever-ghoulish *Illustrated Police News* showed the graphic finding of the face. The central image shows a Thames Division galley with a suitably horrified inspector watching a constable lift the face from the water. This of course did not happen; the face had washed up on shore. Such tinkering with the facts is typical of the *Illustrated Police News* house style. To the left, the caption reads, 'Finding the First Portion – Battersea' and shows wherries drawn up on the foreshore, a derrick in the background and a train picturesquely steaming over the railway bridge. The image to the right is captioned 'Finding the Second Portion – Putney' and a bystander is leaning over a bridge parapet watching the police galley at work below.

On the same day, various papers carried the information that a £200 reward had been put up by the government and a virtual free pardon was guaranteed to any accomplice not actually guilty of murder.

By 25 September, interest was waning. 'People still come to see the remains,' *The Times* reported, 'and tales, some of them very strange in their mystery and some strange by reason of their stupidity, are brought to the notice of the detectives.' Rumours were flying by now of two lunatics who had escaped from Broadmoor. William Bisgrave had absconded on 13 July and John Walker on 7 August. Both had been seen in the London area and their descriptions were circulated. We shall meet these two again in a later chapter.

The Times waxed lyrical on the case: 'There will be no lack of persons ready to throw blame upon the police and to mention that it is their duty to discover the murderer. It is worth while to point out that policemen, even if they are styled detectives, are only endowed with ordinary senses.' This was not, *The Times* pointed out, an ordinary murder and

> it is not pleasant to reflect that, in our high civilization, any one, however poor or friendless, can thus be made away with; but it is inevitable that the art of detection should remain somewhat in the wake of crime and that the best efforts of the police should be sometimes baffled by the union of vulpine cunning with unscrupulous brutality.'[8]

And no further progress had been made by June the following year. Evidence for what had happened to the body found in the Thames at Putney in June 1874 is almost nonexistent. My original intention was to devote a full chapter to this killing, but the meagre details do not merit it.

Gladstone's Liberals lost the election in January as Benjamin Disraeli labelled the outgoing Cabinet 'a range of exhausted volcanoes'. Irish lawyer Isaac Butt was leading the first of the 'filibustering' campaigns for Irish Home Rule in the Commons. Well-to-do society was fascinated by the fraud carried out by Arthur Orton, a Wapping butcher, who claimed to be the long-lost heir to the vast Tichborne estate. In August, the ten-hour day became a reality for thousands of factory workers, but none of this would account for news of a dismembered corpse found in the Thames being forced off the front pages.

All we do know is that the *News of the World* for 14 June carried the story that a headless body without arms, but with one leg remaining, was taken from the Putney riverbank to Fulham Union Workhouse. At the subsequent inquest, Dr E C Barnes, the police surgeon, stated that he believed the body had been divided at the spinal column and that a covering of lime had been used to aid decomposition. Once again, although today we would have no doubt that a murder had been committed, the letter of the law demanded that an open verdict be delivered; an unknown fate for an unknown woman.

Chapter 10

The Girl with the Rose Tattoo: Tottenham Court Road, 23 October 1884

It was ten years before the torso killer struck again.

Or was it? We now know that serial killers go through cycles in their killing behaviour and there is no standard or rational time-scale for this. Jack the Ripper killed five women in the space of less than ten weeks in 1888. Steven Wright, the 'Suffolk Strangler' murdered the same number in a little over six weeks. We would expect, then, something of an outbreak of torso murders in 1873 or 1874, but they did not happen. How can we explain this ten-year gap?

Dr Joel Norris, one of the world's leading experts on serial killers, has identified seven phases in which such a murderer operates. The aura phase is the one in which the killer withdraws into a private world of perverted fantasy. He cannot focus, becomes slipshod in his everyday work. If he is employed, he will make mistakes. If he has a social life, he will reduce it, become less gregarious, move away from the herd. The pressure grows in his brain to kill and he moves on to the trawling phase. Steven Wright, the Suffolk Strangler; Gary Ridgeway, the Green River Killer; Joel Rifkin, the Long Island Murderer; Jack the Ripper and, I believe, the torso killer, all targeted prostitutes because they were lust murderers and because prostitutes were easy prey. Ted Bundy fits this pattern too, as does Peter Sutcliffe, the Yorkshire Ripper.

The killer selects his victim. Perhaps she has the kind of hair he likes – most of Bundy's targets had long, straight dark hair. Perhaps she is the right size – all of Rifkin's victims were under 5ft 3ins. Perhaps it is their dress or the particular place in which they are standing. *Something* drives the serial murderer on. Into the wooing phase.

Grabbing a woman from a public place is hazardous. There might be an eyewitness to such an abduction. And the victim might fight back. One of the reasons that child-killer Robert Black was caught is that he wrongly estimated the age of his last target. She may have looked 12 but in fact she was 16, struggled loudly when he tried to bundle her into his van and got away, able to give a full – and for Black, fatal – description to the police. The wooing phase involves calm and reassurance, even for a short time. Ted Bundy used the ploy of a broken arm and asked girls for help opening his car door. Ridgeway and Rifkin both appeared to be punters, interested in nothing more than sex.

Wooing quickly turns to capture. The victim is thrown into a car or pickup truck, shoved down an alleyway, silenced by strangulation or a fist. The murder itself is carried out by whatever means the killer is most comfortable with – a slash to the throat; strangulation with or without ligature; a single shot to the head. This is the climax – the all-consuming point which the earlier phases have been building towards. For sexually sadistic killers, this may or may not result in orgasm. Peter Kürten, the Monster of Dusseldorf responsible for dozens of sex crimes against women and children in 1920s Germany admitted that it was the flowing of blood, not sex itself, that excited him.

The totem phase is one in which the killer seeks to relive the thrill of the murder. He will take a trophy of some kind – jewellery, underwear, body parts – which he can use to remind him of the event. Some lust-murderers – Ted Bundy, John Christie – were necrophiliacs; they enjoyed sex with the cadavers they had created.

The final phase is that of acute depression. The murderer can become suicidal, but actual suicides are rare and usually take place only once the killer is caught. The Gloucester murderer Fred West and Dr Harold Shipman, perhaps the most prolific killer of all time, both ended their lives awaiting trial in prison. For most serial killers, the phase passes and the whole cycle begins again.

The problem arises over time-scale. For every burst of frenetic slaughter à la Steven Wright or Jack the Ripper, there are many examples of an altogether slower kill-rate, with months or years between murders. The unidentified murderer known as 'Il Mostro', the Monster of Florence, for example, had a gap of six years between his first and second murders and seven between that and his third. So it is possible that the torso killer was merely biding his time between the summer of 1874 and the October of ten years later. On the other hand, of course, he could have moved away for a time and come back, or he could have been imprisoned on unrelated charges. Or he could have been in a mental institution.

By 1884 of course, the world had turned. Oxford University passed a resolution allowing women to sit examinations and women were able to compete at Wimbledon for the first time. Beatrice Webb founded, with her husband Sidney, the Fabian Society, dedicated to introduce socialist reforms by gradual, peaceful means. In the male-dominated world, Alfred Tennyson, the poet laureate, was made a Lord; Hiram Maxim, the American engineer, invented a machine-gun that fired rapid rounds without reloading. In London, the Circle Line of the Underground was completed and the National Society for the Prevention of Cruelty to Children was set up. There was pressure, in the national scene, to further the extension of the franchise. The international picture was dominated by the potential crisis in the Sudan, where General Charles Gordon had been sent to evacuate Europeans from Khartoum. These last two events alone prove that ''orrible murder' had yet to steal the headlines – that would be the legacy of Jack the Ripper to the nation. In 1884 the potential martyrdom of Gordon and Gladstone's third reform bill meant that 'the discovery of human remains' was relegated to a single half column in *The Times*.

The latest discovery was made almost a mile as the crow flies from the river. The nearest point was the Victoria Embankment just below Waterloo Bridge, but the find itself was made in Alfred Mews off Tottenham Court Road.

'Yesterday,' said *The Times* of 24 October, 'considerable excitement was caused in the neighbourhood of Tottenham Court Road by the discovery of human remains, supposed to be those of a woman, under circumstances suggesting foul play.'[1] On that Friday morning, a carman named Rawlinson and a road-sweeper named Threader were involved in clearing rubbish by emptying dustbins in Alfred Mews, a narrow cul-de-sac almost opposite Goodge Street Underground station. Clearly neither man looked carefully at their cart's contents because it was not until they reached King's Cross railway station, belonging to the Great Northern Railway Company, that they realized what they had. They assumed at first that the body parts were those of a dog or cat. Railway workers sorting the rubbish later that day recognized that at their feet lay a human skull with flesh still clinging to it but no hair and some sort of lime attached. Rawlinson called the police.

At almost the same time, a gardener was making a gruesome discovery in Bedford Square, a few hundred yards to the south-east and only minutes walk from Alfred Mews.[2] Thrown over the railings in the gardens in the centre of the square was a parcel and in it a human arm which had been dipped into lime in an attempt to destroy it. These remains were taken to the police who, under the direction of Chief Inspector Richard Williams and Inspector Hollis of the Great Northern Railway, found more body parts. They were taken to St Giles's Mortuary and the police surgeons went to work.

We have to see all this in the context in which the Victorians did. Even a casual flick through national and local newspapers of the time paints a nightmare world which we cannot imagine. Five years earlier, an Irish maidservant, Kate Webster, had quarrelled with her employer, Mrs Julia Thomas at her house in Park Road, Richmond. The quarrel led to Julia being thrown downstairs and then strangled by Kate, who had the perennial problem of body disposal. She opted for dismemberment, hacking Mrs Thomas's head off with an aptly named cut-throat razor and her arms and legs with a meat saw from the kitchen. She parboiled the limbs and torso in a copper and burned the woman's intestines and internal organs. Nauseated by the process though she was, Kate packed the body parts into a wooden box only to discover there was no room for the head and one foot. Rumours that she tried to sell the fatty scum from the copper as dripping were never substantiated, but she was not the last killer to make such a literal profit from her work.[3] She shovelled the foot onto a dung heap and stuffed the head into a black bag. Neither the foot nor the head was ever found, even though Kate had the nerve to allow two friends, the Porters from Notting Hill, to carry it for her to a railway station. She engaged the help of Robert Porter to help her carry the trunk with the body parts to Richmond Bridge and, when the lad walked off, she threw it into the river.

Here it was found by a coal heaver the next morning and the finds taken to Inspector Harber at Barnes police station. Subsequently, the 'Barnes Mystery' became a source of local fascination and Kate Webster wandered around in her dead mistress's clothes, arranging for the sale of the house and contents before planning to return to Ireland.

When neighbours became suspicious, police searched Mrs Thomas's house and found a razor, an axe and charred bones. Kate Webster was arrested in Ireland and brought back to face trial. Had the Thames torso killer ever been caught, the prosecution would have faced the same problem that Sir Henry Gifford, the Solicitor General, did at Kate's trial. With no head, how was it possible to prove that the separated and half-cooked corpse had once been Julia Martha Thomas? In the event, the evidence against Kate was too strong, largely circumstantial though it was and she was hanged at Wandsworth gaol by the executioner William Marwood.

But the horrors did not end with Kate Webster, whose wax likeness soon appeared at Madame Tussaud's Chamber of Horrors (which was open, by the way, between 8am and 10pm, six days a week). In September 1884, a disgusted 'countryman' wrote to the *Holborn Guardian* to complain about an abandoned graveyard in the area where bones had been removed from desecrated tombs. Parcels containing newborn infants were turning up regularly all over the Metropolis and in November a box was sent through the post to the Home Secretary, Sir William Harcourt. It contained a dead baby and a covering letter from its parents. Inspector Andrews from Scotland Yard (quite possibly Walter Andrews 'a jovial gentlemanly man, with a fine personality and a sound knowledge of his job[4]), was sent to investigate. But there had been no crime. The baby had died of natural causes and the distraught parents wanted to bring attention to the fact that there was no burial space available in their area.

Against this background of brutality and tragedy with headlines of other atrocities reading 'Shocking Case' and 'Extraordinary Outrage', the body parts found at King's Cross merited little space. 'The police', noted the *Clerkenwell Press* routinely, 'are investigating the affair and the coroner has been communicated with'.[5]

And it soon became clear that not one, but two different bodies were involved. Almost a month earlier, on 25 September, Charles Fitch of 179 Barnsby Road found human bones in the Ornamental Gardens of Mornington Crescent. The Crescent lies to the northwest of Alfred Mews along Hampstead Road, a continuation of the Tottenham Court Road. There is about a quarter of a mile between the two finds. A constable who only appears by his collar initials in the *Clerkenwell Press* – PC 559 of 'S' Division – took the remains to nearby Albany Street police station. The police surgeon here, having examined the remains, decided that these bones had been used for anatomical purposes, but beyond that was infuriatingly vague. Does this mean that the Mornington Crescent find was a hoax, the rather unpleasant prank of a medical student, which *The Lancet* back in 1873 assured its readers could not happen? Or could the police surgeon have been wrong? He had only a left arm, hand and two feet to work with, but was convinced they belonged to a female and she was young.

There was a delay as a result of deciding which body parts belonged to which victim and the inquest was not held until 11 November. Dr Danford Thomas opened the proceedings at St Giles coroner's court on all the remains found, including the portion located by police officers from the pavement outside 33 Fitzroy Square, which was a drill hall and armoury (and is today, with a certain irony, part of the London Foot Hospital!).

The first witness was George Peck, the Bedford Square gardener who explained his finding of the 'pieces of flesh' on the ground. Questioned by the coroner, Peck told the jury that the parts were wrapped in brown paper and the package had been thrown over the railings. The lime that covered the flesh also ended up on the iron spikes. A constable from Tottenham Court Road police station had collected the parts in a basket.

William Meager was employed as scavenger by the St Giles Board of Works and was sweeping Alfred Mews on the morning of 23 October when he saw a newspaper parcel some 15 yards away from the dustbin of a family called Thexton. He simply scooped it up, not checking the contents. That pleasure fell to Inspector Summers of the Met who found a quantity of a woman's hair in the rubbish dumped by Meager at the King's Cross refuse tip.

Constable 305E John Watts was on his beat on the southwest side of Fitzroy Square when he noticed a 'quantity of human flesh' outside number 33. This was clearly placed beyond the iron gate and railings that led to the building's semi-basement because the officer had to ask a caretaker to let him go down to investigate. Here he found the 'lower parts' of a body at a distance of about a foot apart. They were covered in a strongly smelling white powder. The *Pall Mall Gazette* was adamant that this drop was done with great coolness and in a tiny window of opportunity: 'The side walk in front of the house is constantly patrolled by police ... it is believed that the parcel was deposited between ten o'clock and ten fifteen, when the police relief takes place.'

Dr Samuel Lloyd told the inquest jury that the body parts found in Alfred Mews, Fitzroy Square and King's Cross station all came from the same individual. His next observation was odd however. He believed, from the shape

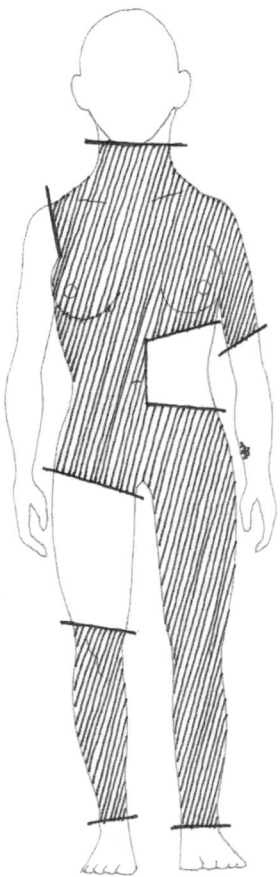

The thick black lines represent the cuts made to dissect the body. The shaded areas are the parts that were never found.

of the delicate arms, hands and well-manicured nails, that the victim was a gentlewoman. The face was smooth and the hair long and fair.

The scant information on this murder – or was it, including the Mornington Crescent find, two murders? – is not helpful. There is nothing like the detail of the 1873 torso, but of course more than that of 1874. If this victim was not a prostitute, but a woman of refinement as the appearance suggested, why did no one come forward to report her missing? I think the answer lies in the tattoo which was found on the dead woman's arm. It was a rose and in the 1880s, the only sort of women who had themselves tattooed were those who tended to the exotic and avant-garde. At the upper end of such an echelon were society beauties such as Jenny Jerome, the American heiress who had married Lord Randolph Churchill in 1873. At the lower end were the relatively well-to-do street walkers we met in Chapter 7. It may be of course that Dr Lloyd had little experience of such ladies of the night (although as a divisional police surgeon, that is hardly likely). Lloyd believed her to have been between 25 and 50, but if there was a head, albeit a decaying one, why was he not able to paint a clearer picture or estimate a rough time of death and its cause? The body had been dissected by 'some one skilled, but certainly not for the purposes of anatomy'.

The Mornington Crescent finds had lain in the St Pancras Mortuary for some time and had been buried. Lloyd wanted these exhumed to see if they were the missing parts of the Alfred Mews corpse. Inspector Langrish from Bow Street was in charge of the case and told the jury that his investigations were ongoing. *The Times* of two weeks earlier had quoted Lloyd as saying that two different bodies were involved, then he retracted and said one. He guessed that the murder probably took place sometime around April (though he would not be drawn on that at the inquest). Dr Danford Thomas promised to ask the Home Secretary, while arranging for the exhumation, whether a reward should be posted.

One curious facet of the case was that many of the body parts appeared to have been slightly crushed by being piled at some stage on top of one another; some of the 1873 finds exhibited similar characteristics. Each had been placed in some sort of receptacle and, as with virtually all the other torso murders, dismemberment had been carried out soon after death.

If Langrish and his assistant, Detective Sergeant Roman, were hoping for someone to come forward to identify the victims or to provide some clue, they were hoping in vain. In what is probably the most bizarre of all the torso killings, the body parts found off the Tottenham Court Road were never given a name. But I believe we can be certain that they were victims of the same man.

And he would strike again, as we have seen, in 1887, 1888 and 1889, before vanishing into the river mist for ever.

Chapter 11

Men Behaving Madly

Whoever the torso murderer was and whatever his motivation, he must rank as a serious contender for the world's first serial killer. The term and the concept were unknown to the Victorians, but everybody from the ranks of the police, doctors and journalists expected someone who dismembered people in this way to be a literal monster. They thought exactly the same about Jack the Ripper. Both killers would be certifiable lunatics, with wild, rolling eyes, irrational behaviour and would literally be dripping blood. This is why, in 1873, the press made great play of the two Broadmoor escapees. We now know enough about serial killers to know that they never exhibit these tendencies, but there were many men at the time who did and if several of them were once considered potential Rippers, they could have been the torso killer too.

The extraordinary social spotlight thrown on the East End as a result of the Whitechapel murders revealed disturbing facts about some of the men who lived there. None of them was Jack, but they all bore watching.

Aaron Davis Cohen was 23 when he was arrested by Constable 91H John Patrick. He was brought before Thames Magistrates Court the next day, charged with being, in the unkind legal language of the time, 'a lunatic wandering at large'. It may be mere coincidence that Gertrude Smith, Mary Jones and Ellen Hickey, all prostitutes, were arrested at the same time. Or it may be that Cohen was rounded up with them in one of the Met's periodic brothel raids. On the same day, 7 December 1888, he was taken to the Whitechapel Workhouse Infirmary and admitted under the name of David Cohen. He gave his address as 86 Leman Street, but that was a Boys' Club at the time and this may be an example of his irrationality.

For the next fortnight, Cohen stayed in the Infirmary in Baker's Row and the medical officer, Dr Larder, noted that he was violent and noisy, threatening other inmates, damaging property and dancing. The Infirmary had its share of 'imbeciles' as they were called, usually harmless, sad introverts, but Cohen was too much of a handful and was transferred to Colney Hatch Lunatic Asylum on

21 December. Here he had to be force-fed and spent the next nine months being destructive and dirty. By October 1889 he was ill and confined to bed and died of phthisis (tuberculosis) on the 20th. To those who believe that Mary Kelly was the last of the Ripper's victims, the removal of Cohen from the streets a month later explains why the Whitechapel murders stopped. There is of course no evidence against the man at all. As a Jew, he would be most unlikely to kill a gentile, let alone five; inter-racial killings are a rarity among serial murderers.[1]

Another 'lunatic at large' was Thomas Hayne Cutbush. He was the nephew of Superintendent Charles Cutbush who shot himself in 1896 after several years of depression. Thomas lived in Albert Street, Kennington, and may have contracted syphilis in 1888. Since the disease takes several years to affect the brain, it is unlikely that it triggered the paranoid delusions which led to him abandoning his job and wandering at night. He often returned home with muddy clothes.

On 5 March 1891 he was detained as a lunatic in Lambeth Infirmary but escaped, staying on the run for four days. During this time, with a knife he bought in Houndsditch, he assaulted Florence Johnson and Isabelle Anderson in Kennington, by prodding them in the bustles. In this, he was almost certainly emulating a sadist named Colicott who had stabbed six women earlier in the year in the Kennington area. Astonishingly, Colicott got off on a technicality and it was as well that none of the women was seriously hurt. Cutbush was arrested on 9 March and committed to Broadmoor where he died in 1903. The *Sun* newspaper, on 13 February 1894, suggested Cutbush as a possible Whitechapel murderer, but in his famous 'memoranda', Sir Melville Macnaghten quite rightly pointed out that no one capable of the appalling slaughter in 1888 would be content merely to prick girls' bustles three years later.

On 11 September 1888, when the Whitechapel murders were escalating and the torso killer had already claimed four victims, Sir Charles Warren, Commissioner at the Yard, wrote a memo to Evelyn Ruggles-Brise, private secretary to Henry Matthews, the Home Secretary. He mentioned three suspects and complained that his officers were being constantly hampered by reporters who followed them everywhere and compromised leads by badgering potential witnesses before the police could do their job properly. Two dangerous men were mentioned by name; the third was simply a description of a blood-stained man in a brothel and proved a dead end. Warren wrote of his second suspect: 'A man called Puckeridge was released from an asylum on 4 August. He was educated as a Surgeon – has threatened to rip people up with a long knife. He is being looked for but cannot be found as yet.'[2]

Oswald Puckeridge was actually a chemist. He was born in 1838 and married Ellen Puddle thirty years later. He was admitted to Hoxton House private asylum in Shoreditch on 6 January 1888 and released, as Warren says, on 4 August. No further information is forthcoming. If the police found him and questioned him they could not link him to the Whitechapel killings. All we know is that he died on 1 June 1900 in Holborn Workhouse in the City Road.

Warren's first suspect is Jacob Isenschmid 'the Holloway lunatic': 'The lunatic Isensmith [sic] a Swiss arrested at Holloway ... is now in an Asylum at Bow and arrangements are being made to ascertain whether he is the man who was seen on the morning of the murder in a public house by Mrs Fiddymont.'[3]

On 11 September, three days after Annie Chapman was murdered and the day Elizabeth Jackson's arm was found near the sluice by Ebury Bridge Road, two doctors, colleagues from Holloway, reported the peculiar behaviour of a local tenant in Mitford Road. This was a pork butcher named Isenschmid and his wife, who had not seen him for two months, told police that he carried knives with him wherever he went. Found and arrested the next day, it became clear that Isenschmid suffered annual bouts of insanity towards the end of each summer and had been in and out of Colney Hatch for a while. He had classic delusions of grandeur, calling himself 'the king of Elthorne Road', and could be very threatening, ostentatiously honing his knife blade. He seemed a likely Ripper for a while, although he had no definite links with Whitechapel, but he was still under psychiatric care when the later murders took place and was effectively off the hook as a result. For the rest of his life he was mostly in institutions and, despite his profession, cannot have been the torso killer either.

Henry James was far less likely to attack anyone than either Puckridge or Isenschmid but he had his collar felt in the Ripper case anyway. He was seen on the day of Annie Chapman's death on Cambridge Heath Road, moving in a peculiar way. Thomas Ede, a railway signalman, reported him to the police because he had seen a blade protruding some four inches out of his pocket. James was discounted as a 'harmless lunatic' according to local press reports and it was probably his wooden arm that made him move oddly. This is typical of the mindset of the average Victorian working man, who paid to gawp at freak shows like the Elephant Man, Joseph Merrick.[4] Anyone with a physical deformity was likely to own a sick mind too.

'Innocent or guilty,' say the authors of the incomparable *Jack the Ripper: A to Z* cryptically, 'it is research centred on Aaron Kosminski ... which will most likely lead to the identification of Jack the Ripper, if it has not done so already.'[5]

If we assume that all the torso murders were carried out by the same man, then that man is not the Polish-Jewish hairdresser Kosminski who did not come to England until 1882. Eight years later he was removed from his brother

Wolf's house in Sion Square and admitted to the Mile End Old Town Workhouse Infirmary. This was 12 July and three days later he was released into his brother's care. By early February 1891 he was readmitted to another infirmary in Greenfield Street, examined by Dr Edmund King and committed to Colney Hatch where he stayed until April 1894. From there he was sent to the Leavesden Asylum near Watford where he died in 1919. His delusions included hearing voices. He never washed, refused to work and only ate scraps from gutters because he believed fresher food might be poisoned. Kosminski's involvement in the Ripper case is beyond the scope of this book, although it is likely to be an example of a misidentification by senior police officers not sufficiently au fait with the minutiae of the investigation. He appears as No. 2 in the infamous Macnaghten Memoranda probably written in 1894: 'He had become insane owing to many years indulgence in solitary vices. He had a great hatred of women, with strong homicidal tendencies.' Another variant of the same document adds that his hatred was directed at 'the prostitute class'.

Since the Colney Hatch records also refer to self-abuse as the cause of Kosminski's madness, we cannot blame Macnaghten for following the scientific orthodoxy of the day. The fact is, of course, that the doctors were wrong. Masturbation does not cause madness, although other causes may give rise to a lack of inhibitions on that score. Like Isenschmid, Kosminski claimed to be rather superior, knowing 'the movements of all mankind' according to Dr Edmund Honchin, police surgeon to H Division. Although his mental and physical health declined at Colney Hatch, he fluctuated between quiet apathy and noisy hysterics. 'Demented and incoherent' he only once offered violence by threatening a (male) guard with a chair leg.

Charles Ludwig was a deranged hairdresser from Hamburg, Germany. He lodged in the Minories, not far from Pinchin Street, and came to the attention of the police on the night of Tuesday 18 September 1888 when he pulled a knife on one-armed prostitute Elizabeth Burns in Three King's Court. She screamed and patrolling City policeman John Johnson came to her rescue. The attacker vanished in the darkness but was soon causing trouble at a coffee stall in Whitechapel High Street. In the eternal parlance of the street thug, then as now, he asked innocent bystander Alexander Frieberg what he was looking at. Ludwig flashed his knife again and another policeman, Constable 221H Gallagher, arrested him. He was charged at the Thames Magistrates Court with being drunk and disorderly and using threatening behaviour, but since this was not an isolated incident, he was probably in need of psychiatric help.

On Sunday 9 September 1888, two days before Elizabeth Jackson's body parts began turning up, the landlady of the Pope's Head pub at Gravesend contacted the police. Superintendent Berry took charge of what followed, talking to William Henry Pigott, himself a former policeman in Hoxton. Pigott had arrived at the Pope's Head about four in the afternoon, having walked, he said, from Whitechapel. In his bag was a blood-stained shirt and his shoes seemed to have been recently wiped. He had been loudly proclaiming his hatred of women in the bar and he had an injury to his hand which he said had been caused by a bite from a woman in the backyard of a lodging house, probably in Brick Lane. He was interviewed by Inspector Abberline of H Division who was convinced he was not the Ripper and was released. It is not clear what happened to Pigott, but an institution of some sort seems likely.

Much of the police paperwork on John Sanders has been lost to time but he may have once been a serious Ripper suspect. The son of an Indian Army surgeon, Sanders was born in 1862 and joined the London Hospital, Whitechapel, at the age of 17. In 1880 he is described as an outpatient dresser, implying that he was a houseman entrusted with fairly mundane tasks. This may be because he was already showing signs of mental illness. Ordinarily shy and retiring, he became increasingly domineering and violent, threatening even his closest friends. He was transferred from one asylum to another until his death at Heavitree, Exeter, in 1901. Extraordinarily, Sanders seems to be one of three medical students at the London Hospital who were thought to be insane and all could be accounted for, the other two having gone abroad. The odds against *three* such men being in the same institution at the same time seem astronomical, but selection procedures for hospitals were vastly different in Victorian England.

In the context of the torso murders, G Wentworth Bell Smith is altogether more interesting. He believed prostitutes should be drowned. Smith was a Canadian who worked for the Toronto Trust Society in Finsbury Square and moved to 27 Sun Street, off the square, from Canada at some time in 1888. He suffered from religious mania, dashing off pages of his thoughts about God, vice and the appalling state of the world. He had noticed prostitutes walking through St Paul's during divine service[6] and his nocturnal wanderings took some explaining. He wore galoshes so that his tread was virtually silent, talked to himself and kept three loaded revolvers in his rooms. He often lay on the sofa and 'foamed'.

On 7 August 1888, the night that the Ripper killed Martha Tabram, Smith arrived home at four in the morning with the story that his watch had been stolen in Bishopsgate. He told his landlord, Mr Callaghan, that he had to return to Canada urgently and left his lodgings, although he was known to be still in London a month later. Smith's later whereabouts are unknown. Presumably he returned to Canada still railing about prostitution. He was certainly odd, but he was neither the torso killer nor the Ripper.

Neither was Alois Szemeredy, the first man to be named as the Whitechapel murderer in a full book written in 1908. He described himself variously as an American surgeon and an Austrian sausage-maker and probably deserted from the Austrian army before sailing to Buenos Aires where he may have carried out a series of armed robberies and perhaps even murder. He was committed to a lunatic asylum in 1885 and returned to Vienna seven years later. He committed suicide while in police custody there on further robbery charges. There is no link with London, let alone Whitechapel, but rumours of his being Jack were circulating via the *Daily Graphic* in 1892.

The men we have met so far have been odd, even dangerous, but they were not (with the possible exception of Szemeredy) murderers. James Kelly was. An upholsterer by trade, he moved to London in 1878 when he was 18, living with a family called Lamb in Collingwood Street, Bethnal Green. Three years later he met 20-year-old Sarah Brider and moved in with her and her family at 21 Cottage Lane. The pair were married on 4 June 1883 and they lived unhappily ever after. He was suffering from an abscess on the neck and violent headaches which caused unpredictable mood swings. In a row with Sarah in June 1883, Kelly stabbed her below the left ear. Treated at St Bartholomew's Hospital, she died on 24 June and Kelly stood trial for her murder at the Old Bailey in August. He was reprieved three days before his execution date and sentenced to life imprisonment in Broadmoor, despite the fact that examining doctors could find no evidence of insanity.

On 23 January 1888 James Kelly escaped from that institution and extraordinarily remained on the run for the next thirty-nine years, including a brief return to England in 1896 when he again got away from the authorities in Liverpool Docks. On 11 February 1927 he turned up at the gates of Broadmoor and asked to be readmitted. He died there in September 1929. Author James Tully has tried to convince the world that James Kelly could be the Whitechapel murderer[7] but the actual evidence is very thin. If not Jack, then could Kelly have been the torso murderer? Emphatically not. Two of the murders took place while the mad upholsterer was a child. For the 1888 and 1889 murders we have no idea where he was, but bearing in mind his correspondence in connection with this 1896 return came from New Orleans, it is unlikely that he was hanging around in London. Above all, James Kelly seems to have acquired an evil reputation out of all proportion to his crime. The only person he is known to have killed is his wife and that was in the heat of the moment. There was no attempt to conceal the crime, no attempt at dismemberment and little hard evidence to suggest that Kelly had murderous intents against anyone except the unfortunate Sarah.

Dr Thomas Neill Cream was in a different category altogether. Born in Glasgow in May 1850, Cream moved with his family to Quebec when he was 4.

The boy worked with his father in the lumber business until 1872 when he enrolled in McGill College, Montreal, to study medicine. Richer than most students, he led a flash life, glittering with jewellery and driving a carriage and pair. In line with what may have been borderline schizophrenia he also taught in a Sunday school. Cream graduated MD in March 1876 but the theme of his farewell address was, oddly perhaps, 'the evils of malpractice in the medical profession'. In two examples of unscrupulous behaviour before he left Canada, Cream started a fire in his Montreal lodgings in order to claim the insurance. Having got Flora Brooks pregnant, he was forced by her father to marry the girl but promptly left for Britain to further his medical studies. When he heard that his wife had died of consumption in August 1877, Cream demanded $1,000 under the terms of the marriage contract. In the end, he accepted $200.

Cream's name first appears in London in October 1876 when he attended a course of lectures at St Thomas's Hospital. He probably lodged in Lambeth Palace Road. On 13 April 1877 he obtained a double qualification in medicine and surgery from the Royal College of Physicians in Edinburgh. No sooner had he obtained his degree than he was back to Canada, this time Ontario. The death of a chambermaid, Kate Hutchinson, may have been Cream's first murder. His story was that she approached him for an abortion (illegal of course in both Canada and Britain) and that she had committed suicide when he refused. Since her body was found in a privy behind Cream's lodgings, it seems highly likely that he killed her with chloroform. He moved to Chicago to avoid the limelight.

Here he carried out a series of abortions and in 1888 came under police suspicion over the death of Julia Faulkner. There was insufficient evidence against him and he embarked on a career of blackmail the following year. It was then that he took up with a married woman, Julia Stott, whose aged husband Daniel suffered from the epilepsy that Cream claimed to be able to cure. The old man died twenty minutes after taking Cream's medicine, but a coroner might well have passed this off as coincidence and the cause of death natural had not Cream made a big fuss about the incompetence of the chemists who made the mixture up. He demanded an exhumation and four grains of strychnine were found in the dead man's stomach. He and Julia Stott were charged with second degree murder. She was acquitted; he became Prisoner No. 4374 at Joliet, Illinois's State Penitentiary.

After applying pressure on the system, Cream obtained a reduction of sentence and was released at the end of July 1891, obtaining the fortune his dead father had left him. He arrived in London on 5 October 1891, comfortably after all the crimes attributed to Jack and the torso killer were over. He moved into lodgings at 103 Lambeth Palace Road near St Thomas's Hospital and the river 'finding there', as W Teignmouth Shore wrote in 1927, 'the victims whose slaughter brought him to the scaffold'.

We are not concerned with the details of Thomas Neill Cream's crimes; he was not the Ripper nor the torso killer. What is important is the ease with which he picked up prostitutes and their vulnerability. His first victim was 19-year-old Ellen Donworth who lived at 8 Duke Street off Westminster Bridge Road. Inevitably, in the journalese of the time, her death became 'the Lambeth Mystery'. Interestingly, Cream's technique was to write to these victims, asking them to meet him at a certain time and place. Unlike the Ripper's targets who were random, Cream's were personally chosen by him and 'groomed' to an extent before he struck. Ellen died of strychnine poisoning but not before she was able to describe her attacker – 'a tall gentleman with cross eyes, a silk hat and bushy whiskers gave me a drink out of a bottle with white stuff in it'.[8]

Four days after Ellen's death, Cream wrote to the deputy coroner for East Surrey, George Wyatt, to the effect that he could provide evidence as to who killed her, in exchange for £300,000. It was signed 'A O'Brien, detective'.

The next target was Matilda Clover. She was 27 and lived in a room in Lambeth Road, with her 2-year-old child. She had recently separated from the boy's father – or rather he had abandoned her; an all too familiar picture. She was an alcoholic and at first it was assumed that her death on 20 October 1891 was due to a lethal mix of drink and the bromide of potassium prescribed for her by her doctor. She was buried in Tooting Cemetery on the assumption that death was due to natural causes. If Cream had not written two anonymous letters to total strangers that Matilda had died by strychnine poisoning, he might have got away with the perfect murder.

Emma Shrivell, 18, and Alice Marsh, 21, shared lodgings in Stanford Street. They were both from Brighton and, typical of girls lured to London by the 'Whittington Syndrome', found that the streets were not, after all, paved with gold; in fact they took to those streets to make a living. They had a room each and paid 7s 6d a week rent. Comparing this with Mary Kelly's 4s 9d we have some understanding of the hierarchy among prostitutes. They were both poisoned by Cream on 11 April 1892 when he shared a meal of beer and tinned salmon with them. What he did not share were the three capsules of strychnine he passed to them both.

On 30 April, it was decided to exhume Matilda Clover. There was strychnine in her stomach. From the middle of May onwards Cream was being watched by the police but he continued to pick up prostitutes, even offering what he called 'an American drink' to Violet Beverley of North Street, Kensington Road. Luckily for her, she refused. His peculiar behaviour, including attempts to implicate others, led to Cream's arrest by Inspector Tunbridge of the CID who had been in charge of the Rainham Mystery case five years before. The doctor was formally charged with the murder of Matilda Clover on 18 July and subsequent charges included Ellen Donworth, Alice Marsh and Emma Shrivell. He was also charged with sending threatening letters and the attempted murder of Louisa Harris aka Lou Harvey, whom Cream probably assumed he had actually killed. It turned out that Cream had picked the woman up on 20 October and after a couple of evenings at music halls and hotels, he gave her two capsules which she pretended to take but actually threw into the Thames near Charing Cross underground station.

Cream was found guilty at the Old Bailey and hanged by Thomas Billington at Newgate on 15 November 1892. His alleged last words before the hangman jerked the lever and cut him short were 'I am Jack the ...', which has led the poisoner to be suggested as a potential Ripper. He was certainly a disturbed and twisted character, but the phrase, if he said it at all, is very in keeping with his extraordinary arrogance and the need to continually draw attention to himself. He was an abortionist, would-be blackmailer and arsonist before he ever embarked on a career of murder. He was almost certainly addicted to morphine and possibly pornography, in that he carried lewd photographs with him. He was also a sadist. While his actual relations with prostitutes were probably 'normal', his use of strychnine was calculated to cause maximum pain. Other poisons, to which he had access and whose properties he must have known, were less appalling in their effects.

W T Shore summed Cream up in the way only 1920s writers could:

We may picture him walking at night the dreary, mean streets and byways of Lambeth, seeking for prey, on some of whom to satisfy his lust, on others to exercise his passion for cruelty; his drug-sodden, remorseless mind exalted in a frenzy of horrible joy.

Whatever exactly he was, the halter was his just reward.[9]

The halter was also the just reward for George Chapman, another killer walking dreary, mean streets. And Chapman has been put in the frame as the torso murderer. But then, he has also been suggested as Jack the Ripper ...

Chapman's real name was Severin Klosowski, although the original spelling was probably Severiano, the name on the murder warrant against him for the death of Maud Marsh. He was born in 1865 in Nagornak, Poland, the son of Antonio and Emile and became an apprentice surgeon at the age of 15. Between 1885 and 1886 he was a student at Praga Hospital, Warsaw, and qualified as junior surgeon in 1887. He reached England in the June of that year. Like Cream, Klosowski was a child at the time of the Battersea and Putney murders, which fact alone rules him out as a viable suspect in the torso case. The Rainham corpse had also been found by the time Klosowski got to London. The only other writer on the torso case, R Michael Gordon, implies that Klosowski is both the Ripper and the torso killer, even though the MO of the two are totally different and only the most prurient tabloids of the time tried (largely unsuccessfully) to link the two. Klosowksi's importance here is that his arrival in 1887 means that at the end of the decade and into the next there was not one, but four serial killers at work in one city, even if that city was the largest in the world.

We have no clear indication why an apparently promising medical student should suddenly leave his native home and travel west. R Michael Gordon suspects some scandalous malpractice and he is probably right. In the long tradition of barber-surgeons stretching back to the Middle Ages, Klosowski worked for Abraham Rudin, a hairdresser in the India Dock Road. Between 1888 and 1890 when the Ripper and torso killings were taking place, he ran his own barber shop in a basement below the White Hart, a pub which still stands on the corner of Whitechapel High Street and George Yard where Ripper victim Martha Tabram had met her end in August 1888.

By this time Klosowski was living with Lucy Baderski from Walthamstow. He may have gone through a form of marriage with her and a son was born in April 1890. The family moved frequently in these months, from Greenhill Street to Commercial Street to Cable Street, around the corner from the site of the body drop in Pinchin Street. On 3 March 1891 the little boy died and the parents emigrated to America. This was of course *the* time for Eastern European Jewish migration; both Britain and America were seen as lands of golden opportunity. By February 1892 however, Lucy was back after a row with Klosowski and she was pregnant again. Although he soon joined her, the relationship was not a happy one. Klosowski was a serial philanderer and almost certainly already had a family back in Poland. The birth of a daughter in May did nothing to improve things and Lucy left him soon after. She was lucky.

By the end of 1893 Klosowksi had taken up with Annie Chapman (no relation to the Ripper victim of the same name) and he used her surname as his own from now on. This may have been to make himself more acceptable in an alien land or it may have made his philandering easier. Annie had left him by December 1894 and he took up with a fellow lodger in Tottenham, Isabella Spink, whose husband had just deserted her. On the rebound, Isabella moved to Hastings with 'Chapman' in March 1896 where he opened a successful barber shop in George Street. By September of the following year they were back, with Chapman now running the Prince of Wales pub off Old Street. Isabella Spink died of phthisis (tuberculosis) on Christmas Day 1897.

Within months, Chapman had taken on a new barmaid and lover, Bessie Taylor, and after a brief stay in Bishop's Stortford, returned to London to run the Monument pub in Union Street. It was here that Bessie died, of intestinal obstruction on 13 February 1901. By October, Chapman had met and married Maud Marsh and the following summer saw them at the Crown pub in the Borough High Street. By the summer of 1902 Chapman had grown tired of Maud as he had of so many other women and killed her, using the same tartar emetic poison he had used on Isabella and Bessie.

Coincidences do not extend this far and police suspicion of Chapman led to his arrest by Inspector George Godley in December 1902. For four days in the following March, Chapman stood his trial. He was found guilty and executed on 7 April, gibbering on the scaffold and having to be supported by warders.

It is inconceivable that Severin Klosowski aka George Chapman was Jack the Ripper. The myth has come about because Inspector Frederick Abberline, one of the foremost detectives on the Ripper case, wrote an article for the *Pall Mall Gazette* in which he admitted that Chapman's behaviour and antecedents fitted well with 'the man we struggled so hard to capture fifteen years ago'.[10] That statement shows the huge gulf that existed between reality and the minds of the men charged with hunting Jack. Klosowski was a poisoner, using his medical knowledge to good effect in that the deaths of two of his victims were put down initially to natural causes. Yes, he was once a junior surgeon. Yes, he lived briefly in Cable Street, but there, the links and coincidences end.

Klosowski was merely one of a whole range of men behaving madly at the time. Most of those discussed in this chapter came to light because of the Ripper murders and are inevitably located in the East End. As Cream and Klosowski show however, dangerous insanity was not confined to the adjacent parishes of Spitalfields and Whitechapel.

Nor were serial killers confined to the London of the 1870s and 1880s.

Chapter 12

Other Times, Other Crimes

The trunk of a body was discovered by Regent's Canal, Edgware Road, London on 28 December ... A few days later the head was recovered and 'matched' with the body and eventually the remaining parts were found. The head was made available for public inspection and in March ... Hannah Brown's brother came forward to identify her. It took a while to trace Hannah's betrothed, James Greenacre, who by this time was living with Sarah Gale in the Kennington Road. Despite denying any connection with the murder, remnants of a cotton dress matching the original wrappings of the body were discovered in their lodgings, together with many personal items belonging to Hannah. Greenacre was subsequently sentenced to death and Sarah Gale was transported for life.[1]

This is not another example of the torso murders, although the MO was depressingly similar. It happened back in 1836 when the Met was only seven years old and there was not even a Detective Branch at Scotland Yard. Three days after Christmas, Constable Pegler of S Division was on his beat along the Edgware Road when he met an hysterical man who had spotted a parcel tucked behind an up-ended pavement flagstone. In the parcel was a naked female body without head or legs. Pegler took the remains to the nearest workhouse in a wheelbarrow and discovered mahogany shavings and a piece of patched nankeen cotton in the sacking parcel. Technically, the body was found in T (Kensington) Division and Inspector Feltham led the inquiry. Doctors speculated that the victim was between 40 and 50 and had 'an unusual interior malformation'.[2] Ten days later the head was found floating in Regent's Canal. It was preserved in spirit of alcohol and put on display in the workhouse, although by now it must have been almost unrecognizable, battered and bloated. The canal was dragged in search of the legs, but these would be found seven miles away in the Camberwell marshes. They were wrapped in hessian and an extraordinary piece of police work led to the producer of the material in Covent Garden. Here however the trail went cold.

Among those who came forward to identify the deceased was a Mr Gay whose sister, Hannah Brown, had gone missing shortly before Christmas. He recognized the head from a torn earlobe, an old injury caused years before in a fight with a fellow servant. Hannah had been due to marry a Mr Greenacre, whom Gay had not met, on Christmas Day but disappeared on Christmas Eve apparently en route to a friend's house. James Greenacre was telling friends on the same day that the wedding was off. The reason he gave was that Hannah was horribly in debt and had run away in shame.

At Greenacre's lodgings in Camberwell, Constable Pegler found not only a live-in lover, Sarah Gale, but a child's frock of nankeen, patched in the same way as the fragment found with Hannah's body. The mahogany shavings had come from the carpentry shop next door. Greenacre's story now was that Hannah had accidentally fallen backwards at a drunken party on Christmas Eve and had hit her head. Since the most obvious wound was to the face, almost removing an eye, this was patently a lie.

What is fascinating about the Greenacre case, apart from its similarity to the later torso murders and the first-class detective work by a man (Pegler) who was not even a detective, is that we have the murderer's confession as to how he disposed of the parts. Presumably, Greenacre panicked. He had had a row with his fiancée, quite possibly over Sarah Gale and had killed her. Body disposal in a confined or public place is difficult and speed is of the essence. A narrative of 'The Paddington Tragedy' was published by Orlando Hodgson of Fleet Street, featuring the lives and trial of James Greenacre and 'the woman Gale'. In typical 'Penny Dreadful' style, the artist showed Greenacre at work, a demonic look on his face, a bloody, curved knife in one hand and Hannah's decapitated head in the other. On the table behind him, in a cheerful little room with a roaring fire, lies the bleeding torso and on the floor, lying stockinged foot to stockinged foot, her legs. Greenacre confessed that he had taken the wrapped head to Stepney by bus and dropped it into the canal. On Christmas Day he wandered out onto the Camberwell marshes to drop the legs and then, on Boxing Day, the trunk was taken by cart and cab to the Edgware Road. What Greenacre was doing was exactly what the torso killer did half a century later; he was scattering the body parts to confuse the police. But one major difference was that James Greenacre was not a skilled surgeon or a butcher. His sadism existed only for a few seconds in what was almost certainly a spur of the moment attack.

One hundred years and three and a half thousand miles away from the Thames torso murders, somebody else was cutting up bodies and dumping them to be found. The Kingsbury Run was an area of wilderness on the edge of industrial

Cleveland in Ohio and in the 1930s it was home to the most vulnerable victims of the Depression. Every bit as hopeless as the inhabitants of Whitechapel in the days of the Ripper, the hobos of the Run lived in shanty towns of scrap iron and timber, hitching rides on freight trains in their desperate search for work. When author James Badal was a child, his history teacher told the class stories of a series of murders carried out in the Run, with an effective dose of gallows doggerel: 'Floating down the river, chunk by chunk by chunk, Arms and legs and torsos, hunk by hunk by hunk.'

Between September 1935 and August 1938, the Cleveland Torso killer claimed twelve victims, male and female, although it is possible that his spree did not finally end until 1950. The first victim – the lower half of a woman's torso, severed at the knees – was found on the shores of Lake Erie by Frank LaGassie, who had been searching for firewood. Some sort of preservative had been poured over the body which left the skin red and leathery. The forensic experts decided that this was probably chloride of lime. The dead woman had been in the water for about four months; her death had occurred two months before that. She would have been in her late thirties, about 5ft 6ins tall and had had a hysterectomy about a year before she died. Such operations were common during the Depression, so what may have been a promising lead ultimately led nowhere. Over the next few days, the lake yielded other body parts and a photograph printed in the local *Plain Dealer* newspaper on 14 September shows just how little integrity of a crime scene mattered in 1930s America. An upper arm lies on the foreshore and two or three policemen, two sailors and civilians including five children are all standing nearby. Three years later a police photograph shows detectives sifting the rubble where anonymous victims No. 11 and No. 12 were found, surrounded by a huge crowd of men swarming all over a potential murder site. When the coroner, Dr Samuel Gerber, arrived, he was photographed in his everyday suit, handling the grisly skull with ungloved hands.

Theories that the body may have been a suicide subsequently sliced by a boat's propeller were exploded by coroner Arthur J Pearce who concluded that a butcher's knife was probably used and the job was skilfully done except for the right arm which had been botched. Pearce supposed that disposal of the body on dry land where the murder took place was difficult so that the parts were placed in boxes in the lake where wave action had brought them to the surface. He believed that the lime used was the wrong sort in that it preserved the body rather than destroyed it. The lake's currents meant that the parts could have been deposited as far away as Canada or even thrown from a light aircraft.[3]

On 23 September 1935 the decapitated body of a man, later identified as petty criminal Edward Andrassy, was found at the bottom of Jackass Hill in the

Kingsbury Run. His genitals had been removed and his head was found nearby. Not far away a second headless corpse was found. It would never be identified and remains on record as Victim No. 2. At the time, the police were unsure whether the 'lady in the lake' was the first in a series or not.

The following June, a head wrapped in trousers was found by Louis Checley and Gomez Ivey, two kids out playing and the rest of the body turned up near East 55th Street. Despite the fact that the body carried clear tattoos with the name 'Jiggs' and the head, suitably cleaned up, was put on public display for identification, the corpse was never identified and remains as Victim No. 4.

At least Victim No. 3 had a name. She was 43-year-old prostitute Flo Polillo and parts of her were found stuffed in baskets behind the Hart Manufacturing building on the east side of Central Avenue in the freezing January of 1936. These and the later portions found the following month were wrapped in burlap bags, stained with blood and sticky with chicken feathers. Flo had a rap sheet, having been arrested for prostitution in Washington, DC, in 1934 and three years earlier in Cleveland itself. In the era of prohibition, she was also arrested for selling alcohol on St Clair Avenue in the city in October 1935. Her mug shot, the only known photograph of her, shows a plump, half-smiling woman with a double chin and erratic hair. She had been murdered only two days before her body was found.

The press at the time confirmed that the police did not seem to be making any connection between these victims; nor did they see their deaths as part of a series. In this they shared the myopia of the London police of the 1870s and 1880s. Even by the time of the Cleveland killings of course, the term serial killer and even the concept of murder of this type, was unrecognized. Forensic science had its blood groupings and its fingerprints and in 1935, in Britain, Professor Glaister was making excellent progress in corpse identification in the case of Dr Buck Ruxton, who murdered his wife and housekeeper.[4] In terms of actual psychoanalysis however, the nearest that the police could come was that they were probably looking for a 'pervert'. The fact that the Cleveland killer's victims were male and female pointed to an unusual kind of murderer – at the time Peter Kürten, the monster of Dusseldorf who was executed in 1931, was probably the most notorious example. The removal of heads and genitals however was not necessarily sex related. In the prohibition era, the Mob sent such messages to anyone who crossed them in various eastern cities. Bodies were frequently fished out of New York's East River in the 1930s, some identifiable, some not.

The most high-profile policeman hunting the Cleveland killer was Eliot Ness. In 1928 he had hand-picked nine special Prohibition agents from the Chicago Police Department who went to war with Al Capone's bootleg and narcotics racketeers for six years. Named the Untouchables because neither bribery nor intimidation worked against them, Ness's men made a serious financial dent in Capone's organization before the gangster himself was sent to prison on tax evasion charges. In Cleveland, Ness's role was that of public safety director and he scored more successes here against syndicate boss Moe Dalitz. But the torso killer beat him. Cynics said that Ness was the murderer's thirteenth victim in that he retired from law enforcement soon afterwards and his later business ventures were failures.

Huge amounts of money and police time went into catching the Cleveland killer. Some detectives went underground as hobos, riding the freight trains that rolled through the Kingsbury Run, believing the corpses could have been thrown from a cattle truck. On 18 August 1938 Ness launched his own Prohibition-style raid, rounding up the vagrants sleeping rough in the Run and burning their shanty towns to the ground. Many people believed that the killer was smoked out in that the murders apparently ceased. Victim No. 12 had been found along with No. 11 at the corner of East 9th and Lake Shore Drive near the Lake Erie docks two days before Ness's conflagration. Was it a copycat twelve years later who dumped the body parts of Robert Robertson along Davenport Avenue, only a few yards from the dump site of Victims 11 and 12? Robertson's prints were on file as a habitual drunk who had often been arrested. In every respect, he was typical of the John and Jane Does who became the Cleveland killer's victims.

The police of course had their suspects and it was standard procedure to beat confessions out of people in the days before human rights and political correctness. Frank Dolezal was a predatory homosexual who fitted the pattern in police eyes; he hanged himself in police custody in August 1939. Eliot Ness had several interviews with a suspect he called Gaylord Sundheim, who conveniently committed suicide in a mental institution shortly afterwards. Black cab driver Willie Johnson murdered and dismembered 19-year-old prostitute Margaret Wilson in June 1942 and he went to the chair for that on 10 March 1944; all attempts to connect him with the other killings failed. Kentucky butchers, New Castle Railroad men, male nurses and Dr Francis Sweeney all came under the suspicion of one or more of the detectives working the case, but hard evidence, that one final piece of the jigsaw which would link all the Cleveland murders of the Kingsbury Run, was never found.

Coroner Sam Gerber wrote, in the 1930s version of profiling:

> He is a person of more than average intelligence, with definite professional knowledge of anatomy but not necessarily a man of surgery. He is large and strong. He probably lives in the section bordering Kingsbury Run where he

comes and goes without attracting attention. In all probability he belongs to a higher social stratum than his victims, but can mingle with vagrants without arousing their suspicion. His murders are committed mostly in a laboratory near the Run. He is a pervert who sometimes drugs his victims and may lead a normal life when not absorbed with his sadistic passion.[5]

Detective Peter Merylo, who worked the case on the ground for years, went further:

the murderer is a sex degenerate suffering from necrophilia, aphrodisia or erotomania who may have worked in the pathology department of some hospital, morgue or some college where he had the opportunity to handle a great number of bodies, or may have been employed in some undertaking establishment and that he had a mania for headless and nude bodies ... the murderer procured his [sexual] gratification while watching the blood flow after cutting the jugular vein of his victim.[6]

While Merylo may have been spot on with this analysis he wrote in reply to a letter in October 1938:

In your letter you mention Jack the Ripper in London, but this killer only committed crimes upon one sex, while the [Cleveland] Torso Murderer has changed from one sex to another, apparently without discrimination. Therefore we are of the opinion that we have to deal with a person whose mental processes are so far unknown to scientists.[7]

Fast forward thirty years. 1960s London was the heart of the swinging scene. Carnaby Street was the centre of the world for anybody under 30. And crimes not unlike those of the torso killer were being carried out along the Thames. They did not involve dismemberment, but the victims were prostitutes and the river bank was their resting place.

Hannah Tailford, Irene Lockwood, Helen Barthelemy, Mary Fleming, Margaret McGowan and Bridie O'Hara were the heiresses of Elizabeth Jackson – West End prostitutes who met the wrong client at the wrong time. The tallest was only 5ft 2ins and they all died within one year – January 1964 to January 1965.

Hannah Tailford aka Terry Lynch was found on the dark mud of the foreshore near Hammersmith Pier on 2 February. She was naked except for her stockings which were round her ankles. Her panties had been stuffed into her mouth. The last time anyone saw her was nine days earlier when she left her home in Thurlby Road, West Norwood. Her clothes were never found; nor was the handbag containing her diary, which may well have listed her clients and possibly, her murderer. Originally from Northumberland, Hannah had a 3-year-old daughter. Her flat was found to contain photographic equipment which she may have used for blackmail purposes. There were rumours of kinky parties in Belgravia involving foreign diplomats. A glimpse of the scale of police operations at the time is evidenced by the fact that DCI Ben Devonald interviewed nearly 700 people on this case; it all led nowhere.

Extraordinarily, Assistant Commissioner 'Big John' du Rose who spearheaded what became known as the Nudes or Jack the Stripper murders, believed for a time that Hannah Tailford might have been a suicide. In the 1960s about a hundred bodies were fished out of the Thames each year and it was not unknown for suicides to strip and push a gag into their mouths to make breathing impossible or to prevent calling out for help. If that were the case, where were Hannah's clothes? Did she walk naked through London without attracting attention? It did not help that one of the foremost pathologists of his generation, Dr Donald Teare, could only find bruising on the jaw which could have been the result of a fall. With the official weight of evidence so undecided, coroner Gavin Thurston could only direct the inquest jury to deliver an open verdict.

Two months later, Irene Lockwood's body was found on the river's foreshore at Duke's Meadows, Chiswick, not far from the pier. This was only a few hundred yards upstream from the Hannah Tailford dump site. Irene, aka Sandra Russell, had lived in Denbigh Road, Ealing. Like Hannah, she had a flat to entertain clients – the rent was £12 10s a week. Like Elizabeth Jackson eighty years earlier, Irene was pregnant. Like the anonymous Bedford Square victim of 1884, she had a tattoo; hers read 'John in Memory'.

Irene, from Lincolnshire, was involved in the 'blue film' industry that provided cheap super 8 movies for home consumption or were shown in Soho 'theatres'. A friend of hers in the same racket, Vicki Pender, had been murdered the previous year, proving, if proof were needed, what a dangerous game these girls played. Vicki aka Veronica Walsh had been battered and strangled to death by a client who was subsequently jailed for life.

Superintendent Frank Davies now led the enquiry, as clearly there was a pattern emerging here. Vicki Pender was a one-off, but Davies now had two dead prostitutes found in similar attitudes along the river bank and within yards of each other in space and two months in terms of time. In the middle of all this, Kenneth Archibald confessed to Irene's murder, saying he had killed the woman and pushed her body into the river. He signed a confession twice before retracting it and a whole pantomime was played out as Archibald was tried and acquitted in a court of law. He admitted later that he had been 'on a bender' with friends and that it was alcohol that made him spin the murder yarn. Astonishingly, so many of the points he made fitted reality that the police believed him.

The river pattern was broken by the next murder, rather as the London Squares killing broke the torso pattern in 1884. Helen Barthelemy, from Talbot Road, Willesden, was found sixteen days after Irene Lockwood, in a driveway behind houses at Swincombe Avenue, Brentford, about a mile from the Thames. She was naked, the dark ring round her waist proof that her panties had been removed after death and four of her teeth were missing, one lodged in her throat. Helen had been educated in a convent in Scotland and had literally run away to join a circus. She worked as a waitress and stripper along Blackpool's Golden Mile for a time and she used the aliases Teddie, Thompson and Paul. Her forearm bore the tattoo 'Loving You'.

Helen operated in the Notting Hill and Shepherd's Bush areas, newly filled with a growing West Indian population, and kerb-crawlers and cars in those streets were checked. This was light years away from CCTV on every corner and pleas by the police for the girls to be extra-vigilant and to cooperate largely fell on deaf ears.

It was not until 14 July that Jack the Stripper struck again. Scottish-born Mary Fleming of Lancaster Gardens, Ealing, was found dead, sitting upright near a garage door in Berrymead Road, Chiswick. She was naked and her clothes were never found. Neither was the denture which had been torn out of her mouth. The body was found at 5am by a chauffeur, George Head, on his way to the garage complex to pick up his car. Painters working through the night on a rush job had seen a car or small van reversing in the cul-de-sac in Lancaster Gardens two hours earlier. They also saw its driver, but the angle was not clear and, aware that he was being watched, he drove off.

Forensics now came to the aid of the police. The latest victims had minute traces of car-body paint sprayed on their skin and the search was on for premises near the dump sites. Manpower was increased on the case, but no real headway was made before the next killing. Margaret McGowan, a Notting Hill prostitute, was already something of a celebrity before her body was found, partly decomposed, in a rubbish dump in a car park at Hornton Street, Kensington. One of her teeth was missing and she had tattoos on one arm, including 'Helen, Mum and Dad'. Under the name of Frances Brown, Margaret had given evidence in the vice trial of Dr Stephen Ward, the osteopath linked to call-girls Christine Keeler and Mandy Rice-Davies, whose association with War Minister John Profumo helped to bring down Harold Macmillan's government.

Margaret was living in Shepherd's Bush and had given birth to three illegitimate children. Together with Kim Taylor, she had been soliciting in

Portobello Road on the night she vanished. Kim was able to give police a description of the man who had picked Margaret up, but no one, understandably, came forward.

The Stripper's next – and final – victim was Bridget O'Hara, known as Bridie. She paid £3 10s a week for her flat in Agate Road, Hammersmith, and was last seen alive at the Shepherd's Bush Hotel on the night of 11 January 1965. The next person to see her, other than her killer, was Ernest Beauchamp, who came upon what he first took to be a shop mannequin lying largely hidden under shrubs on the Heron Trading Estate[8] on 16 February. She had not been there all that time, the pathologist believed, but had been kept somewhere indoors before being dumped. The Irish girl was naked, with the name 'Mick' tattooed on her arm. She had died, as had all the others, from asphyxiation and her front teeth had been knocked out. There were once again paint-spray particles on the skin.

It is useful to compare police tactics in the Stripper case with those of eighty years earlier. Policewomen dressed up as prostitutes with tiny tape recorders hidden in gloves and scarves to lure clients. Even the police had no real idea of the enormous range of perversions that call girls were asked to provide. Sado-masochism was paramount and the detectives leading the case were particularly interested in anyone with a penchant for fellatio, which might explain the missing teeth in so many victims. Kerb-crawlers were interviewed, sometimes at home on flimsy excuses like minor road accidents so that wives should not become suspicious and marriages fall apart. Focusing on paint-spray workshops, squads of uniformed men and women combed the twenty-four square mile area north of the Thames. Such was the press coverage of the Stripper murders that a total of 500 policemen, uniformed and plainclothes, worked on the case.

The Heron Estate became the focus of police activity and one paint-spray shop in particular had been the temporary resting place of Bridie O'Hara. Seven thousand people worked on the estate and there was open access to it to any number of outsiders. The rapid rebuilding which has characterized London since the end of the Second World War meant that buildings were demolished during the Stripper's spree, destroying perhaps valuable evidence.

Unlike the hunters of the Thames torso killer, the police had mass communication at their disposal. Not only did newspapers give the case a huge coverage by comparison with that of the 1870s and 1880s, but the police held twice-daily press conferences that were broadcast on radio and television. It was as though John Du Rose's men were talking directly to the man they were after.

In what may well be the most disappointing end to a murder investigation in the history of true crime, du Rose wrote in his autobiography in 1971 that the psychological pressure brought to bear by the police drove the prime suspect to suicide.

> We had done all we possibly could but faced with his death no positive evidence was available to prove or disprove our belief that he was in fact the man we had been seeking. Because he was never arrested or stood trial, he must be considered innocent and will therefore never be named.[9]

Subsequent theories pointed to the apparent suicide of night-club owner and former boxing champion Freddie Mills who was found blasted by a rifle bullet in his car outside his own club, the Nite Spot, in Charing Cross Road, on the night of 25 July 1965. A recent book claims that Mills was Jack the Stripper and that the missing teeth were the result of his boxer's right hook. The evidence is flimsy, but probably no more outrageous than Home Office Pathologist Keith Simpson's claim that Mills's wound may well have been self-inflicted. Since the only wound was a bullet's entry in the inner angle of the right eye and the weapon was a .22 rifle, this must have been one of the most awkward and unlikely suicides on record. I have no doubt that Mills was murdered. I also have no doubt that he was not Jack the Stripper. Another killer of women along the river had got away with murder.

Gary Ridgeway would not get away, but the killer of women along the Green River in Washington State enjoyed a twenty-year run before he was caught. Just as the Thames torso killer operated in a criminal nightmare world dominated by Jack the Ripper, so Ridgeway's hunting ground was very similar to that of serial killer Ted Bundy. At one point in fact, while Bundy was on Death Row for his crimes, he offered to help police in their enquiries into the Green River case on the dubious grounds that he understood how the man's twisted mind worked.[10]

Unlike the Thames, the Green River runs through wild, open countryside for much of its sixty-five-mile length, through the state of Washington. It is popular with anglers and kayakers and some of its stretches are dangerous, with fast-flowing currents and rapids. In July 1982 the first victim of the Green River killer was found. She was 16-year-old Wendy Coffield and her naked body was fished out of the water by detective Dave Reichart, who would spend half his working career trying to find out who killed her. Although only the first three victims were found beneath the water's surface, an estimated fifty more would appear over the next twenty years, hidden mostly in the thick scrub woodland that forms the river's hinterland.

Most of the killer's victims were prostitutes, picked up along the Pac HiWay, known locally as the SeaTac Strip. The area's ribbon development provided everything for the passing motorist on his or her way to Seattle or Tacoma and that included drugs and prostitution.

The first three bodies elicited various clues. Their clothes had gone, but dental records, not kept in the 1870s and 1880s, could prove useful. The water had removed all traces of semen, but two of the three had triangular shaped stones stuffed into their vaginas in what seemed to be symbolic rape. All three women were identified and there had been no attempt at dismemberment.

The 1980s saw something of an upsurge in the serial killer in the United States. That was essentially the first full decade in which the term was used of a murderer who kills again and again, choosing similar targets and using a similar, but constantly developing MO. Ted Bundy began his murderous spree in the Seattle area in 1974, killing seven women in seven months. With his cool arrogance and exceptional cunning, he lured pretty, dark-haired teenagers into his VW before raping and murdering them. So assured was he, he even gave his real name – Ted – and continued to kill in three more states before he was finally arrested. He confessed to twenty-eight murders and often returned to the corpses to have sex with them. Two other necrophiliacs whose *folie à deux* led to the death penalty, Henry Lee Lucas and Otis O'Toole exaggerated the number of young girls they killed, but they were certainly seriously deranged sociopaths whose total killings have been notched up at anything between three and sixty-nine (the notoriously vague Lucas claimed nearly three hundred!). The Hillside Stranglers, Kenneth Bianchi and his cousin Angelo Buono egged each other on to commit murders across California in the 1970s and Bianchi's attempt to fool psychiatrists into believing he was suffering from multiple personality disorder failed.

Against high-profile monsters like these, Gary Ridgeway comes across as 'normal', even humdrum. And it was this very ordinariness that allowed him to notch up over fifty murders. His battered pickup truck was spotted several times along the Pac HiWay. He was known to be a kerb-crawler. The police talked to him more than once. But each time, Gary Ridgeway walked away, as slippery as mercury, to kill again.

His list of victims makes depressing reading. Wide publicity, the advancing technology of media and the anxiety of distraught relatives meant that most of the Green River killer's targets were identified. Some, however, despite forensic techniques to reconstruct faces that Doctors Kemper, Hebbert and Bond could only dream about, remain mere numbers. Many were runaways, nice kids who fell out with moms and dads and stepmoms and stepdads, whose grades began to fall at school, who wanted independence and the good life. Such women were as notoriously vulnerable in Washington State in the 1980s as their counterparts were in London a century earlier. The only difference was that they tended to be younger.

The enquiries made by the Green River Task Force, a beleaguered team faced with dwindling funds and waning public interest as time went on, revealed a huge variety of sexual oddities among ordinary people. One travelling salesman returned home with variously coloured samples of pubic hair. A husband took a macabre delight in cutting up the centrefolds of porn mags and rearranging the dismembered heads, arms and legs.

And the killer seemed to be taunting the police. At one point he staged a carefully constructed murder scene, as when Carol Christensen was discovered fully clothed with false clues nearby. At other times, the bodies were almost literally thrown away. And again, others were systematically hidden in dense undergrowth. They were black and white, making a nonsense of the usual serial killer's pattern of intra-racial murder only.

Time and again the police had to break the worst news to frantic parents. The reactions varied, but the quiet dignity and extraordinary courage of these parents is best summed up by the mother of 16-year-old Kimi-Kai Pitsor last seen getting into an old pickup truck in downtown Seattle. She was only identifiable through dental records. 'She's not hurting now,' her mother said. 'She's not cold. She's not hungry. She's no longer in any kind of pain.'[11]

Forensic technology was coming to the aid of the police during the long years of the Green River Killer's reign of terror. Ted Bundy had been nailed by bite marks he left on one of his victims and in 1985 Colin Pitchfork became the first murderer to be caught by matching his DNA with semen found on the underwear of his teenaged victims. Criminal profiling had not only established the term 'serial killer', but a great deal was known about the mindset of such people – how they operate and what drives them to kill. When Gary Ridgeway was finally caught he exhibited all three of the 'triad' symptoms in childhood which marks a high percentage of multiple murderers. He was obsessed with lighting fires, carried out torture on animals and was still wetting the bed at 13. Profiler John Douglas of the FBI's Behavioural Science Unit at Quantico got the killer's age range right (mid-twenties to early thirties) and said prophetically: 'These homicides reflect rage and anger ... He will not stop killing until he is caught.'[12]

But Gary Ridgeway did not fit the usual pattern. In fact, a deep study of him since his arrest has helped establish new norms of behaviour for serial killers. In 1984 he passed a polygraph test when interviewed over the murders. He was regularly employed, painting trucks for the Kenworth Company for twenty years. He did not come from a broken home and had several lasting relationships, most recently with an unsuspecting wife whose presence almost certainly slowed down his killing rate. His workmates even joked about the fact that Gary Ridgeway's initials were the same as the killer's sobriquet and for a while he was 'Green River Gary'.

On 16 November 2001 Gary Ridgeway was arrested on a routine charge of loitering for prostitution. The girl was a policewoman and for the Green River Killer it was the end of the line. Weeks, then months of interviews, DNA testing, arraignments and the whole palaver of bringing a twenty-year killing spree to an end, followed. When he appeared before the flashing cameras of the media for the first time, he was, in Ann Rule's words, 'medium height, medium build, totally average-looking, a man who scarcely resembled what they believed him to be – the most infamous and prolific serial killer ever known in America'.[13] He told police flatly and without emotion how he had killed various women, strangling them usually from behind. 'Some went easily,' he said, 'and some fought hard. But they all died.'[14]

'Adam' was seen floating past the Tower of London on the afternoon of Friday 21 September 2001. A passerby on Tower Bridge saw a bright orange object bobbing on the water's surface and he realized they were shorts wrapped around the body of a black boy. Once the police had been alerted, Thames Division's marine search unit went into action and recovered the corpse. There was huge and almost immediate media coverage and in the absence of a name, the police called the boy 'Adam'.

The subsequent post-mortem revealed that Adam was between 4 and 7 years old. His head, both arms and both legs had been removed, but there were no obvious signs of sexual assault and the body did not seem malnourished which would have been the case in the event of neglect. His stomach contents contained British food but pollen traces in his lungs was from African trees. More sinister was the fact that the stomach also contained a mixture which the Met knew was used in African ritual magic. Bone analysis proved that Adam came from the Yoruba Plateau area in Nigeria. The pollen implied that he had been in England only a few days.

Met officers travelled to Yoruba, working with the Nigerian police who had their own missing children file and trawled villages and primary schools in the forlorn hope of locating Adam's parents. They drew a blank.

Ten months after Adam's body was found, a Nigerian woman turned up in London from Germany with an extraordinary claim that she had fled Yoruba where a cult was involved with the ritual murder of children. Orange shorts like the pair Adam was wearing were found at her flat and one of her associates, Kingsley Ojo, had several ritual items in his apartments, but no DNA links with Adam. He was sent to jail for four years in 2004 for child trafficking. Like the victims of the torso killer, Adam was never identified. With all the scientific advances available to the police and all the worldwide media coverage of the case, the little boy in the Thames essentially remains unknown and his killer has got away with murder.

In this chapter we have looked at other examples of dismemberment following murder. We have looked at dangerously deranged men who targeted prostitutes; at crimes committed near the banks of the Thames; at murders carried out and bodies dumped underwater. James Greenacre was caught by astute detective work and luck. Gary Ridgeway evaded police investigation for twenty years. The victims of the Cleveland Butcher and of Jack the Stripper still await justice. And little Adam may be the tip of a terrifying iceberg no one wants to uncover.

Different times; similar crimes. No happy ending.

Chapter 13

The Habitual Homicide

One of the most disturbing facts about the arrest of Long Island murderer Joel Rifkin in June 1993 is that many policemen in the area had no idea that a serial killer of prostitutes was at large. The arrest had been for a traffic violation, but the arresting officers grew suspicious of a smell emanating from a tarpaulin in the back of Rifkin's pickup truck and discovered a dead body, one of seventeen he had murdered over a period of time.

All this took place at a time when the concept of 'serial killer' was fully understood, when mind-mapping and geographical profiling were already cutting edge in the hunt for the seriously disturbed. A century earlier, the men hunting the torso killer had no chance. In looking for a madman, they were looking in the wrong direction altogether. We have already examined the various 'men behaving madly' who wandered the streets of late Victorian England and some of them conformed to the stereotypical dribbling lunatic who ranted and raved and frightened the children. London's asylums, like those all over the world, were full of such people and if it was no longer fashionable to poke these sad cases with sticks to see how they would respond, the exact nature of their illness was usually woefully misunderstood. Restraints and cruelty were all too often the order of the day rather than kindness and understanding.

In the sixteenth century, the 'scientific' rage was physiognomy. External appearance – sizes and shapes of noses, ears, lips – spoke volumes about the appearance of a man's soul. This is why Shakespeare and his audiences were quite happy to accept as truth the behaviour of the greatest stage villain of all time – Richard III. Since Richard, according to gossip, was born prematurely with hair, teeth, a humped back, withered arm and deformed leg, *of course* it was possible for him to kill eleven people, including his own nephews, to get to the throne. And in some people's minds, the physical-moral link never went away. In one of the scores of 'helpful' letters sent to the City Police during the Ripper scare of 1888, A Mason of the Union Bank of Scotland in Chancery

Lane wrote to warn of 'a repulsive man at Smith's bookstall at Cannon Street Station' on the night that Mary Kelly was murdered.

The spin-off of physiognomy by the early nineteenth century when James Greenacre was frantically distributing dismembered parts of Hannah Brown over London, was phrenology, essentially, the pattern of skulls. The Austrian doctor Franz Gall believed that the brain was composed of thirty-three 'organs'. Some of these controlled essential human characteristics; others controlled sentiments; the third group recognized higher complexities such as cause and effect. One of these organs – which could be felt through the cranium – was what another age might call the criminal gene. Identify this in infants and criminals could be stopped even before their careers began. Gall was not admired in Austria, but Britain, France and the United States were impressed. In America in particular phrenologists joined the scores of quacks who toured the fairs selling potions to cure anything from love-sickness to snake bites.

By the decade of the torso murders, Professor Rudolf Virchow of the Berlin Pathological Institute was making some interesting discoveries. His notes for guidance on autopsies became a bible across Europe. Drs Bond and Hebbert, who worked on both the torso and the Ripper victims, shared their faith in this man along with the more enlightened of the Met's police surgeons. Virchow studied some 6,000 criminals over a twenty-year period, making careful measurements of their skulls in particular and came to the conclusion that criminal heads tended to the prehistoric, with relatively small crania and pronounced eyebrow ridges and muzzles.

Cesare Lombroso took up this torch with alacrity. He had served as an army surgeon with the Italians in the late 1860s and was appointed Professor of Mental Diseases at Pavia University. His 'eureka moment' came when carrying out a post-mortem on an executed thief: 'At the sight of that skull, I seemed to see, all of a sudden, lighted up as a vast plain under a flaming sky, the problem of the nature of the criminal – an atavistic being who reproduces in his person the ferocious instincts of primitive humanity and the inferior animals.'

Three years after the torso killer first struck, Lombroso was made Professor of Forensic Medicine and wrote his seminal work *L'Uomo Deliquente* (Criminal Man) which made him a star almost everywhere except England. His division of criminals into 'occasional' and 'born' still strikes a chord today, but he could not escape from the myth of physiognomy. His sequel, written twenty years later (*Criminal Anthropology*, 1895) led to very specific identifications of criminal types. Pickpockets had long hands (no surprises there!) but they were also tall and had black hair and thin beards. Arsonists were light with small heads; rapists had short hands and narrow foreheads, they had abnormalities of the genitals (of course!) and of noses; assassins had wide cheekbones, thick hair and prominent jaws.

In France, Alexandre Lacassagne, Professor of Forensic Medicine at Lyon University, disagreed with Lombroso. With an argument that still finds favour today, Lacassagne regarded crime as a social manifestation. Poverty breeds despair and despair leads to crime, be it theft, rape or murder. The huge scale of physical differences between serial killers over the past forty years would certainly tend to prove Lombroso wrong, even if the jury is still out on Lacassagne's argument. In France, too, the Bertillons, father and son, were taking physiognomy to a new – and vital – level. Louis Bertillon was President of the Paris Anthropological Society in the 1870s and by the time the torso killer had struck for a third and fourth time, leaving body parts in the squares of Bloomsbury, his son, Alphonse, was with the Parisian *Prefecture de Police*. Over a five-month period, the younger Bertillon assembled physical measurements – 'portraits parlé' (the speaking likenesses) – of 1,600 criminals on a cross-referenced card file system at the Sûreté. 'Bertillonage' proved highly successful, especially with the increasing use of photography, central to a crime scene today, and its use spread widely. Eliot Ness's cops in Cleveland were still using the system to track down the butcher of Kingsbury Run in the 1930s.

The Italian criminologists Enrico Ferri and Napoleone Colajanni were interested in motivation for crime. 'Cosmic' causes included temperature and diet; 'biological' referred to anatomy, physiology, psychology; the 'social factor' reflected Lacassagne's belief in 'the price of alcohol' and 'the price of wheat'. Another Italian, Figerio, lectured on the largest ears he had ever seen which were on a woman charged with murdering her husband. Ottolenghi noted that sex offenders had rectilinear noses; Marro found most of them to be full-bearded.

The problem was that no one in the 1870s and 1880s had the nerve to dismiss the clap-trap of earlier generations. 'I do not need to see the whole of a criminal's face,' wrote François Vidocq, the early nineteenth-century thief-taker, 'to recognize him as such; it is enough for me to catch his eye.' This classic piece of braggadocio is fine for a dodgy character writing his memoirs; but for an earnest policeman trying to catch the torso killer in the 1880s, it is of no use at all.

Lombroso had written:

The eye of the habitual homicide [scrial killer] is glassy, cold and fixed; his nose is often aquiline, beaked, reminding one of a bird of prey ... the jaws are strong; the ears long; the cheek-bones large; the hair dark, curling, abundant; the beard often thin, the canine teeth much developed ...

One man who could have proved him wrong was Richard von Krafft-Ebing. An eminent Austro-German psychiatrist at a time when that science was in its infancy, he ran a number of asylums in Germany before going into print with his *Psychopathia Sexualis* in 1886. The book broke new territory and polite society was appalled by it. It introduced all sorts of perversions to the great and good of Europe, including sadism, masochism (terms which Krafft-Ebing invented) and bestiality. A later edition of his work (probably published in 1892) refers to the Whitechapel murders. This is disappointing in that it contains various factual errors, presumably because the author was working from scrambled newspaper accounts and, among 238 cases he discusses, some distortion is inevitable.

Only one of Krafft-Ebing's 'lustmurder' cases involves dismemberment. It is the rape-murder of little Fanny Adams, whose name became part of folklore, in 1867. Krafft-Ebing notes the chilling diary entry by killer Frederick Baker, a solicitor's clerk from Alton, Hampshire: 'Killed today a young girl. It was fine and hot.' Having raped Fanny in a cornfield, Baker hacked her body into pieces and scattered them over a wide area. Some pieces, including the genitals, were never found.

The year after the last torso killing, Henry Havelock Ellis went into print with *The Criminal*. In terms of criminal psychology, he lamented the fact that Britain had fallen far behind Europe – 'no book, scarcely a solitary magazine article dealing with this matter, has appeared among us'. In 1890, Ellis told his readers that about 100 people imprisoned yearly were found to be insane. He acknowledged just how in the dark doctors – and policemen – were:

> The lunatic may be influenced by the same motives that influence the sane person, but he is at the same time impelled by other motives peculiar to himself and to which we may have no means of access.

It was not strictly true that all policemen were clueless. John Littlechild had been an inspector with Special Branch at the time of the Ripper killings and had been sent out to the United States in search of a possible suspect 'Doctor' Francis Tumblety. Answering a letter about this peculiar charlatan years later, Littlechild wrote:

> He was an American quack ... and was at one time a frequent visitor to London and on these occasions constantly brought under the notice of police [for acts of indecency with men] there being a large dossier concerning him at Scotland Yard. Although a 'Sycopathia Sexualis' subject he was not known as a 'sadist' (which the [Whitechapel] murderer unquestionably was) ...[1]

The great psychoanalysts of the twentieth century were born too late to have any effect on the hunt for the torso killer. Sigmund Freud was 17 and still at school in Vienna when the first finds were made along the river at Battersea. Alfred Adler was only 3. Carl Jung would not be born until two years later. But one of the first men to work as a profiler, nearly a century before the term was coined, was Dr Thomas Bond, whose expertise we have seen in the physical sense of carrying out post-mortems on the torso victims. He was asked by Robert Anderson, Assistant Commissioner at Scotland Yard, what sort of man the Whitechapel murderer was and this was his response:

> The murderer must have been a man of physical strength and of great coolness and daring. There is no evidence that he had an accomplice. He must, in my opinion, be a man subject to periodical attacks of homicidal and erotic mania. The character of mutilations indicate that the man may be in a condition sexually that may be called satyriasis.[2] The murderer in external appearance is quite likely to be a quiet, inoffensive-looking man, probably middle aged and neatly and respectably dressed ... he would probably be solitary and eccentric in his habits. Also he is most likely to be a man without regular occupation, but with some small income or pension. He is possibly living among respectable persons who have some knowledge of his character and habits and who may have grounds for suspicion that he is not quite right in his mind at times.

Bond was describing, in modern psychiatric terminology, a disorganized 'blitz' killer, experiencing the grim cycle of homicidal mania outlined by Dr Joel Norris. Such men do not quite kill on impulse, in that they plan their crime and stalk their prey to an extent. But they are risk-takers, killing in public places, often (but not in Jack's case) leaving behind the murder weapon which they found to hand. There is no attempt to conceal the crime and escape is largely a combination of low cunning and luck. The pity for us is that no one asked the prescient Dr Bond to give his thoughts on the torso killer.

If we fast forward to 1988, Special Agent John E Douglas of the FBI's Behavioral Science Unit at Quantico, Virginia, was asked to provide a new profile of Jack for a television programme marking the centenary of the Whitechapel murders. It is fascinating to compare his work with Bond's. The language may be more terse, in the bullet-point style to which we have become accustomed, but the similarities are extraordinary:

> An asocial loner. Employment in positions where he could work alone and experience vicariously his destructive fantasies, perhaps as a butcher or

hospital or mortuary attendant. Dress, neat and orderly. Sexual relationships mostly with prostitutes. May have contracted venereal disease. Aged in his late twenties. Employed since the murders were mostly at weekends. Free from family accountability and so unlikely to have been married. Not surgically skilled. Probably in some form of trouble with the police before the first murder. Lived or worked in Whitechapel area and his first homicide would have been close to his home or place of work. Undoubtedly the police would have interviewed him.

By the time he wrote his book *The Cases that Haunt us* in 2000, Douglas modified his views and went into greater detail. The most telling change of mind is that the profiler now believed Jack to have had 'some anatomical knowledge or curiosity'.

It is difficult to know on what Thomas Bond based his ideas, but in the case of John Douglas, it was the culmination of years of experience in dealing with serial killers, 74 per cent of whom are American and many of whom have spent years in prison explaining their every move to psychiatrists. 'We serial killers are your sons,' wrote Ted Bundy chillingly, 'we are your husbands, we are everywhere. And there will be more of your children dead tomorrow.'

There is no doubt that the serial killer – along with the paedophile – is the new bogeyman. Thanks to novels by Thomas Harris, Val McDermid, Kathy Reichs and many more, we, the public, treat them almost as old friends. In the film *Silence of the Lambs*, cannibalistic madman Hannibal Lecter, played with an eerie Gothicism by Anthony Hopkins, is employed by the FBI who are hunting an even more grotesque nutcase, 'Buffalo Bill' (Ted Levine). Harris borrowed bits from many of the real-life monsters of our time. Cannibalism was the stock-in-trade of the German killers Fritz Haarmann, Georg Grossmann and Karl Denke. Jeffrey Dahmer, the 'Milwaukee Monster', showed similar tendencies, as did Albert Fish when he roasted and stewed the body parts of 10-year-old Grace Budd. Russian killer Andrei Chikatilo ate the genitals of several of his child victims. As for 'Buffalo Bill', the man dresses up in the skin of his victims, a characteristic of serial killer Ed Gein. We are so inured to the bloody behaviour of serial killers that we think we know all about them. Yet with each one there seems to be a new angle, a different twist and we are really no further forward in understanding them or able to stop what sometimes seems like an epidemic! In the United States in 1988, the National Institute of Justice defined serial murder as 'a series of two or more murders, committed as separate events, usually, but not always, by one offender acting alone. The crimes may occur over a period of time ranging from hours to years.'

An analysis of American serial killers provides a pattern which is often faithfully woven into fiction. Eighty-seven per cent are the 'asocial loner' which

John Douglas associated with the Ripper. Ted Bundy followed this pattern. So did David Berkowitz, the 'Son of Sam'. That of course still leaves 13 per cent who do not follow the convention. Ten per cent work in pairs, such as the Hillside Stranglers, Bianchi and Buono. The term applied to them, 'social killers', seems particularly rich in irony. Three per cent vary their approach, working either alone or with a partner. An unlikely gender combination is that of Douglas Clark and Carol Bundy, who targeted prostitutes.

Killer types have been divided into: the territorial, who kill within a 'circle of comfort', a defined area they know well; nomadic, who travel widely in search of prey; and stationary, those who draw victims to a lair as a spider might catch a fly. Motivation varies. Some are vision killers, believing that God or the Devil has chosen them to carry out their work. Peter Sutcliffe, the Yorkshire Ripper, claimed to hear voices from God: 'The women I killed were filth – bastard prostitutes who were littering the streets. I was just cleaning up the place a bit.' In his warped mind, he was just doing us all a favour. This makes him a mission killer too (the definition boundaries blur), where prostitutes, homosexuals, ethnic groups become the target. Pleasure killers are the thrill-seekers; Leopold and Loeb killed little Bobby Franks just to prove they could in 1924. They also kill for profit – John George Haigh who dissolved his victims in drums of acid before selling their furniture and houses is a classic example. The type most usually found in fiction is the killer who murders in order to exercise power or control. Harvey Glatman photographed his pretty female victims bound and gagged before he raped and killed them. Neville Heath thrashed Margery Gardner with a riding crop and almost bit her nipple off in the course of her murder.

David Wilson is one of Britain's leading authorities on serial murder. His book *A History of British Serial Killing* (2009) cites the examples of thirty-one murderers and their 375 victims over a 120-year period. The figures fall far short of American statistics of course, and I have to take issue with Wilson's contention that 'The phenomena now known as serial killing – in Britain and elsewhere – formally begins on the night of 31 August 1888, when Mary Ann Nichols' was murdered. Even allowing for the fact that I believe that she was Jack's second victim (his first being Martha Tabram three weeks earlier), it is clear from the factual record that the torso killer beat Jack by fifteen years.

Analyst Professor Danny Dorling of the University of Sheffield has studied British murder during the twenty years 1980–2000 and has come up with some fascinating observations, especially on motivation.

> Behind the man with the knife is the man who sold him the knife, the man who did not give him a job, the man who decided that his school did not need

funding, the man who closed down the branch plant where he could have worked, the man who decided to reduce benefit levels ...³

And very quickly, the whole fraught question of what makes a serial killer descends into political name-calling. Even the briefest of comparisons with a century earlier gives us a grimmer picture than anything we have known. When the torso killer walked London, there was no welfare state. School boards were only just being set up in school-less areas. Medicine was expensive, hospitals still centres of disease. Social benefits extended only to the dreaded workhouse for the poor, a place where only the truly desperate went. Consumption and diphtheria killed thousands and cholera and typhus fever were only yesterday. Men and women worked to the rhythm of giant, soulless machines. Too many of them became lost in a downward spiral of poverty and vice. Most of them, somehow, coped. Some of them succumbed, dying alone in the scum-smeared alleyways of Spitalfields and Whitechapel. One or two of them became serial killers.

Chapter 14

The Cat's Meat Man

The starting point for the investigation of any murder is the crime scene. Thanks to our current obsession with serial killers and cop shows on television, we are very familiar with the men in white suits, hoods and overshoes. We understand that everything must be photographed, measured, bagged and tagged. What is not observable to the naked eye can nevertheless be analysed in the laboratory, where the microscope and DNA analysis are vital tools of the trade. Even in the 1870s and 1880s when policemen walked all over crime scenes in hob-nailed boots, they at least looked for alien footprints, carriage or cart tracks and items in the vicinity which may have a bearing on the case. Sometimes, in fact, these casual finds, which were not crime-related, caused problems. The leather apron found near the body of Ripper victim Annie Chapman in the yard behind 29 Hanbury Street, led to a vigilante obsession to find 'Leather Apron' and the arrest of the innocent John Pizer, whose nickname that was. In fact the apron belonged to one of number 29's residents who had washed it and left it there to dry.

Police surgeons called to crime scenes followed the precepts of Professor Virchow to the letter. Once they had satisfied themselves that the victim was actually dead, they checked for body warmth, noted the position of the corpse in relation to its surroundings, blood patterns, disarrangement of clothes and so on. Dr George Brown, called to the Ripper's handiwork in Mitre Square, made very accurate drawings of the position of the body in a corner of the Square, the obvious external wounds and even a close-up of the unusual mutilations of the face.

The police themselves made a complete list of the clothes and belongings of Annie Chapman so that we know exactly what she was wearing on the night she died. They also took photographs at the crime scene in 13 Miller's Court, the dingy room rented by Mary Kelly. Other photographs may have been taken in situ of other victims, but there is no mention of them and none has survived.

The problem with the torso killings is that there is no crime scene. It would be ludicrous to suggest that the murderer killed his victims and cut them into pieces along the riverbank. But the nature of the dismemberment means that considerable time and care was taken. The torso killer must have had relatively secure premises where he knew he would not be disturbed. This makes him a very different kind of killer from Jack, an opportunistic murderer who took huge chances and could easily have been caught in the act. In the murder of Katherine Eddowes in Mitre Square, if we are to believe the official time-keeping, Jack overpowered the woman, cut her throat, slashed her abdomen, removed uterus and one kidney and disfigured the face, all in the fifteen minutes between police patrols of the square. The torso killer is cool and suave by comparison. He kills indoors and has leisure to carry out his dismemberment.

It is this cold, unemotional act that is the most unusual aspect of the torso cases and, to Professor Laurence Alison, the most interesting. Professor Alison is Academic Director of the National Centre for the Study of Critical Incident Decision Making in Liverpool University's School of Psychology. His core of interest lies in 'processes by which individuals make sense of ambiguous, complex or contradictory information'. In the context of this book I am the individual and they do not come any more ambiguous, complex or contradictory than the torso killings! Professor Alison is perhaps best known outside purely academic circles for his book on Robert Napper, the killer of Rachel Nickell in 1992 which he co-wrote with colleague Marie Eyre.[1] He is familiar with sexual assault in all its grim manifestations and we worked together on a recent television documentary on Jack the Ripper.[2]

What strikes Alison as odd is what is *not* there in terms of motive. Where is the frenzy, the removal of sexual organs, the focus on genitalia which we associate with sexual killers and which was very obvious in the Ripper murders themselves? We will return to this later.

Disposal of a body is one of the most difficult problems for any murderer. David Whitelaw wrote in the 1930s:

> One can hardly picture a worse fate for even the most callous of murderers than that they should be doomed throughout eternity to carry with them portions of their victims, seeking resting places for their grim burden and finding none.[3]

In 1869 the tailor Pierre Voirbo killed a man with whom he had quarrelled over money, dismembered his body and filled the head with molten lead before throwing it into the Seine in Paris. Other body parts he stashed under his floor tiles however and these were discovered by clever detective work on the part of

Gustave Macé. Donald Hume hired a biplane eighty years later to scatter bits of Stanley Setty whom he had killed in a fight. He mistook the Essex marshes of the Thames Estuary for the open sea and the body parts were found. Even so, Hume could only be charged at the time with accessory to murder – the actual crime being the dumping of the portions. One of the most famous cases was that of Louis Voison, a Belgian butcher who lived during the years of the First World War in a basement at 101 Charlotte Street, virtually across the road from the torso finds in Alfred Mews and its neighbouring squares. Something of a ladies' man, Voisin found himself caught in a love triangle with his two mistresses and with the help of one of them, Berthe Roche, battered the other, Emilienne Gerard, to death. As a butcher, Voisin had no problem dismembering Emilienne. Her torso was wrapped in her underwear and forced into a sack. The legs were wrapped in brown paper. He loaded them onto his cart and wheeled them across Bloomsbury to Regent Square, where he dumped them behind railings. The body was identified via the underwear and the dead woman's head and hands were found in a barrel of sawdust in Voisin's apartment. He was hanged at Pentonville in March 1918.

The key to concealment through dismemberment is to leave no traceable clue on the bodies. This may be why the torso killer removed wedding rings; it may also be why he removed heads. In the case of Elizabeth Jackson, he was taking a calculated risk by wrapping her body parts in portions of her own clothes, although, as we have seen, the laundry label L E Fisher led nowhere. Nor did scars on the torso victims help. True, Elizabeth Jackson was eventually identified by scars on her arm, but the burn scar on the 1873 victim was wrongly attested to by Mary Cailey's family and the rose tattoo on the Bedford Square corpse produced no results at all.

What can the various post-mortems on the torso victims tell us? There is no doubt that by the standards of the time – and using the Virchow method by 1887 – the police surgeons did a first-rate job. They were able to match up body parts accurately, make intelligent guesses at the height and age of the deceased and hint at least, because of the good condition of the hands, that the victims were prostitutes. They were hampered of course by two things. First, the immersion of body parts in the Thames caused damage in the form of post-mortem bruising which obscured what on dry land would be obvious. Tar on one body portion almost certainly came from mooring ropes or planking on the sad, ghastly journey downriver. The skin distorts in water to such an extent that features are unrecognizable. No one going through the awful experience of viewing Drs Hayden and Kempster's reconstructed head in 1873 saw anyone they knew and the face found on the foreshore in 1888 was equally anonymous. Elsewhere, in the case of the Scotland Yard torso and that found in Pinchin

Street, decomposition had set in which caused its own problems. Second, the real breakthrough in forensic science lay just around the corner. Fingerprint evidence, which might have been forthcoming from the bruises on body parts, on parcel wrappings and string, lay only three years in the future, but it would not be until 1905 that a guilty verdict by a jury was delivered on this evidence alone.[4] And, impressive though Dr Thomas Bond was in terms of his autopsy work, the truly outstanding pathologists – Bernard Spilsbury, Keith Simpson, Donald Teare, Francis Camps – belonged to later generations.

What the post-mortem evidence can tell us loud and clear is that whoever dismembered these eight women – and we can legitimately say, murdered them too – was skilled with both knife and saw. This is why the 1902 torso killing in Salamanca Place, Lambeth, is not part of the series. The road lies just off the Embankment between Lambeth and Vauxhall Bridges, but the cuts were done roughly and badly, with none of the precision of the 1870s and 1880s murders and some of the flesh was parboiled. Virtually every book on the Whitechapel killings raises the same issue of dexterity with the knife. Was Jack the Ripper a doctor? Certainly, a medical man would have the skills to commit both the Whitechapel and the torso murders, but the fact is that this kind of murder by medical practitioners is extremely rare. There have been plenty of homicidal doctors – Harold Shipman probably holds the world record for the largest number of victims[5] – but they tend to kill with that far easier method at their disposal, poison. Alone of murderous medics, Buck Ruxton used dismemberment of his wife and maid to disguise his killing of them near Moffat, Scotland, in 1935 and came up against a formidable forensic team in Professor James Brash of Edinburgh University and Professor John Glaister of Glasgow. Their brilliant deductive work, coupled with the fact that Ruxton wrapped the body parts in newspaper which could date the murders fairly precisely, led to the doctor's execution in May 1936.

It was much more likely that the torso killer was a butcher. Such a man would have the skill with which to separate limbs neatly at the joints and would have somewhere in which to carry out not only the murder, but the dismemberment as well. If we refer back to *The Lancet*'s detailed discussion of the 1873 murder, we find an interesting tell-tale observation:

> It is not a little remarkable, however, that although the right leg between the knee and ankle is perfect, on the left side the leg has been sawn in two and only the upper part has been found. It is possible that there may have been some mark on the lower portion of the leg, the murderer has taken the precaution to destroy.[6]

This could of course have been some scar or foot malformation which would have identified the victim, but it could also have been the mark of a rope by which the woman was suspended from a meat hook while her body drained of blood before the joint cutting began. A butcher could target prostitutes as well as anyone else. Once again, in the 120 years of discussion on the identity of Jack the Ripper, slaughtermen, especially shochets or Jewish slaughtermen, are often high on Ripperologists' lists. We have already met Jacob Isenschmid, the mad pork butcher of Holloway. Around the corner from the murder site of Polly Nichols in Buck's Row were the operating abattoirs in Winthrop Street. In fact, as Jack was cutting her throat, the slaughtermen there were already at work in the early morning of 31 August 1888.

Several of the letters purporting to be written by the Whitechapel murderer referred to butchers and others offering advice to police carried the same notion. On 24 September 1888, the very first one, a letter with a SE London postmark came from someone who wrote, 'I am a horse slaughterer and work at [name blacked out] address [name blacked out.]'.[7] On 3 October, W Longley of Yalding, Kent, had heard from hop-pickers' gossip that Jack might be a slaughterman. J W Causier of Yetminster, Sherborne, went even further to say that Jack was a Jewish slaughterman. E W Clark from Addiscombe narrowed it down to one of the Winthrop Street slaughtermen who gave evidence at the inquest on Polly Nichols; and Charton and Legrange from the Royalty Theatre in Dean Street, Soho, even added a name, that of a man called Bluendenwall, derived from the table-rappings of a séance.

Of the 220 letters and postcards sent to newspaper offices and the Met and City police in the 'Autumn of Terror', all are now believed to be hoaxes.[8] But we are not looking for Jack the Ripper; we are looking for the torso killer. We have already heard from the religious maniac who promised death and destruction to the women of Moab and Midian in connection with the Whitehall Mystery, but are there any other tangible clues? On 4 October, 'Jack' wrote to Vine Street police station (although the letter was found, unposted, in Vincent Square, Westminster) – 'I have written this on the embankment, near Waterloo.' The following day, 'Jack Ripper' wrote to Sir Charles Warren, 'Head Police Officer': 'I have done another one and thrown it in the river ...' Two days later, 'Jack' wrote 'again' to Warren, this time at the correct address of 4 Whitehall Place. 'Just a few lines to tell you I shall begin my knife operations again on or near Blackfriars Bridge ...' On 15 October 'Dear Boss' received a note to the effect that yet another body had been dumped in the river. October of course was the month in which the various parts were found in the foundations of Scotland Yard; only one arm came from the Thames.

A week later, 'Good bye ta ta' wrote 'One of the two women I told you about is a Chelsea girl and the other is a Battersea girl. I had to overcome great difficulties in bringing the bodies where I hid them. I am now in Battersea.' The next day, in an unusually long missive, 'H.I.O. Battersea' assured the police that the leg found at Whitehall 'does not belong to the trunk you found there'. C Division received a brief, ill-written note three months later, in January 1889: 'I chucked some old wo[man?] in the thames because [she] began to squeal ...' It was signed Jack Bane.

A butcher perhaps, but can we get closer? One vital clue lies in the way the body parts were distributed. The torso killer had to be able to pass through London streets carrying portions of a human body and not arouse suspicion. One of the most bizarre facts that we find if we look at the social history of London – indeed, any major city – in the nineteenth century is the sheer number of people who keep odd hours. Bank Holidays were still a novel idea; the concept of 'nine to five' unknown. Shopkeepers lived above their shops and were literally open all hours for their customers. The great markets of London opened at four or five in the morning, so carmen, costers, flower sellers, draymen and a whole host of street sellers were out and about early. But the torso killer was not merely a distributor of body parts; he had the skill to create the parts in the first place. That means in all probability he was a travelling butcher, with his meat on a handcart or in a pony-drawn trap. And the most likely candidate that fits that bill is the cat's meat man.

A children's nursery book from the time shows a maid opening a door to the Cat's Meat Man while a rosy child and cats and dogs scamper round his feet.

> He calls 'Meat, meat!'
> All down the street;
> And dogs 'bow wow',
> And cats 'mi-ow'
> While kittens sly
> Come purring by,
> As if to say –
> 'Do serve us, pray,
> The first of all,
> For we're so small.'
> The man throws bits
> Of meat to kits,
> And cats, and dogs;
> Then on he jogs,
> And down the street
> Still cries 'Meat, meat!'

All very jolly. In reality, cat's meat men had a hard life peddling their wares door to door all over London. A photograph from 1901 by John Galt now in the Museum of London shows a moustachioed man with an apron and billycock hat standing by his two-wheeled hand-cart. In 1853, Charles Manby Smith in *Curiosities of Life* remembered as a child that the cat's meat man was always on time and always welcome. The one he remembered had a pony and trap and the cat's breakfast cost a halfpenny. In the year that Victoria was crowned (1837) there were said to be about 2,000 of them in the capital, but the social commentator Henry Mayhew believed this had fallen to about 300 by 1851. Their cries of 'Co! Mee-att!' would bring every stray in the neighbourhood onto the streets. For reasons he does not explain, social analyst Charles Booth said that cat's meat men were most addicted to the showy funerals which, by 1889, were frowned upon as passé and rather vulgar.

What kind of killer are we looking for among the cat's meat men? His profession meant that he could wheel his cart, day or night, along embankments, across bridges, down alleyways, under railway arches. He could even have been a regular visitor among the workers on the Scotland Yard building site or perhaps he was allowed there to feed the strays who no doubt haunted the building as they haunted most of London. It was worth the builders' while to pay the man to feed the cats in order to keep them there to reduce the rat population from the river. This is highly likely because we know from the Whitehall torso finds that he must have made at least two visits, both to bury and to dump. Beneath the upper, acceptable layers of horse meat in his cart lay human body parts that once were Elizabeth Jackson and the other unknown victims he had created.

More than that, we know that the torso killer was what profilers today call an organized killer. The FBI's explanation of such a man is as follows. He is likely to be of 'average or above average intelligence'. This is not a mere wheeler of carts; he sells his wares and handles money. He will be 'socially competent'; if he wants to make a living at all he has to be able to engage people in conversation, to gain their trust. He will be dealing with maidservants and walking the same streets as the prostitutes he targeted. He would have been on equal terms with Elizabeth Jackson. He is 'likely to be a skilled worker'. All the doctors who examined the body parts are agreed on this. The dismemberment was slick and highly proficient as would be the case in a man who cut up horses for a living. It is the next three categories which remain unanswerable. 'High in order of birth', 'father's employment stable', 'inconsistent childhood discipline' is unknown because we have no name. 'Controlled mood during crime.' We cannot be sure of this, partly because the doctors at the time could not find an actual cause of death. It is likely that the 1873 victim died as a result of a blow to the head and if this method worked well, then the torso killer would have continued to use it.

It may well explain why the heads were usually missing. Horse slaughterers killed their animals with a single, powerful axe blow to the head. It may also explain the apparent lack of frenzy in the murders. If that frenzy was directed at the head, for whatever reason, then all the torso killer's angst would have been vented on that; the actual dismemberment was done coolly when the frenzy had passed and for other reasons.

Some of the forensic experts working on the Cleveland torso case believed that there were signs of life in the Kingsbury Run victims *after* dismemberment began, but there is no sense of that here. However frenzied the attack to the head may have been and whatever sexual assault the cat's meat man carried out on his victims before or after death, there is no sign of any of that in the body parts themselves. 'Alcohol use associated with crime.' Again, we do not know. *Somehow* the cat's meat man lured his victims to his slaughterhouse, won them over, perhaps with alcohol, before he went to work – and not in the way they expected. Dr Neill Cream, as we have seen, went so far as to write invitations to some of his victims and was usually careful enough to destroy the letters afterwards. 'Sexually competent.' Once more, we are in the dark. Many serial killers have some sort of sexual dysfunction and the frustration and anger this causes leads them to blame and hurt what they conceive to be the source of the problem – women. Rapists are not interested in sex per se; they crave power and control over their victims. On the other hand, some serial murderers have more or less conventional sex lives – Gary Ridgeway for example or Joel Rifkin, both of whom visited prostitutes for regular sessions before they killed them. Did the cat's meat man have sex with seven-months-pregnant Elizabeth Jackson? We can only assume that that is what she thought he was going to do. 'Living with partner' is again, an unknown. 'Mobility'; the cat's meat man was free to roam in theory all over London, selling his wares. 'Interest in news media reports of crime'; this is a difficult area, but I believe it likely. We must always, in the nineteenth century, consider the problem of literacy; could our killer read? I do not believe he wrote silly, taunting letters to the police about Jack the Ripper, but I do believe he cashed in on police activity twice, rather as modern killers sometimes 'help' the police with their enquiries to keep close to events. Soham murderer Ian Huntley, for example, joined the search for two missing schoolgirls in the area in 2002, knowing full well where their bodies were because he had dumped them there. Otherwise, the torso killer's dump site in the foundations of Scotland Yard and Pinchin Street are the most bizarre coincidences. Norman Shaw's opera house was widely reported in the press as being converted for police headquarters use. Pinchin Street was only hundreds of yards from the murder scene of Ripper victim Liz Stride in Berner Street; it was in the heart of Jack's territory – what better way to cause the total confusion which has extended right down to R Michael Gordon's analysis of 2001?

The last characteristic of the organized serial killer is that after the crime has been committed the murderer might change occupation or leave the area. Is this why we have the strange shift to the Tottenham Court Road? All the other body parts were found in the river, on the foreshore or at least in water (the legs of the 1873 victim in Regent's Canal). Even the Pinchin Street torso is less than a quarter of a mile from the river. But Alfred Mews, Bedford Square, Fitzroy Square – these are land-locked areas and a relatively long way away. Had the horse slaughterer changed direction? And had he returned, with a vengeance, by 1887?

We cannot answer the question whether our killer lived with a partner. It was the convention of the time for men, whether heterosexual or not, to marry or at least live with a woman. In the case of Gary Ridgeway, his final marriage did not end his Green River killing spree, but it certainly slowed it down. Does this explain the ten-year gap between the Putney murder in 1874 and the gruesome finds of the rose tattoo in Bloomsbury? Did the killer's wife die or leave him and is that why he came back to his old haunts?

So we have, in the cat's meat man, an organized killer. The crime committed by such a person, writes Brian Innes,

> Is premeditated, not committed on the spur of the moment. The planning forms part of the offender's fantasies, which have probably been dwelled on for years before they find violent expression. The victims are mostly strangers, of a particular type that the offender has in mind and that he has been hunting for. Since the crime has been planned, the offender will have figured out ways to approach the victim, win over their confidence and so gain control over them ... [such killers] show an intelligent ability to adapt to a changing situation ... and they learn as they progress; from crime to crime, they 'improve' on what they do.[9]

But there were hundreds of cat's meat men in London. Is there any way of narrowing the field? Ripperologists will be familiar with Mrs Harriet Hardyman, a woman of medium height 'with a curiously rounded chin' according to one newspaper report, who was a witness at the inquest on Annie Chapman. She lived with her 16-year-old son on the ground floor front of 29 Hanbury Street and, in the early hours of 8 September 1888, Annie and her killer walked past her window and down the passageway next to Harriet's apartment. The room at the back was used to cook the cat's meat, but it is not clear whether the Hardymans sold the produce from their door or whether young Hardyman had a cart. In the 1891 census, Mrs Hardyman called herself, rather grandly, a 'purveyor of horseflesh'.

A trawl through all the horse-slaughterers, butchers and sellers of horseflesh in London ('cat's meat man' was only ever the colloquial term for such occupations) takes months of research and inevitably focuses on Smithfield and the East End where they tended to proliferate. But there is one tool of modern psychology which reduces the search and that is geoprofiling. A more useful term for this process is murder-mapping, a systematic study of where the murders occur. Of course our job is complicated by the fact that we do not have any actual murder sites. We know that the Whitechapel murderer killed in certain streets forming a pattern within a stone's throw of each other because his victims' bodies were found there. All we have in the case of the torso killer is dump sites, which are not the same thing at all.

Perhaps the best known geoprofiler in Britain today is Dr David Canter, who always asks himself two basic questions in relation to murder sites: where is the likely home or base of the killer and how far is he prepared to travel in search of his prey? The Ripper killed in a tight 'circle of comfort' in an area he knew like the back of his hand, the neighbouring parishes of Whitechapel and Spitalfields. A modern serial killer like child-murderer Robert Black was unusual in that he drove in his white van, committing crimes between Oxford and Edinburgh and dumping his victims' bodies far from where he abducted them. Professor Laurence Alison wrote:

> Today's geoprofilers would break down the sub-tasks the offender needed to accomplish in order to escape and examine the exit points from the scene of each attack. They would systematically consider the most likely route home, including temporal (time) and topographical (detailed lay of the land) patterns that may influence the choice the offender makes in targeting crime scenes.[10]

With the torso killer, the problem is a little different because I believe he killed his victims in the same place. The risk element came with his 'wooing phase'. He must have had the social skills to persuade them to go with him in the first place. We do not know what premises any of the women lived in. There is a suggestion that Elizabeth Jackson lived in a common lodging house in or near Turk's Row, but that is not proven and anyway such places would not tolerate open prostitution. If the victims worked out of a brothel, then they certainly had an available bed, but the torso killer was not interested in that; he would have invited them back to his. A far greater risk was involved when he got rid of body parts, wheeling them around London. Much of this was probably achieved in the early hours, before the river was too busy, although such was the lifestyle of the street-traders, that there was never a truly quiet time.

Geoprofiling has shown that a serial murderer's first kill will take place nearest to his home, the place he feels safest. Later kills will radiate out as he gets bolder, more experienced and also, perhaps, there is a need to avoid places where he might have been seen previously. Looking at the map of the dump sites, even allowing for the tidal action of the river, there is undeniably a focus on Battersea. Of the twenty-five body parts found along the river, eight of them turned up between Battersea and Victoria Bridges. If we widen our search slightly, the figure is fourteen – over half the total. Geoprofiling is an imprecise science – some say it is actually an art – but it *does* give us a pattern. Let us remind ourselves of the view of the police at the time of the first murder, back in 1873. They believed that the body parts had been deposited in the river somewhere near the point where the Wandle tributary runs into it. Is there anything relevant to the cat's meat man in this area? Draw a line southeast from the Wandle estuary. Just over half a mile away, lies Garratt Lane. 'In Garratt Lane, Wandsworth,' wrote W J Gordon in 1893, 'is the largest horse-slaughtering yard in London.'[11]

Despite the positive article about life for London's horses written in G R Sims's *Living London* in 1903, many of them ended up broken by fatigue and bad treatment – Anna Sewell highlighted their plight in *Black Beauty*. Some 26,000 horses a year died at the hands of Harrison Barber Ltd, of Garratt Lane. In 1873, when the torso killings began, the slaughterhouse was owned by M Wallis, who by 1886 had gone into partnership with a Mr Milestone. The following year the company had been bought up by a social climber, John Harrison, who was the official horse slaughterer to Her Majesty and did regular trade with the Dukes of Teck and Edinburgh, as well as the Household Cavalry and Royal Horse Artillery. Harrison's original premises were along York Road in North London and these he retained, adding by 1887 other companies' premises in: Queen Victoria Street; Brandon Road, King's Cross; Westcott Street in the Borough; Green Street, SE; Parliament Street, Bethnal Green and Coventry Street in the East End. Intriguingly, he also owned the abattoirs at 19, 21 and 23 Winthrop Street around the corner from the murder site of the Ripper's first 'canonical' victim, Polly Nichols. These premises had belonged to a Mr Barber who now became Harrison's partner in what by 1889 was something of a monopoly.

William Gordon wrote:

No horse that enters [Harrison's] yard must come out again alive, or as a horse. The moment it enters those gates it must be disfigured by having its mane cut off so close to the skin as to spoil its value and though it may be put in a 'pound' on the premises, which might better be called a condemned cell or moribundary, it must not remain there for more than three days.

Gordon describes Harrison's yards as having stood there for over a hundred years, 'by the banks of the winding Wandle'. It was 'practically odourless' with a field in front of the building and a firework factory next door. Mr Milestone himself showed Gordon the killing process; it was all over in two seconds: 'Maneless he stands; a shade is put over his eyes; a swing of the axe, and with just one tremor, he falls heavy and dead on the flags of a spacious kitchen.' In a little over half an hour, the hide was added to a nearby pile, hoofs in a second heap, bones dumped for boiling into oil and flesh 'is cooking for cat's meat'.

Slash, slash go the knives and the hide is peeled off about as easily as a tablecloth and so clean and uninjured is the body that it looks like the muscle model we see in the books and in the plaster casts at the corn-chandlers.

The rest of the process was almost mass-production. The bones were pulped into a huge 'digester' and the oil produced was pressed out between sheets of paper, white cakes for the candle makers. Surplus oil was used for lubrication and leather-dressing. Other bones were crushed ready to be sent to manure merchants, in rows 'like flour-sacks at a miller's'. Still others were ground to powder and mixed with sulphuric acid to make fertilizer. The skin and hoofs were sent to the glue-makers and button makers, the shoes recycled if they were in good enough condition or melted down by farriers and rehammered into shape. Tails and manes ended up in sofas or as fishing lines. Hides became whip-lashes, carriage roofs and even the leather inserts on cavalry troopers' overalls. The problem of smell was minimized by a complex ventilation system of pipes passing over a furnace, so that by the 1890s, the noisome stench associated with the 'stink' industries was, at least, reduced.

The horse meat was boiled in coppers 'with just the central tint of redness and rawness that suits the harmless, necessary cat'. Tripe was available for the 'palate of the less fastidious dog'. The work of slaughter went on endlessly – 'Go to any of their depots between five and six o'clock in the morning and you will find a long string of the pony traps and hand-carts, barrows and perambulators' of the cat's meat men. The meat was often placed on skewers of wood and William Gordon estimated that 182½ tons of deal a year was used by Harrison Barber Ltd. 'Here is another item,' he said prophetically of the 'greens' of the next century, 'for the forest conservation people.'

And the Garratt Lane branch had cold storage. Two hundred and fifty carcases could be stored there: 'A door is opened and shut ... a shiver of cold runs through us as a match is struck and a candle lighted ... around us are piles of meat, all hard as stone and glittering with ice crystals ...' William Gordon was describing an abattoir. He was also, unknowingly, describing a murder scene.

Let us consider the known facts again against the background of a slaughterer/cat's meat man employed by Messrs Wallis later Harrison Barber along Garratt Lane. He stalks prostitutes on either side of the river, which is half a mile away from the slaughterhouse. We certainly know that this was the patch worked by Elizabeth Jackson. He is experiencing the traumatic phases of the serial killer. He selects a woman, on what basis we do not know. Perhaps she is short, dark-haired, a little on the plump side. Perhaps he takes her for a drink in one of the many waterside pubs they both know so well. He invites her back to his. But it is not his home, it is a large building overlooking open fields. He assures her they will not be disturbed. Perhaps he has a wife at home or children. Or nosy neighbours who will disapprove. He has probably already handed over the cash, done the necessary deal. He has his own key because he is a trusted, perhaps relatively senior, employee and lets them both in. Does she strip? Do they have sex? It is impossible to say. Impossible to say, too, how long it is before the axe comes crunching down on her head. There were one or two blows on the temple of the 1873 victim. 'It was all over in two seconds' for the horses; perhaps it was the same for her. She falls 'heavy and dead on the flags of a spacious kitchen'.

What happens next depends on the exact type of killer he is. He does not mutilate, unlike Jack. He seems to have no fixation with a woman's genitals or internal organs. But it is possible he has sex with her as she lies there. He cannot afford to wait too long. The place is lit with the candles made from the animals who usually die here. It will not be long before his colleagues arrive for the day's work so he goes to work with speed and confidence. If the police and medical men were right about the projected times of death, at least two of them are highly likely to have been committed on a Sunday, the day the slaughterhouse was closed. 'Slash, slash' goes the knife to disarticulate flesh and sinew. He uses the fine saw for the rest of the work, dumping the portions into the anonymous flour sacks to hand or wrapping them in other bags, bound with equally anonymous string. On one occasion, we know, he used a copy of the *Echo* that someone had left lying around. On another, he used Venetian blind cord. On two occasions, and we do not know why, he used the victims' clothes – the chemise of the Pinchin Street woman and the dress, drawers and Ulster of Elizabeth Jackson. How he chose the number of pieces into which he cut the body we do not know. Nor do we know what he does with the head.

Does he, like Voison, fill the skull with molten lead and sink it in the Thames? Does he, like Jeffrey Dahmer, find an isolated corner of the cold store where he can keep them, reliving the thrill of the murder experience? Perhaps he has the coolness to wait until the other deliverymen arrive or perhaps he goes out first, ahead of them, the bodies drained of blood and the blood washed away down the channels in the kitchen floor. We know from the testimony of Constable Pennett that he dumped the torso under the arch in Pinchin Street between five and five thirty. And in the mist curling along the river, he rumbles his cart, chooses his moment and drops his ghastly cargo – 'chunk by chunk by chunk'.

There are no employee lists of Messrs Wallis in the 1870s nor of Messrs Harrison and Barber in the 1880s. So our killer is untraceable, exactly as he hoped he would be. And one of the premises bought up by Harrison in 1887, the year of the Rainham Mystery, is that of Henry A Currell, slaughtermen of Brandon Road, King's Cross. Brandon Road that is fifteen minutes walk from Alfred Mews. Did the torso killer take flight after his butchery in 1874 and find a similar day job in Brandon Road? And did the Harrison buy-up in 1887 mean that he found himself redeployed once again to his old haunts in Battersea?

Did the police investigate the premises of Harrison Barber? We do not know because details of the minutiae of the investigation have not survived; but it seems likely that they did. What would they have found? The kind of knives and saws which *could* have been the murder weapons, but there was no way of proving that. Sacks and string of the type in which the body parts were wrapped but which were so anonymous they could be found all over the country. The body parts of horses waiting for disposal. A lot of animal blood which could not be differentiated from human and would have been washed away continually as the working day progressed. And a lot of horse slaughterers and cat's meat men who had seen nothing, heard nothing and simply, but for very different reasons, could not help.

And if one of these men was the man who had worn the unidentifiable uniform who had prophesied the finding of the torso near Pinchin Street to Mr Arnold the news vendor, how were the police supposed to recognize him?

There are more questions than answers in the Thames torso case. Laurence Alison finds it odd, as do I, that most of the victims remained anonymous. Remember, however the loss of life aboard the *Princess Alice* when 160 corpses remained unclaimed. Could they *all* have been solitary individuals with no family and no friends? If the torso victims were all prostitutes, especially if they worked out of a brothel, or were kept by some dubious gentleman leading a double existence, it was clearly in someone's best interests *not* to identify the deceased.

Time and time again, we come back to the heads. Why go to the lengths, in 1873, of removing the skull and not the face? Is the deliberate dumping of body parts a message to someone? After all, the killer could have destroyed the bodies totally in his workplace, grinding the bones to powder. Is the killer taunting the public and the police, saying, 'Look how clever I am. I can leave these ghastly objects where I like and you can't catch me.' This is certainly the tone of many of the Ripper letters and if none of these is genuine, the 'spirit' of the message might well have been shared by the torso killer.

Or is the cat's meat man simply carrying out a job for someone? Is he, in fact, that most beloved stalwart of the modern thriller, a hitman, carrying out contracts, which may have been the clue to the Cleveland torsos of the Kingsbury Run. Or is all that in the realms of fiction?

Whoever he was, the torso murderer was a new breed of killer and the police were at a loss to know where to start. I have traced the man as far as I can and that is much nearer than anyone else has got. But he has, nevertheless, got away with murder, then and for all time.

Like most of the women he killed, he has no name and no face.

As R Michael Gordon was putting the finishing touches to his book on the torso murders in 2002, a series of prostitute killings was being investigated by police in London. One of the victims was Zoe Parker, who had a red rose tattoo on her arm. As I write this final paragraph of my book, police have arrested a man calling himself the 'Crossbow Cannibal' believed to be responsible for the murder of several prostitutes in Bradford's red light district. The eighty-one body parts of one of them, Susan Blamires, have been found floating in the River Aire …

We serial killers are your sons, we are your husbands, we are everywhere. And more of your children will be dead tomorrow.

Notes

Chapter 1: Messing About on the River
1. Rudyard Kipling, *The River's Tale*.
2. Where I refer to him, it will be by surname only to avoid confusion.
3. Charles Dickens, *Dictionary of the Thames* (1887), p. 45.
4. In *The River's Tale* that begins this chapter.
5. Thomas Traherne, *Shadows in the Water*, quoted in Peter Ackroyd, *Thames, Sacred River* (London, Vintage, 2008), p. 353.
6. Because of the alteration of the Thames's course since 1215, Runnymede is now part of the bank and is no longer an island.
7. Dickens, *Dictionary*, p. 216.
8. Ibid.
9. John Gay, *Epistle to the Earl of Burlington* (1712), quoted in Ackroyd, *Thames*, p. 434.
10. Dickens, *Dictionary*, p. 118.
11. Ibid.
12. Quoted in Ackroyd, *Thames*, p. 435.
13. Dickens, *Dictionary*, p. 26.
14. Ibid., p. 26.
15. Samuel Pepys, *Diary*, quoted in Ackroyd, *Thames*, p. 438.
16. Technically, it is the bell inside the clock tower and not the tower itself that has this name.
17. Quoted in Ackroyd, *Thames*, p. 438.
18. Quoted ibid., pp. 294–5.
19. Quoted ibid., p. 17.
20. Ben Jonson, *The Devil is an Ass* (1616).
21. Quoted in Ackroyd, *Thames*, p. 203.
22. Virginia Woolf, *The Docks of London*, quoted in Chris Ellmers and Alex Warner, *London's Lost Riverscape*, introduction by Gavin Stamp (London, Guikd Publishing, 1988).
23. Such a plan was actually in existence during the 1660s when Britain was at war with the Dutch three times. The writer Aphra Benn was a government

agent for Charles II at the time and passed vital information from the Low Countries to London.
24. Legal quays were set up officially during the reign of Elizabeth I with a monopoly on taxed goods. The sufferance quays, by contrast, were originally only on the south bank of the river and were necessary because of the increasing congestion of river traffic. They were essentially temporary in nature.
25. Quoted in Ackroyd, *Thames*, p. 442.
26. Quoted in Dickens, *Dictionary*, p. 88.

Chapter 2: River of Death
1. Quoted in Ackroyd, Thames, p. 157.
2. Dio Cassius, *Historiae*, quoted in John Peddie, *Conquest: The Roman Invasion of Britain* (Stroud, Sutton, 1987), p. 84.
3. Dio Cassius, *Epitome* 62, quoted in M J Trow and Taliesin Trow, *Boudicca, the Warrior Queen* (Stroud, Sutton, 2003), p. 176.
4. Ackroyd, *Thames*, p. 370.
5. Quoted ibid., p. 380.
6. Quoted ibid., pp. 388–9. All details on this accident from Ackroyd.
7. Tr. Swanton, *Anglo Saxon Chronicle Peterborough (E) text* (London, Phoenix, 2000), p. 138.
8. Admiral John Byng was shot on the deck of his own flagship for failing to face the enemy during the Seven Years' War. Recognized then and now as a gross miscarriage of justice, it was not seen that way by the cynical François Voltaire who claimed that the English 'shot an Admiral now and again to encourage the others'.
9. M J Trow and Taliesin Trow *Who Killed Kit Marlowe?* (Stroud, Sutton, 2001).
10. Thomas Hood, *The Bridge of Sighs* (1844). It was the favourite poem of murderers Charlie Peace and Henry Wainwright.
11. Ackroyd, *Thames*, p. 374.
12. Quoted ibid., p. 376.
13. Henry Mayhew, quoted in Peter Ackroyd, *Dicken's London* (London, Headline, 1987), p. 121.
14. Both these phrases are taken from the full title of Colquhoun's treatise.
15. For an excellent survey of the chaotic and overlapping duties of these medieval forces, see T A Critchley and P D James, *The Maul and the Pear Tree* (London, Sphere, 1987).
16. Molly Lefebure, *Murder on the Home Front* (London, Grafton, 1990), p. 25.

Chapter 3: Found Dead

1. R Austin Freeman *London Below Bridge* from George R Sims, *Living London* (London, Cassell & Co., 1903), p. 256.
2. The Anatomy Act was passed in 1831 as a direct result of the murders by Burke and Hare in Edinburgh. It provided far more bodies legally for the purposes of medical study.
3. *The Times* (16 May 1887).
4. Ibid.
5. Quoted in R Michael Gordon, *The Thames Torso Murders of Victorian London* (Durham, NC, McFarland & Co., 2002), p. 40.
6. *The Times* (21 July 1887).
7. Quoted in Gordon, *Thames Torso Murders*, p. 44.
8. And the numbers of murderous doctors historically are very high – Pritchard, Palmer, Bodkin Adams, Ruxton, Shipman, etc.
9. Gordon, *Thames Torso Murders*, p. 44.
10. Charles A Hebbert, *An Exercise in Forensic Medicine* (1888). There was always a slight problem for an exclusively male police force (and quite possibly doctors too) in telling one female garment from another. When Molly Lefebure was secretary to one of the most famous pathologists, Dr Keith Simpson, during the Second World War, she found it amusing to have to explain to officers cataloguing crime scenes of female victims what bits of underwear were called.
11. Ibid.
12. Ibid.

Chapter 4: Jack

1. Ann Rule, *Green River, Running Red*, New York, Pocket Star Books, 2004, p. 447.
2. Gordon, *Thames Torso Murders*, p. 73.
3. See Chapter 8.
4. In *Jack the Ripper: Quest for a Killer* I identified the Whitechapel murderer as Robert Mann, the mortuary assistant attached to the Whitechapel Workhouse Infirmary. To avoid confusion and not to veer too far off the point of this book, I simply refer to the killer as Jack the Ripper, preserving his anonymity yet again!
5. For reasons why the mutilations on Alice McKenzie seem different, see my *Jack the Ripper: Quest for a Killer*.
6. R Michael Gordon does not mention the Battersea, Putney nor Tottenham Court Road murders at all.

Chapter 5: The Whitehall Mystery
1. Hebbert, *Exercise in Forensic Medicine.*
2. Quoted in Gordon, *Thames Torso Murders,* p. 67.
3. Quoted ibid., p. 68.
4. Quoted ibid., p. 71.
5. See Chapter 4.
6. Lees diary for those dates, quoted in Stewart P Evans and Keith Skinner, *Jack the Ripper: Letters from Hell* (Stroud, Sutton), 2001, p. 143.
7. *Illustrated Police News* (20 Oct. 1888).
8. *The Times.*

Chapter 6: The Frankenstein Connection
1. Dickens, *Dickens's Dictionary of the Thames* (1887), pp. 25–6.
2. Hebbert, *Exercise in Forensic Medicine,* pp. 151–7.
3. *Weekly Herald* (June 1889).

Chapter 7: The Women of Moab and Midian
1. George R Sims, *London At Dead of Night* from *Living London* (1902), vol. 3, p. 355.
2. Letter to Central News Agency, 5 Oct. 1888, quoted in Evans and Skinner, *Jack the Ripper: Letters from Hell,* p. 223.
3. The generic slang term for a prostitute, probably from *motte*, French for a hill, referring to the genital area.
4. Quoted in Paul Begg, Martin Fido and Keith Skinner, *Jack the Ripper A–Z* (London, Headline, 1991), p. 10.
5. William Booth, *In Darkest England and the Way Out* (London, Salvation Army Publications 1890), p. 51.
6. Quoted in Graham Ovenden and Peter Mendes, *Victorian Erotic Photography,* New York, St Martin's Press, 1973, p. 87.
7. Quoted in Ronald Pearsall, *The Worm in the Bud,* London, Pelican, 1971.
8. Black Sarah.
9. Quoted ibid., p. 351.
10. Ibid., p. 323.

Chapter 8: The Pinchin Street Torso
1. Israel Lipski poisoned Miriam Angel in June 1887 and was hanged at Newgate for the murder in August of the same year.
2. Hebbert, *Exercise in Forensic Medicine.*
3. James Monro to J S Sanders, 11 Sept. 1889. HO File 144/221/A49031K.

Chapter 9: Dealers in Horror

1. Arthur Appleton, *Mary Ann Cotton: Her Story and Trial,* London, Michael Joseph, 1973, pp. 131–2.
2. In 1811, two families living along the Highway were bludgeoned to death in two separate incidents within weeks of each other. A sailor named Williams was charged with the murders but was found dead in police custody before he came to trial.
3. Quoted in Pauline Chapman, *Madame Tussaud's Chamber of Horrors* (London, Grafton, 1986), p. 95.
4. It was never certain whether the Thames Mystery corpse was that of a prostitute but it seems highly likely. In later cases involving prostitutes both in Britain and the United States, the police were often accused of not working hard enough to solve the murders because of the victims' lifestyles. This does not appear to have happened in the torso cases of the 1870s and 1880s.
5. The term means anatomist, one who, before the Anatomy Act of 1831 obtained corpses by illegally exhuming bodies for dissection in the medical schools. William Burke, the unlucky half of the murderous duo Burke and Hare, went a stage further and murdered victims which were then sold to the nearest hospital. He was hanged in Edinburgh in 1829.
6. *The Lancet* (1873).
7. *The Times* (16 Sept. 1873).
8. Ibid.

Chapter 10: The Girl with the Rose Tattoo

1. *The Times* (24 Oct. 1884).
2. As I write (March 2010) the Met are investigating the suspicious death of a young man found in Bedford Square's garden near a shed used by gardeners. The Homicide and Serious Crime Command, descendants of the men who hunted the torso killer, believed they knew the man's identity. Scores of office workers must have walked straight past the body on their way to work.
3. Fritz Haarmann was a predatory homosexual who picked up young men near his local railway station in 1920s Germany and dismembered the bodies, selling their flesh in his market stall around the corner.
4. Chief Inspector Walter Dew's description of him in *I Caught Crippen* (1935).
5. *Clerkenwell Press* (Saturday, 25 Oct. 1884).

Chapter 11: Men Behaving Madly

1. Although Gary Ridgeway, the Green River Killer, murdered black and white girls indiscriminately.
2. Sir Charles Warren to Evelyn Ruggles-Brise, 19 Sept. 1888, quoted in Stewart P Evans and Donald Rumbelow, *Jack the Ripper: Scotland Yard Investigates* (Stroud, Sutton, 2006), p. 86.
3. Ibid.
4. Joseph Merrick was exhibited in various freak shows in London before he was 'rescued' by Dr Frederick Treves of the London Hospital. Merrick suffered from the extremely rare condition of neurofibromatosis Type 1, possibly linked with another, undiagnosed condition.
5. Begg, Fido and Skinner, *Jack the Ripper A–Z*, p 152.
6. He would have been right 300 years earlier!
7. In *The Secret of Prisoner 1167*, London, Robinson, 1997.
8. Quoted in *The Trial of Neill Cream*, p. 9.
9. W T Shore, *Introduction to Trial of Thomas Neill Cream* (London, William Hoyle & Co., 1923), p. 40.
10. *Pall Mall Gazette* (1903).

Chapter 12: Other Times, Other Crimes

1. Clifford Elmer, *Synopsis of the Edgware Road Tragedy, Fairbairn's Edition of the Trial of Greenacre and Gale for the Horrible Murder and Mutilation of Hannah Brown.* Catalogue entry, 2010.
2. Quoted in Joan Lock, *Dreadful Deeds and Awful Murders* (Taunton, Barn Owl Books, 1990), p. 29.
3. Donald Hume killed Stanley Setty in a fight and dismembered his body which he then took up in parts in a light aircraft he had hired for the purpose. The parts themselves were located scattered over the Essex marshes and a brilliant piece of forensic science led to the killer's door.
4. Bukhtyar Rustomji anglicized his name to Buck Ruxton when he moved to England. He killed his wife and the family maid in December 1935 and dismembered their bodies before dumping them in a tributary of the River Arran near Moffat, Edinburgh.
5. Quoted in James Badal, *In the Wake of the Butcher* (Kent, Ohio, Kent State University Press, 2001), p. 168.
6. Quoted ibid., p. 169.
7. Quoted ibid., p. 170.
8. By an odd coincidence, serial killer of prostitutes John Christie had worked here fifteen years earlier.

Index

Abberline, Inspector Frederick, H Division 111, 117
'Adam' 130–2
Adams, Fanny 136
Adler, Alfred 137
Ainger, Constable, V Division 59
Albert Embankment 6, 7
Albrook, Lizzie 71
Aldgate 71
Aldgate High St 40
Alfred Mews 101, 103, 104, 143, 149, 154
Allen, Inspector, Essex Constabulary 26, 27
Anderson, Dr Robert 42, 65, 71, 137
Anderson, Isabelle 108
Andrassy, Edward 121–2
Andrews, Inspector Walter, Scotland Yard 42, 102–3
Angel Alley 36, 69
Angle, Mr, journalist 55
Archibald, Kenneth 125–6
Arnold, John 80
Arnold, Supt Thomas, H Division 77, 80
Audray, Madame 73–4

Baderski, Lucy 116
Baker's Row 107
Bankside 61

Barking Creek 12
Barnaby and Burgho 50
Barnes 2, 4, 5
Barnes Mystery 102
Barnes, Dr E C 97
Barnett, Joseph 41
Barthelemy, Helen (Teddie) 124, 126
Battersea 6, 23, 58, 86, 91, 92, 95, 115, 137
Battersea Park 6, 65, 67
Battersea Reach 14, 29, 59
Battersea Waterworks 86
Baxter, Wynne, Coroner, SE Middlesex 58–9, 65, 71, 81, 82, 83
Bazalgette, Joseph 6, 7, 8, 45, 86
Bedford Square 101, 103, 125, 143, 149
Berkowitz, David 139
Bermondsey 10–11, 41, 57
Berner St 40, 50, 76, 148
Berry, Supt 110–11
Bertillon, Alphonse 135
Bertillon, Louis 135
Bianchi, Kenneth 129, 139
Billingsgate 8, 41
Billington, Thomas 115
Bishopsgate 111
Bishopsgate Police Station 40
Black, Robert 99–100, 150
Blackwall 12, 22

Bodden, George 46–7, 48, 53
Bond, Dr Thomas 30, 31, 32, 33, 42, 43, 46, 47–8, 49, 52, 53, 54, 55, 58, 59, 61, 65, 71, 134, 137, 138, 144
Booth 'General' William 69, 70, 71–2
Booth, Charles 70, 147
Bowyer, Thomas 41
Brash, Professor James 144
Brentford 4, 9
Brett, Isaac 57, 59
Brick Lane 37, 111
Brider, Sarah 112
Bridges: Albert 28, 57, 59, 60, 61, 92; Battersea 22, 23, 28, 151; Blackfriars 28; Charing Cross 8; Chelsea 6, 86, 93; Kingston 1; Lambeth 144; London 1, 4, 7, 8, 9, 11, 15, 16–17, 19, 22; Richmond 102; Southwark 64; Tower 10, 18; Vauxhall 58, 87, 144; Victoria 93, 151; Wandsworth 60, 86; Waterloo 8, 18, 19, 28, 101; Westminster 7
Briggs, Sergeant William, V Division 57
Brough, Edwin 50
Brown, Dr Frederick 41
Brown, Hannah 119, 120, 134
Brown, William 47, 53, 54
Brown's Stable Yard 37
Buck's Row (Durward St) 37
Budd, Grace 138
Bugsby's Reach 25
Bulling, Thomas 51–2
Bundy, Ted 99, 100, 128, 129, 130, 138, 139
Buono, Angelo 129, 139
Burns, Elizabeth (One-Armed Liz) 71, 110

Cable St 116, 117
Cailey, Mary 91, 93–5, 143
Calcraft, William 85

Camberwell Marshes 119, 120
Camps, Dr Francis 144
Cannon Row 51, 54
Carter, Mrs 27
Carter, W, Coroner 87, 88, 91, 94
Cassius, Dio 13, 14
Cassivelaunus 2, 13
Castle Alley 42, 43
Central News Agency 40, 51, 68
Chapman, Annie 116, 149
Chapman, Annie (Dark Annie) 38–9, 40, 41, 45, 70, 79, 109, 141
Charing Cross 8
Charlie, pimp 67, 68, 72
Charrington, Frederick 38
Chelsea Embankment 6, 53, 61
Chelsea Reach 28, 40
Chelsea 6, 46, 68, 92
Chikatilo, Andrei 138
Chiswick 5, 20
Chiswick Ait 5
Christensen, Carol 130
Christian, Benjamin 93
Christian, Mary 93–5
Christie, John 100
Churches: Chelsea Old Church 6; St Helen & St Giles, Rainham 25; St Magnus the Martyr 9; St Mary's, Putney 5; St Mary's, Teddington 2; St Paul's Cathedral 9; St Peter's, London Docks 19
Church Passage 41
City Police 40–1, 75
Clark, Dr Percy, Police Surgeon 77, 81
Clarke's Yard 71
'Cleary, John' 76, 80, 81
Cleveland Torso Killings 120–4, 135
Clover, Matilda 29, 114–15
Coffield, Wendy 128
Cohen, Aaron 107, 108
Colajanni, Napoleone 135

Coles, Frances (Carrotty Nell) 71
Colney Hatch Lunatic Asylum 107, 109, 100
Colquhoun, Patrick 21
Commercial St 116
Connolly, Mary 36
Conway, Thomas 40
Coram St *see* Great Coram St Murder
Corder, William 89
Cortis, Captain 8
Cotton, Mary Ann 85, 89
Cream, Dr Thomas Neill 29, 112–15, 148
Criminal, The 136
Criminal Anthropology 134
Criminal Man 134
Cross, Mrs 27
Cross, Charles 37
Crossingham's Lodging House 38
Crossness 15
Curiosities of Life 147
Cutbush, Supt Charles 108
Cutbush, Thomas 108

Dahmer, Jeffrey 138, 154
Davis, John 39
Davis, Joseph 59–60
Dead Man's Hole 18
Dead Man's Island 18
Dead Man's Steps 18
Denke, Karl 138
Deptford 11, 22
Deptford Strand 17
Dickens, Charles, Snr 3, 15, 20, 90
Dickens, Charles, Jnr 1, 2, 4, 5, 6, 7, 9, 10, 11, 12, 13, 22, 59
Diemschutz, Louis 40
Dobson, Supt, Essex Constabulary 27
Docks *see* Quays
Donovan, Timothy 38
Donworth, Ellen 114, 115

Dorset St 41, 71, 82
Douglas, John, FBI Agent 130, 137–8, 139
Druitt, M J 19, 20, 28, 42
Duke's Shore 87
Dunlap, Chief Supt Joseph, C Division 49, 72
Du Rose, John, Assistant Commissioner, Metropolitan Police 125, 127–8
Dutfield's Yard 40

East London Cemetery 83
Ebury Bridge Rd 45, 109
Eddowes, Katherine (Kate) 29, 40–1, 42, 50, 70, 81, 142
Ede, Thomas 109
Edgware Rd 119, 120
Eel Pie Island 3
Ellis, Henry Havelock 136
Exercise in Forensic Medicine 77

Faircloth, John 67, 68, 72
Fall's Point, Rainham 12
Ferrett, Inspector Arthur, H Division 71
Ferri, Enrico 135
Fiddymont, Mrs 109
Figerio 135
Fish, Albert 138
Fish, William 65
Fisher, Constable, Herts Constabulary 64
'Fisher, L E' 58, 63, 66, 67, 143
Fisher, L E (barmaid) 64
Fisher, L E (Mrs Wren) 64
Fitzroy Square 103, 104, 149
Flower and Dean St (Lolesworth Close) 37
Frame, Constable Richard, Thames Division 86

Franks, Bobby 139
Freshwater, Constable, Thames Division 57
Freud, Sigmund 137
Frieburg, Alexander 110
Frobisher, Martin 4, 11

Gale, Sarah 119, 120
Gall, Dr Franz 134
Gallagher, Constable, H Division 110
Galleon's Reach 15
Galloway, Dr Edward 26–7, 28, 29, 30, 31, 33
Gardner, Margery 139
Garratt Lane 151, 153
Gein, Ed 138
George St 116
George Yard 36, 116
Gerber, Dr Samuel, Cleveland Coroner 121, 123
Gerrard, Emilienne 143
Gerrard, Joseph 90, 92
Gibbon, Charles 75–6
Gladstone, William 70, 96, 101
Glaister, Professor John 122, 144
Glatman, Harvey 139
Godley, Inspector George, H Division 80, 83, 117
Gordon, William 151–3
Goulston St 41
Gravesend 9, 15, 91
Great Coram St Murder 95
Great Prescott St 75, 76
Great Stink 7
Green River Killer *see* Ridgeway, Gary
Green River Murders 128–30
Greenacre, James 119, 120, 130, 134
Greenwich 11–12, 16, 86
Greenwich Reach 11–12
Grossmann, Georg 138
Grosvenor Rd 40, 45–6

Haarmann, Fritz 138
Haig, John 139
Hamerton, Dr, Assistant Police Surgeon 28
Hammersmith 5, 14, 90, 92
Hampton Court 2, 6
Hanbury St 39
Hardyman, Harriet 149–50
Hare, Inspector Arthur, Scotland Yard 29, 32
Harris, Louisa (Lou Harvey) 115
Harrison Barber Ltd, horse slaughterers 151–4
Harrison, John 151
Hart, Lydia 81
Hawke, Richard 77, 82
Hayden, Dr Edmund 89, 92, 93, 95, 143
Heath, Neville 139
Hebbert, Dr Charles 32, 33, 46, 48, 49, 52, 53, 55, 61, 62, 77, 78, 87, 134
Hempleman's Factory, Rainham 25, 26
Henley 19
Henry VIII 6, 11
Heron Trading Estate 127
Hickey, Ellen 107
Hicks, A Braxton, Coroner, SW London 29, 65
Holland, Ellen 37
Holland, Emily 65
Honchin, Dr Edmund, Police Surgeon, H Division 110
Hood, Thomas 18, 19
Hughes, Edward 25, 26, 27
Hume, Donald 143
Hutt, Constable George 40

Ilford Cemetery 29
In Darkest England and the Way Out 69
India Dock Rd 116
International Working Men's Club 40
Isenschmid, Jacob 109, 110, 145

Jack the Ripper 35–43, 79, 81, 82, 99, 100, 101, 107, 111, 117, 139, 141–2, 144, 145, 148, 150
Jack the Stripper 126, 127, 128
Jackson, Annie 66
Jackson, Catherine 66, 67
Jackson, Elizabeth 66, 67–8, 71, 72, 79, 109, 110, 124, 143, 148, 150, 153
Jackson, May 66
Jacob's Island 11
Jerome K Jerome 1
Johnson, Constable John, City Police 110
Johnson, Willie 123
Jones, Mary 71, 107
Jung, Carl 137

Keating, Michael 77, 82
Kelly, James 112
Kelly, John 40
Kelly, Mary 41–2, 70, 71, 79, 82, 108, 114, 134, 141
Kempster, Dr, Divisional Police Surgeon 29, 58, 60, 61, 64, 87–8, 90, 92, 94, 95, 143
Kew 4, 6, 14
King, Dr Edmund 110
King's Cross Refuse Tip 103
Kingsbury Run 120–4, 135, 148, 155
Kingston 1, 2, 17
Klosowski, Severin (George Chapman) 115–17
Kosminski, Aaron 109–10
Kosminski, Wolf 109–10
Krafft-Ebing, Richard von 136
Kürten, Peter 100, 122

Lacassagne, Alexandre 135
Lagassie, Frank 121
Lambeth Mystery 114–15
Lambeth 7, 92

Lambeth Palace Rd 6, 113
Lammas Hard, Chelsea 60
Langham, S F, Coroner 29
Langrish, Inspector 105
Lansdowne, Sergeant, Scotland Yard 87, 92
Larder, Dr, Medical Officer, Whitechapel 107
Leary, John 80
Lees, Robert 50
Leman St 107
Leopold, Nathan 139
Lewis, C C, Coroner, South Essex District 26
Limehouse 10, 30, 87, 90
Lipski, Israel 77
Littlechild, Inspector John, Special Branch 136
Living London 151
Llewellyn, Dr Rees 37
Lloyd, Dr Samuel 104, 105
Locke, Constable Henry 87
Lockwood, Irene (Sandra Russell) 124, 125
Loeb, Richard 139
Lombroso, Cesare 134
London, Jack 36
London Hospital 111
London Labour and the London Poor 69
Long, Elizabeth 39
Long Island 133
Lower Pool 80
Lucas, Henry Lee 129
Ludwig, Charles 71, 110

Macé, Gustav, detective 143
McGowan, Margaret (Frances Brown) 124, 126–7
Macnaghten, Melville 19, 36, 42, 43, 108
Macnaghten Memoranda 19, 108, 110

Madame Tussaud's Waxworks 89, 102
Man of Pleasure's Pocket Book 70
Marler, Inspector, Thames Division 87
Marro 135
Marsh, Alice 114, 115
Marsh, Maud 115, 117
Marshall, Inspector, A Division 52, 53
Marwood, William 102
Mason, A 133
Matthews, Henry, Home Secretary 29, 78, 108
Mayhew, Henry 20, 69, 70, 147
Meager, William 103
Merylo, Peter, detective 124
Metropolitan Police: A Division 30, 47, 50; Albany St Police Station 103; B Division 46; Barnes Police Station 102; Battersea Police Station 87; Greenwich Police Station 91; H Division 77; Kennington Lane Police Station 92; King David Lane Police Station 76; King St Police Station 47; Leman St Police Station 75, 76, 77, 80; R Division 26; Scotland Yard 22, 41, 45, 46, 54, 83, 87; T Division 4, 22, 119; Thames Division (River Police) 10, 20–3, 28, 58, 80, 86, 90, 92, 95; Thames Lower Station 22; Thames Middle Station 22; Thames Upper Station 22; Tottenham Court Rd Police Station 103; V Division 4, 22; Vine St Police Station 145; Wapping Police Station (Thames Division HQ) 23, 57, 87; Waterloo Police Station 23
Mile End Old Town Workhouse Infirmary 110
Milestone, Mr 151, 152
Miller's Court 41, 71, 141
Mills, Freddie 128

Minories 110
Minter, Mary 66, 68
Mitre Square 41, 82, 141, 142
Monsell, Colonel Bolton, Chief Constable, Met 80
'Monster of Florence' 100
Moore, Frederick 45–6, 53
Moore, Henry, Inspector 81, 82, 83
More, Thomas 6, 16
Mornington Crescent 103, 105
Morris, George 41
Morris, J 28
Mortlake 4, 5, 15
Mortuaries: Battersea 59, 60, 61; Clapham and Wandsworth Workhouse 88; Millbank St 47–8, 52, 53, 54; St George's in the East 20, 27; St Giles 101; St Pancras 105; Westminster 48; Whitechapel Infirmary Workhouse 20
Munro, Assistant Commissioner James 31, 78, 79, 80
Mylett, Rose (Fair Alice) 58, 71

Napper, Robert 142
Neckinger River 17
Ness, Eliot 122–3, 135
Newgate Gaol 115
Newspapers: *Clerkenwell Press* 103; *Daily Graphic* 112; *East London Advertiser* 38; *Eastern Argus* 38; *Echo* 49, 153; *Essex Times* 27; *Holborn Guardian* 102; *Illustrated London News* 23; *Illustrated Police News* 51, 95; *Morning Advertiser* 83; *New York Herald* 76, 80, 81; *News of the World* 96; *Pall Mall Gazette* 104; *Plain Dealer* 121; *Preston Herald* 65; *Star* 38; *Sun* 108; *Telegraph* 38; *The Lancet* 39, 86, 92, 95, 103, 144; *The Times* 29, 30, 38,

Index 173

50, 54, 58, 60, 62, 86, 87, 88, 89, 90, 91, 94, 95, 96, 101, 105; *Weekly Despatch* 75; *Weekly Herald* 64
Nichols, Mary Anne (Polly) 27–8, 45, 70, 139, 145, 151
Nickell, Rachel 142
Nine Elms 87

O'Hara, Bridget (Bridic) 124, 127
Ojo, Kingsley 131
Old Bailey (Central Criminal Court) 81, 112, 115
O'Toole, Otis 129
Ottolenghi 135

Paddington Tragedy 120
Parker, Constable John, Thames Division 87
Parker, Zoe 155
Patrick, Constable John, H Division 107
Pearce, Arthur J, Cleveland Coroner 121
Pegler, Constable, S Division 119–20
Pender, Vicki (Veronica Walsh) 125
Pennett, Constable William, H Division 76, 81, 154
Pepys, Samuel 7, 19
Phillips, Dr George Bagster 39, 42, 43, 77, 80, 81, 82
Phoenix Hotel, Rainham 26
Pickle Herring Stairs 10
Piers: Battersea Park 28, 61; Temple 8, 28, 60; Waterloo 29, 60; West India Dock 67; Westminster 46, 51
Piggott, William 111
Pimlico 46, 49, 53
Pinchin St 36, 75–83, 85, 110, 116, 144, 148, 149, 153
Pinhorn, Inspector Charles, H Division 77, 81, 82

Pitchfork, Colin 130
Pitsor, Kimi-Kai 130
Pizer, John 141
Polillo, Florence 122
Port of London Authority 9, 13
Psychopathia Sexualis 136
Puckeridge, Oswald 108–9
Public Houses: Bear, London Bridge 19; Coach and Horses, Kew 4; Crown, Borough 117; Duke of York, Docks 73; Frying Pan, Whitechapel 37; Greyhound, Kew 4; Griffin, Kingston 2; Half Moon, Docks 73; King Lud, Ludgate St 80; Lamb Tap, Chiswick 20; London Apprentice 4; Monument, Borough 117; Pope's Head, Gravesend 111; Prince of Wales, Whitechapel 116; Princess Alice, Whitechapel 114; Rising Sun, Whitechapel 38; Seven Stars, Docks 73; Ship and Shears, Docks 73; Star and Garter, Battersea 65; Star and Garter, Kew 4; Sun, Kingston 2; White Hart, Whitechapel 116
Putney 5, 96, 97, 115
Putney Murder 149

Quays: Albert Dock 12, 25; Baltic Dock 11; Black Eagle Wharf 10; Brunswick Wharf 87; Butler's Wharf 17, 57; Cock's Quay 9; Cole's Wharf 57; Copington's Wharf 60; Deal Wharf 35; East India Dock 11, 12; Eastern's Wharf 92; Execution Dock 18; Gowland's Coal Wharf 37; Hammersmith Docks 90; Hammond's Quay 9; Hay's Wharf 10; Humphrey's Dock 10; Irongate Wharf 10; Mark Brown's Wharf 10; Old Aberdeen

Wharf 10; Oliver's Wharf 10;
Orchard Wharf 11; Palace Wharf
60; Pickle Herring Wharf 10;
Regent's Canal Dock 30; Shadwell
Dry Dock 37; St Catherine's Dock
(Howland Great Dock) 10, 18; St
Olave's Wharf 10; Sun Wharf 10;
Thorneycroft's Wharf 20; Victoria
Dock 12, 25; Wapping Dock 10;
West India Dock 12, 30, 60, 87;
White Hart Docks 92; Wilson's
Wharf 10; Woolwich Dockyard 91
Railways: Great Northern 101; Great
Western 4; London and
Southwestern 2, 87; Tilbury and
Southend 76
Railway Stations: Cannon St 134;
Charing Cross 115; King's Cross
101, 103, 104; Waterloo 3, 8
Rainham 12, 13, 25–33, 85
Rainham Mystery 25–33, 46, 48–9, 60, 79, 115, 116, 154
Ratcliffe Highway 73, 88
Red Barn Murder 88
Regent's Canal 29, 32, 119, 149
Reichart, Dave, detective 128
Reid, Inspector Edmund, H Division 75–6, 77, 81
Richmond 2, 3, 15
Ridgeway, Gary 35, 99, 100, 128–31, 132, 148, 149
Rifkin, Joel 99, 100, 133, 148
Roche, Berthe 143
Rose Tattoo Murder 99–105, 149
Ruggles-Brise, Evelyn 108
Ruxton, Dr Buck 122, 144
Ryan, Inspector John, Thames Division 58

Sadler, James 71
Salamanca Place 144

Sayer, Inspector, Scotland Yard 87, 91, 94
Setty, Stanley 143
Shaw, Supt John, Scotland Yard 29
Shipman, Harold 100, 144
Ships: *Alert* 23; *Bywell Castle* 15; *Investigator* 22; *Margery* 8; *Port Mahon* 22; *Princess Alice* 15–16; *Royalist* 22, 86, 91
Shrivell, Emma 114, 115
Simpson, Dr C Keith 23, 128, 144
Sims, George R 67, 151
Skeats, Supt, Thames Division 22
Smith, Charles Manby 147
Smith, G Wentworth Bell 111
Smith, Gertrude 71, 107
Somerset House 22, 28, 86
South St 91, 93
Southwark 9, 23
Spilsbury, Dr Bernard 144
Spink, Isabella 116
Spitalfields 35–43, 73, 117, 139
St George's Stairs 57
St Giles's Coroner's Court 103
St Pancras Lock 29
Starkey, Inspector, Thames Division 87
Stott, Daniel 113
Stott, Julia 113
Stride, Elizabeth (Long Liz) 40, 50, 70, 76, 77, 148
Sundheim, Gaylord 123
Sutcliffe, Peter 99, 139
Swallow Gardens 71
Swanson, Chief Inspector Donald 80
Sweeney, Dr Francis 123
Szemeredy, Alois 112

Tabram, Martha 36–7, 38, 43, 70, 111, 116, 139
Tailford, Hannah (Terry Lynch) 124–5

Taylor, Bessie 117
Taylor, Kim 126–7
Teare, Dr Donald 125, 144
Teddington 2, 22
Temple Stairs 28–9
Thames Magistrates' Court 107, 110
Thick, Sergeant William, H Division 36, 80–1
Thomas, Dr G Danforth, Coroner, Central Middlesex 30, 103, 105
Thomas, Julia 102
Thorney Island 7
Thrawl St 37
Threader, road sweeper 101
Three Kings Court 110
Thurston, Gavin, Coroner 125
Tottenham Court Rd 99–105, 148
Tower of London 19
Treatise on the Police of the Metropolis 21
Troutbeck, John, Coroner 53, 54, 55
Tumblety, 'Dr' 136
Tunbridge, Inspector, Scotland Yard 58, 65, 114
Turk's Row, Chelsea 66, 67, 68
Turner, Constable Henry, W Division 87
Turner, J M W 3, 7
Twickenham Ait *see* Eel Pie Island

Upper Pool 10

Victoria Embankment 6, 27, 101
Vidocq, Francois 135
Vincent, Howard 22
Virchow, Professor Rudolf 134, 141, 143
Voirbo, Pierre 142,
Voisin, Louis 143, 154

Wallis, M 151
Walters, Catherine (Skittles) 69
Wandle, River 6, 28, 86, 90, 151, 152
Wandsworth 6, 23
Wapping 18, 21, 22, 64, 80
Wapping Old Stairs 8, 10
Waring, Jasper 53, 55, 65
Warren, Commissioner Sir Charles 38, 50, 108, 109, 145
Waterloo Tragedy 95
Watts, Constable John, E Division 104
Webb, Beatrice 73, 100
Webster, Kate 101–2
Wentworth St 42
West, Frederick 100
Westminster 7
Wharfs *see* Quays
Whitechapel High St 42, 76, 110, 116
Whitechapel Rd 37, 69
Whitechapel Workhouse Infirmary 38, 107
Whitechapel 1, 19, 35–43, 64, 73, 79, 80, 82, 109, 111, 112, 117, 140
Whitehall Mystery 41, 45–55, 57, 68, 143, 148
Whitelaw, David 142
Willett, Mother 73
Wilson, Margaret 123
Windborn, Frederick 46–7, 48, 49, 50, 53, 54
Winthrop St 145, 151
Woolwich 12, 86, 91
Wright, Steven 99, 100
Wyatt, George, Deputy Coroner E Surrey 114